"The truth and beauty of Catholicism are best imparted not by a textbook but by a living witness. Lenny DeLorenzo offers in this beautiful book a reorientation of the way we think about and implement catechesis and faith formation. This book is a game-changer both in its unique, coherent presentation of the faith and in its provocative and compelling approach to forming others in the faith. This is a book that should be in the hands of every parent, pastor, catechist, and teacher."

—Most Reverend Kevin C. Rhoades
Bishop of Fort Wayne-South Bend

"The Catholic faith, and the person of Jesus Christ who reveals it, is ever new and has the power to fascinate the mind as it sets a heart on fire with excitement about the promise of a life greater than we can imagine. DeLorenzo brings to life the striking beauty of the story of Jesus Christ and offers a method that empowers catechists to share this life-changing truth with young people. This book, firmly based in the principles of the new Directory of Catechesis, has the power to transform an ordinary confirmation program into a life-changing experience, because it helps the catechist become a witness to the transforming power of the Gospel."

—Most Reverend Andrew H. Cozzens, STD, DD
Auxiliary Bishop of St. Paul and Minneapolis

"Leonard DeLorenzo's new book *Turn to the Lord* is an encounter with the Body of Christ! I have often found myself to be without words when trying to explain the fullness of the Catholic faith. Describing beliefs or practices by themselves feels like scattering puzzle pieces. This book will be appreciated by catechists, youth ministers, parents, and anyone who loves the faith and longs to share it. By describing the themes of faith, DeLorenzo paints the big picture of what it means to be Catholic, and to be loved by our generous God."

—Tom East, Director of the Center for Ministry Development and
Project Coordinator for the Certificate in Youth Ministry
Studies Program

"Dr. Leonard DeLorenzo's book articulates a comprehensive approach to faith formation. From exhaustive catechetical content to real life conversational quips, this book is a delight. DeLorenzo possesses a quality of simple explanation of deep ideas found in C. S. Lewis and N. T. Wright. The book reads like an inspiring essay but sticks with you like an excellent keynote speech. It will become a tool on the shelf of anyone in faith formation and a gift for all who pursue a deeper understanding of Catholicism."

—Doug Tooke
Vice President of Mission, ODB Films

"*Turn to The Lord* by Dr. DeLorenzo is a refreshing look at the catechism and our youth. Not only does the text provide important elements of the Catholic faith, but also provides a framework in which to share our rich faith with children and teens. Dr. DeLorenzo takes a modern approach to reach and teach today's generation of students."

—Leslie Lipovski, PhD
Assistant Superintendent, Catholic Diocese of Arlington, Virginia

"I am grateful for Leonard DeLorenzo's new book *Turn to the Lord,* which offers parents and catechists both a theological vision of the life of the Christian and a process for proposing it to others. It will be a great resource in our efforts to re-envision an evangelizing catechesis in our day."

—Katie Dawson, Director of Parish Evangelization and Faith Formation, Diocese of Orange

Turn to the Lord

Forming Disciples for Lifelong Conversion

Leonard J. DeLorenzo

LITURGICAL PRESS
Collegeville, Minnesota

www.litpress.org

Nihil Obstat: Msgr. Michael Heintz, PhD, *Censor Librorum*
Imprimatur: ✠ Most Reverend Kevin C. Rhoades, Bishop of Fort Wayne - South Bend, April 13, 2021

Cover design and mosaic by John Vineyard.

1 2 3 4 5 6 7 8 9

Library of Congress Cataloging-in-Publication Data

Names: DeLorenzo, Leonard J., author.
Title: Turn to the Lord : forming disciples for lifelong conversion / Leonard J. DeLorenzo.
Description: Collegeville, Minnesota : Liturgical Press, [2021] | Includes index. | Summary: "A resource for candidates, sponsors, and parents preparing for Confirmation which fosters a holistic formation of mind, heart, hands, and habits needed for transformation into a source of goodness in the world. Includes direct guidance for creating and facilitating 'Catholic Formation Groups'"— Provided by publisher.
Identifiers: LCCN 2020044032 (print) | LCCN 2020044033 (ebook) | ISBN 9780814665640 (paperback) | ISBN 9780814665886 (epub) | ISBN 9780814665886 (mobi) | ISBN 9780814665886 (pdf)
Subjects: LCSH: Confirmation—Catholic Church.
Classification: LCC BX2210 .D45 2021 (print) | LCC BX2210 (ebook) | DDC 265/.2—dc23
LC record available at https://lccn.loc.gov/2020044032
LC ebook record available at https://lccn.loc.gov/2020044033

To the families of St. Joseph Catholic Church
in South Bend, Indiana,
and especially to the young people
in our first "Catholic Formation Group"

Contents

Preface: The Whole Thing xi

Part I: Power and Wisdom

1 The Way 3
2 Saul of Tarsus and the Witness of St. Stephen 8
3 The Conversion of St. Paul 12
4 St. Paul: The Source of Goodness 16
5 Paul, Apostle of Christ 21
6 The Life of Paul and the Love of Jesus 25
7 Who Is Jesus? The Son of the Father Drawn Near to Us 28
8 Who Is Jesus? I AM 36
9 Who Is Jesus? The Power and Wisdom of God 43
10 Who Is Jesus? The Gift of Beatitude 49
11 Advent: Prepare the Way of the Lord 53
12 Advent: Waiting for the Lord 59
13 Where We've Been, Where We're Going 63
14 Who We Are Created to Be 66
15 Male and Female God Created Them 73
16 Sin and Its Effects 80
17 The Gifts of the Holy Spirit and the Strength of Virtue 87
18 Chastity of the Ears: Inclining Our Hearts 96
19 Chastity of the Tongue: Harnessing the Power of Words 104
20 Chastity of the Eyes: Risking the Joy of Encounter 110

21 The First and Perfect Disciple 115
22 The Mystery and Motherhood of the Church 122
23 Becoming Christ's Body: Baptism, Confirmation, Eucharist 125
24 Healed as Members: Penance and Anointing of the Sick 132
25 At the Service of Communion: Marriage and Holy Orders 138
Epilogue The Keynote of Communion 143

Part II: Reflection and Practice

Introduction: The Conditions of Formation 147
1 The Way 159
2 Saul of Tarsus and the Witness of St. Stephen 164
3 The Conversion of St. Paul 168
4 St. Paul: The Source of Goodness 172
5 Paul, Apostle of Christ 177
6 The Life of Paul and the Love of Jesus 178
7 Who Is Jesus? The Son of the Father Drawn Near to Us 181
8 Who Is Jesus? I AM 187
9 Who Is Jesus? The Power and Wisdom of God 192
10 Who Is Jesus? The Gift of Beatitude 197
11 Advent: Prepare the Way of the Lord 201
12 Advent: Waiting for the Lord 205
13 Where We've Been, Where We're Going 210
14 Who We Are Created to Be 215
15 Male and Female God Created Them 219
16 Sin and Its Effects 225
17 The Gifts of the Holy Spirit and the Strength of Virtue 231
18 Chastity of the Ears: Inclining Our Hearts 237
19 Chastity of the Tongue: Harnessing the Power of Words 242
20 Chastity of the Eyes: Risking the Joy of Encounter 248
21 The First and Perfect Disciple 254

22 The Mystery and Motherhood of the Church 262

23 Becoming Christ's Body: Baptism, Eucharist, Confirmation 267

24 Healed as Members: Penance and Anointing of the Sick 273

25 At the Service of Communion: Marriage and Holy Orders 279

Index 284

Preface

The Whole Thing

Catholicism is about the whole but we often pass it on as a bunch of pieces. What is missing in much of religious instruction, faith formation, and sacramental preparation is the coherence factor. We get bogged down in the tedium of "topics," while the coherence factor has to do with the beauty of the whole. Losing the coherence factor is like studying all the different rules of baseball without learning to appreciate the game itself. Or again, it is like focusing so much on each individual amendment to the Constitution that we fail to see the genius of the document as a whole.

I am interested in the genius of Catholicism as a whole, without sacrificing attention to particular things within that whole.

In this book, I attempt to present the whole while offering instruction about important parts of the Catholic faith. This does not mean that I attempt to present everything about Catholicism in this book. Instead, I want to help others encounter the impact the person of Christ makes on those he claims as his own. I want us to see how being claimed by Christ orders us to communion with God and each other. I want us to discern why the discovery of God leads to the discovery of ourselves, as we are created and called to be.

I am not content to just offer a presentation; I also want to help others present Catholicism in a compelling and substantive way. That is why there are two parts to this book. In the first part, I offer the presentation myself. In the second part, I provide guidance for presenting Catholicism to others.

Formed in Community

Where did this idea come from? It came from practice, in a community. The community was my home parish and, within that community, a community of families who wanted to prepare their young people for the sacrament of confirmation in a new and better way. We did not care for using textbooks for religious formation, so we did not use them. Textbooks present topics and are often deficient in presenting beauty or captivating interest. We wanted to form our young in a living faith that is beautiful.

I developed the content for what we called our "Catholic Formation Group," drawing principally from Scripture and the *Catechism of the Catholic Church,* which stand together as the primary texts for this approach to formation. As a theology professor who has both taught in the classroom and crafted pastoral programming for nearly two decades, I was consistently attentive to forming and not just informing our young people. I thought about how to inculcate habits and not just impart knowledge. I sought to lead them into prayer and not into boredom. I was concerned with the whole.

My approach is to move both narratively and biblically. I begin with the narrative of St. Paul, in multiple parts, whose conversion and transformation into what I describe as "a source of goodness" leads us to the person of Christ. The contemplation of who Christ is serves as the centerpiece of the whole, and leads to the practice of learning how to wait for the Lord. If we were to think of the content of this book as a full-year curriculum, the journey from Paul to Christ and into Advent would be the first semester.

The second semester, then, concerns the study of creation in order to discover who and what human beings are created to be. From there, I give an account of sin and the effects of sin. We explore how recovery from sin takes place through the Spirit, and how we grow in virtue to become capable of being who Christ frees us to be. In the process, we touch on the gifts of the Holy Spirit and why they matter, the meaning of the body and of the sexes, the significance of chastity as a virtue, the conditions of discipleship, and the mystery of the sacraments as building up the Body of Christ.

That might sound like a bunch of different stuff, but it is all presented together upon one keynote. The keynote in all of this is communion, because communion is at the heart of Catholicism, because Christ is at the heart of the faith. Christ brings us into communion with God and unity with one another—that's the Catholic whole. By the end of this exploration, then, people will certainly know more things while also becoming practiced in a Catholic view of life, which is not something you can simply be told about; you have to be persuaded by it and ultimately immersed in it.

Two Parts of the Whole

The first part of this book is me writing to you directly ("Power and Wisdom"). I present everything I just mentioned to you. If you are a parent interested in enriching the formation of your children, I think the best resource is actually you yourself—so I want to help enrich you in your understanding of and confidence in the Catholic faith. The same is true if you are a catechist or teacher. Textbooks are often used *in place of* the catechist, parent, or teacher. I don't want to erase you. I want to further equip and empower you. I hope the first part of the book, where I present this material to you directly, will do just that.

The second part of the book, then, is me sharing how I have taught this same material to those involved in faith formation. The primary group that I lead is the group of young people preparing for confirmation. I believe this is easily adaptable (perhaps without much adaptation at all) for the Rite of Christian Initiation of Adults (RCIA) or even for adult faith enrichment.

We need more leaders in the Church, people who will be able to evangelize and educate in their parishes and homes, as well as in schools. Not everyone is a trained teacher or catechist, and not everyone has a degree in theology or training as a professional minister. So I want to provide a resource to help you become the teacher and catechist your community needs. The second part of this book—dedicated to "Reflection and Practice"—guides you as you lead others.

The two parts of this book ("Power and Wisdom" and "Reflection and Practice") are related to each other in the following way: Each chapter of part 1 presents a facet of Catholicism while the corresponding chapter in part 2 offers guidance in how to teach this to others. This means, therefore, that chapter 1 of part 1 corresponds to chapter 1 of part 2, chapter 2 to chapter 2, and so forth.

Part 1 ("Power and Wisdom") is composed of twenty-five chapters and an epilogue. Each of those chapters has a corresponding chapter in part 2. The epilogue of part 1, however, does not have a corresponding chapter in part 2. Instead, part 2 begins with its own introduction ("The Conditions of Formation"). In the online resource available at leonardjdelorenzo.com/turn-resources you will find the prayers used throughout this book (the Angelus, prayers of specific saints, etc.), testimonies from parents in my parish responding to the question of "Who is Jesus for me?," and other material relating especially to the reflection and practice. Everything in the online resource is referenced in part 2.

The two-part volume you are presently reading is intended primarily for leaders of faith formation groups, especially leaders preparing others for the Sacraments of Initiation. You may well be a director of religious education or a trained and experienced catechist, but you may also be a parent, sponsor, or volunteer who is taking on a new leading role, as was the case with me when I directed the formation group for my eldest son and his peers as they prepared for confirmation. Part 2 of this book is especially relevant for you in a way that it would not be for others who are not leading or co-leading a group. Part 1, however, is relevant for more than just group leaders, since part 1 presents a coherent, compelling, and stimulating introduction to or re-immersion in the beauty of the Catholic faith.

Recognizing that part 1 would be valuable on its own and of benefit to a wider circle of people than just the leaders of faith formation groups, we decided to create a shorter book that only contains part 1. That one-part book appears under the title *Turn to the Lord: An Invitation to Lifelong Conversion*. If you are leading a group of young people in preparation for confirmation, the one-part book will be invaluable to parents of all the students involved in the group as it will enable them to contemplate the same things that their children are contemplating, but in a way appropriate to them. The same is true of sponsors for confirmation candidates, and of spouses, family members, and godparents of RCIA candidates. The one-part book is also well-suited for stand-alone adult or young adult faith sharing groups, as well as for anyone who desires to learn more about and pray more deeply into their Catholic faith.

Especially in a time when we have all become keenly aware of the interruption to the normal rhythm of life that something like a global pandemic imposes upon us, this approach to faith formation offers exceptional flexibility and fosters resiliency. The more we invest in parents, sponsors, family members, and mentors, the more easily we will be able to pivot to alternative forms of instruction, faith formation experiences, and sacramental preparation. It is therefore doubly wise for an entire community to invest in this approach, so that even those parents or sponsors who are not directly leading a Catholic Formation Group will read the one-part book I discussed above and thus be prepared to pivot to temporary or more permanent leadership responsibilities should unforeseen circumstances arise. Even if times like that never come for a particular group, the tremendous benefit of a whole community engaging this material together is that our parishes, schools, and family homes will foster a culture of formation through the studious and prayer-filled attentiveness of a great many disciples.

All of this moves us beyond the consumeristic approach to ministry and education, where the parish or the school (and the ministers and teachers therein) are solely relied upon to provide the instruction and formation for emerging disciples. Instead, I want to help ministers and teachers to draw forth the leadership of a great many. In the Church, we do not leave evangelization and catechesis to "the professionals," because each of us, by virtue of our baptism and as sealed through our confirmation, is directly and personally responsible for the mission of Jesus Christ.

I end this general introduction with a word of hope. We know more people are leaving the Catholic Church every year than coming into it. We know that religion in general is in decline. We know that the fastest growing religious group in the United States and elsewhere in the world is the group known as the "Nones," or the religiously unaffiliated. This is all serious stuff. But I am hopeful, because I believe in God the Father Almighty, Jesus Christ his only Son our Lord, and the Holy Spirit, the giver of life. I believe in the Catholic Church. I believe that we do need new strategies and approaches to passing on and forming people in the faith. I believe that we need to commit ourselves more seriously to what matters most. I believe we have to sacrifice more. But I believe we can and will, by the grace of God.

And I believe this book will help.

Part One

Power and Wisdom

chapter one

The Way

God's Plan

"God, infinitely perfect and blessed in himself, in a plan of sheer goodness freely created man to make him share in his own blessed life."[1] That is the first line of the *Catechism of the Catholic Church*, and it is a stunning claim. It means that the point of everything—from beginning to end—is for God's life to become our life.

To share in God's life means becoming what we were not. "In his Son and through him, [God] invites men to become, in the Holy Spirit, his adopted children and thus heirs of his blessed life" (CCC 1). Those claimed in and through Christ receive a share in the inheritance that properly belongs to Christ alone: his blessed life in communion with the Father. By the Holy Spirit, we receive this communion as a gift, with the mission to share this gift of communion with others. Christ is the gift of God's life for us; in him, God's life becomes our life.

There is drama in God's life becoming our life. It is a drama that reaches to the depths of each person and stretches across the connections between us. It has to do with everything we are and, even more, everything we are called to become. God's life is given to us as a gift, but our task is to grow into the gift we receive. And we are responsible for one another toward that end.

1. *Catechism of the Catholic Church* (hereafter, CCC), 2nd ed. (United States Catholic Conference—Libreria Editrice Vaticana, 1997), 1.

Life Begins at Baptism

The life we receive in Christ is no half measure: it is complete, full, and everlasting. Through the ministry of the Church, Christ confers his life upon us through the sacraments, beginning with the sacrament of baptism. In this sacrament, Christ works through his Church to initiate us not merely into a set of teachings or precepts, but into his *life*. The Rite of Baptism performs the initiation the sacrament effects, so that by paying attention to the rite, we learn precisely what the beginning of this new life entails—namely, renunciation, profession, and immersion.

In order to be freed for life in Christ, a person must first be separated from the old life—the life of sin, bound by death. This separation is performed in a minor exorcism, in and through renunciation of this old way.[2] The act of renunciation is typically made in response to three questions, with either the person being baptized or the godparents on his or her behalf offering the responses:

> [Celebrant:] Do you renounce Satan?
> [Parents and godparents:] I do.
> And all his works?
> I do.
> And all his empty show?
> I do.

God's life cannot be mingled with the way that leads to death. There is no double life; again, no half measure. You cannot be truthful and a liar at the same time; you cannot be both dead and alive. The old way must be driven out before the new way begins.

Second, and following the renunciation, comes the profession of faith. As if having breathed out old, stale air from one's lungs, the new, fresh air can now be taken in. Just so, the three "no" responses of the renunciation are now matched by three "yes" responses:

> [Celebrant:] Do you believe in God, the Father almighty, Creator of heaven and earth?
> [Parents and godparents:] I do.

2. See CCC 1237.

> Do you believe in Jesus Christ, his only Son, our Lord, who was born of the Virgin Mary, suffered death and was buried, rose again from the dead and is seated at the right hand of the Father?
> I do.
> Do you believe in the Holy Spirit, the holy Catholic Church, the communion of saints, the forgiveness of sins, the resurrection of the body, and life everlasting?
> I do.

Third and finally, the person is now baptized into *this* faith, which has just been professed. The baptism effects, at one and the same time, a separation (from sin) and an initiation (into Christ's life). This third moment is the one that contains the other two and makes them true: the person is immersed into the baptismal waters and into the name of the triune God—the person is immersed in a *life*:

> [Celebrant:] I baptize you in the name of the Father [immersion no. 1], and of the Son [immersion no. 2], and of the Holy Spirit [immersion no. 3].

In the sacrament of baptism, *God* accomplishes what he set out to do: he brings us into *his* life, in Christ by the Holy Spirit. Our renunciation of sin and our profession of faith are two sides of our consent to what God is doing in the sacrament. In every baptism, God gives us a share in his life and we receive this gift.

The Way of Life

Since this gift is not some mere *thing* but indeed a *life*, Christians are thus initiated into a way of being to which we must grow accustomed. It is a way of life that must be practiced. In fact, in the early Church, before they were called "Christians,"[3] the followers of the risen Christ were known according to their way of life. As such, "Christianity" was simply called "the Way."

We can see the distinctive marks of this "Way" of life in the Acts of the Apostles, where St. Luke gives an account of the earliest Christian community in Jerusalem:

3. See Acts 11:26 for a note about the beginning of the name "Christians."

> They devoted themselves to the teaching of the apostles and to the communal life, to the breaking of the bread, and to the prayers. Awe came upon everyone, and many wonders and signs were done through the apostles. All who believed were together and had all things in common; they would sell their property and possessions and divide them among all according to each one's need. Every day they devoted themselves to meeting together in the temple area and to breaking bread in their homes. They ate their meals with exultation and sincerity of heart, praising God and enjoying favor with all the people. And every day the Lord added to their number those who were being saved. (Acts 2:42-47, NABRE)

As we can see, the life of the early Christian community was built on four pillars. First, they studied the teaching of the apostles—that is, they dedicated themselves to the Gospel of Jesus Christ handed down to them. Second, they shared all things in common, including serving the needs of the neediest—that is, they gave alms and practiced charity. Third, they broke bread together in their homes—this, no doubt, is the beginning of eucharistic fellowship. And fourth, they committed themselves to the rule of prayer.[4] Upon these four pillars, the first Christians grew into the life they had received.

Notice how this scriptural passage concludes: "And every day the Lord added to their number those who were being saved." In other words, as they lived "the Way," these early Christians contributed not just to their own well-being but also to the well-being of others. By conforming their lives to the good gift they had received, they became a *source of goodness for others.*

In this we can see something of the connection between baptism and confirmation. The latter is the sacramental mission to give what you have received. The fully initiated and mature Christian is more than one who has been converted through the love of God; in Christ and by the Holy Spirit, Christians become a source of the good gift they have received. This is the great dignity of the Christian: to share

4. It is worth noting that these four pillars, as I have called them, are visible as the four pillars of the *Catechism* itself: 1. The Profession of Faith (the teaching of the apostles), 2. The Celebration of the Christian Mystery (the breaking of bread), 3. Life in Christ (the communal life), and 4. Christian Prayer (the prayers).

in God's life so fully as to become an agent of communicating that life to others.

Formation for Life

The Christian life is a lifelong practice in saying "Yes" to the life of God, given to us in Christ. That "Yes" begins in baptism and leads all the way to the communion of saints, in whom the Body of Christ is made complete. Being further confirmed and strengthened in this "Yes" requires formation. Those four dimensions of "the Way" enumerated in Acts 2 are the basic dimensions of Christian formation: study of the faith, practices of charity, eucharistic fellowship, and regular prayer. Whether as preparation for the sacrament of confirmation or through RCIA, or as a way of pursuing a deeper commitment to the mature Christian life, the regular practice of this "Way" makes us receptive to God's gift and responsive to the mission of the Church in sharing the gift of life in Christ.

None of this merely belongs to the world of ideas. These are the mysteries that move in this world: the world in which the Word of God became flesh and dwelt; the world in which Christ died and rose from the dead; the world from which Christ ascended to the Father still clinging to the humanity he shares with us; the world into which the Holy Spirit descended, into which the Church was born, and within which the sacraments heal, strengthen, and nourish those becoming united to Christ. These mysteries have not just changed lives; rather, these mysteries have overturned and transformed lives. Those who were dead in sin have been redeemed through Christ's sacrifice and set free as instruments of God's life for others. Even many who actively opposed God's life and gave everything to obstruct "the Way" have been converted from their death-dealing ways so as to be remade as a "source of goodness" for others. And it is with the narrative of one such man that our narrative exploration of the beauty and drama of Christianity shall begin.

chapter two

Saul of Tarsus and the Witness of St. Stephen

"And every day the Lord added to their number those who were being saved."

There was a man from Tarsus who was not among that number. While those who practiced "the Way" gathered people together, this man broke them apart. While they struggled to live in peace, he wrought violence. While they lived a new life in God, he clung to an old life in spite of God. By grace, though, this man from Tarsus was changed from what he was and became what he had never been. Saul of Tarsus became Paul, apostle of Christ. He was converted and then he converted the whole world. But his conversion was no mere turning from one way to another; it was, instead, a thorough transformation into a "source of goodness." Everything about him was transformed. He, himself, became an instrument of the salvation Christ offers. That is his story, his new story—the story of *Saint* Paul. And this story, the story of the last apostle, begins with the first martyr.

"Now Stephen, filled with grace and power, was working great wonders and signs among the people" (Acts 6:8).[1] He was one of seven disciples appointed by the Twelve to assist in their ministry; Stephen's own ministry was persuasive. As so often happens, though, because Stephen acted and spoke with authority, adversaries emerged. When these rivals sought to debate with him and bring him down, they were repelled because "they could not withstand the wisdom and the spirit

1. All biblical citations from NABRE in this chapter.

with which he spoke" (Acts 6:10). So they did what so many jealous and frustrated people do in situations like this: they twisted what he said to mean something that it did not mean. Stephen had indeed been witnessing to Jesus Christ but not as blasphemy, rather as salvation. Like Jesus before him, Stephen was brought before the Sanhedrin. The members of the "Sanhedrin looked intently at him and saw that his face was like the face of an angel" (Acts 6:15).

There have been far too many tender greetings cards and precious statues by now for us to easily imagine what the face of an angel might really look like. But why do you think the first thing angels usually say is "Do not be afraid"? In the infancy narratives alone, we read about angelic appearances to Zechariah, Mary, Joseph, and the shepherds, and each time the angels say "Do not afraid!" Why would they be afraid? Maybe it has something to do with what the prophet Daniel describes, when he writes: "As I looked up, I saw a man [the angel Gabriel (see Dan 8:15, 9:21)] dressed in linen with a belt of fine gold around his waist. His body was like chrysolite, his face shone like lightning, his eyes were like fiery torches, his arms and feet looked like burnished bronze, and the sound of his voice was like the roar of a multitude" (Dan 10:5-6). His face was like lightning! His eyes were like fiery torches! No wonder this angel said to Daniel, "Do not fear" (Dan 10:12). The angel's appearance to Daniel is not at all unlike the one who sat upon the stone rolled back from Jesus's tomb, whose "appearance was like lightning" (Matt 28:3; cf. Matt 17:2). These do not sound like softly winged, rosy-cheeked, chubby Pampers models whom you want to scoop up and cuddle. Just so, when the members of the Sanhedrin saw Stephen's face "like the face of an angel," the logic of Scripture tells us that they were not comforted. They were looking upon a face that was radiant, fiery, and filled with power. Stephen made quite an impression—his was a face to remember.

All the stunning power of his appearance is translated into words in the next section of the narrative, where Stephen offers his testimony before the Sanhedrin. He presents a full summary of salvation history, beginning with Abraham, continuing through Moses, and all through Israel's history. He testifies to the pattern of persecution of Israel's prophets, who foretold of the coming of the Lord. He testifies before them that the Lord's salvation has now come, but asserts that they have long been unprepared to receive the Savior. Unlike Jesus, who remained silent before his accusers, Stephen is not short on words because he must testify to Jesus as the fulfillment of the "God of glory [who] appeared to our father Abraham" (Acts 7:2). His words carry the same power as his appearance; the Sanhedrin was stunned and infuriated.

As they prepare to execute him, Stephen "looked up intently to heaven and saw the glory of God and Jesus standing at the right hand of God," and as the conclusion to his testimony, he testifies to this vision (Acts 7:55-56). So we should wonder again: What did people see when they looked upon Stephen's face? They saw the glory of the Son of Man that shone upon him. That is what an angelic face is: a reflection of God's glory, the glory made manifest in Christ.

Overseeing this whole affair is Saul of Tarsus; he consented to Stephen's execution (Acts 7:58; 8:1). Saul heard Stephen's final testimony, he witnessed Stephen give over his spirit as Jesus himself had done, and he saw Stephen's angelic face ablaze with the glory of God. The narrative shifts to Saul immediately upon Stephen's death—at the beginning of chapter 8—before it is interrupted by the story of Philip and then returns to Saul's conversion in chapter 9. Without doubt, Stephen's face is impressed upon Saul's memory. The first encounter of the man of Tarsus with Christ is in the reflection of Stephen's face.

We are all so quick to see the narrative of Saul's conversion as the beginning of the story of Paul the apostle. But St. Luke, who was Paul's intimate companion, first introduces the last of the apostles with the death of the first martyr. In doing so, the power of Stephen is juxtaposed to the power of Saul: Stephen's power comes from Christ while Saul's power has another source. In the brief introduction to Saul at the beginning of chapter 8, we hear what kind of man he was and what kind of power he wielded: "Saul, meanwhile, was trying to destroy the church; entering house after house and dragging out men and women, he handed them over for imprisonment" (Acts 8:3).

This is not only how Luke identifies Saul, but also how St. Paul later remembers himself, as he was in his "old life." In at least two places later in the Acts of the Apostles, Luke records Paul's testimony about what he once was:

> I am a Jew, born in Tarsus in Cilicia, but brought up in this city. At the feet of Gamaliel I was educated strictly in our ancestral law and was zealous for God, just as all of you are today. I persecuted this

> Way to death, binding both men and women and delivering them to prison. Even the high priest and the whole council of elders can testify on my behalf. For from them I even received letters to the brothers and set out for Damascus to bring back to Jerusalem in chains for punishment those there as well. (Acts 22:3-5)

> I myself once thought that I had to do many things against the name of Jesus the Nazorean, and I did so in Jerusalem. I imprisoned many of the holy ones with the authorization I received from the chief priests, and when they were to be put to death I cast my vote against them. Many times, in synagogue after synagogue, I punished them in an attempt to force them to blaspheme; I was so enraged against them that I pursued them even to foreign cities. (Acts 26:9-11)

By what power did Saul live? He lived by the power of anger, the power of violence, and even the power of fear. He sought to force those who lived in "the Way" to blaspheme for fear of abandoning his own way of life, the righteousness of which he was so unbreakably convinced.

It is precisely that old way of life that Saul will renounce.

chapter three

The Conversion of St. Paul

Think about what happens when someone is enraged. Their breathing deepens, their pulse quickens, and their body heat rises. They are also really focused on what enrages them; their thoughts sharpen; and their words, if they have any, are pointed. To be enraged is no mere intellectual exercise, nor is it a partial experience. It is as much bodily as it is psychological and emotional; it is all-consuming. When Paul remembers that he was once "so enraged" against the holy ones of Jesus, he is remembering himself as completely dedicated and singularly directed. His whole life—the very essence of who he is—was taken up in this rage.

We are reminded of the character of Saul of Tarsus when the story of his conversion commences in Acts 9. In just two verses, the entire person of Saul is on display in his mission to persecute:

> Now Saul, still breathing murderous threats against the disciples of the Lord, went to the high priest and asked him for letters to the synagogues in Damascus, that, if he should find any men or women who belonged to the Way, he might bring them back to Jerusalem in chains. (Acts 9:1-2, NABRE)

On his own initiative, Saul desires to search out the followers of the Way. His eyes, his ears, and his lips are committed to this quest—he is all in.

With his *eyes*, Saul is looking for Christians in a particular way: with anger, hatred, and suspicion. Even more than what he will see, the way in which he sees is being revealed. We might think of times, for example, when someone has wronged us and we go looking for them. We can go in at least a couple different ways: we could go with a desire to understand and maybe even forgive, or we can go with anger looking to strike out and condemn. The way we will see that person when they appear to us is very much determined in advance. So, too, with Saul.

With his *ears*, Saul is listening for evidence of what he considers the disciples' blasphemous allegiance to Jesus. Remember that the early Christians committed themselves to daily prayer and to the teachings of the apostles, as we learned in Acts 2. Saul will hold their prayers and their teachings as evidence against them, determining in advance that when he hears such things, then those who speak them are deserving of punishment. It is not what he hears that separates Saul from the Christians; it is how he hears that pits him against them.

With his *mouth*, then, Saul discharges the rage that is burning within him. As a dragon breathes fire, Saul breathes "murderous threats against the disciples of the Lord" to burn down their way of life. His words and his actions are in strict alignment—this is a focused and committed person whose passion comes from a deep, deep place within him. He is a man possessed.

In the next seven verses, all this is called into question, which is to say that everything about Saul is thrown into crisis. What does he see? What does he hear? What does he say?

He *sees* a light flash around him so brightly that—like a person walking out of a dark room into the sunlight in the middle of day—he is left unable to see anything at all. He *hears* an unknown voice, which confounds him. It is the voice of one who identifies himself with the very ones Saul is persecuting. What Saul does not hear any longer are the voices of those who join him in his mission to persecute; these companions in his misdeeds are "speechless" before the voice from on high (v. 7). So what can the man of murderous threats now *say*? He is reduced to questioning, as one who is not in control but must grope for meaning. Though no horse is mentioned in the passage, Saul is indeed knocked from his high horse, where he was puffed up on his own authority.

Is this not what Saul feared? The light that blinds him is the same light he saw reflected on Stephen's angelic face. The voice he hears confirms the testimony that Stephen gave. The question Saul speaks is of one who has suddenly lost his way. The leveling of mighty Saul is as stunning as it is sudden: he can see nothing, he neither eats nor drinks for three days, and he—this man of initiative—must now be taken by the hand and *led by others* because his own rage can no longer lead him.

The once mighty Saul will indeed meet one of the very disciples he was seeking, though the meeting will no longer be on Saul's terms. The Lord comes to this disciple, Ananias, and commissions him to lay his hands on Saul, to heal him. Ananias was no less confused than Saul before the Lord's voice, for he knows that this man Saul seeks the ruin of those who follow the Way, and yet with the Lord's assurance, Ananias trusts.

What is the first thing that Saul *hears* when Ananias stands before him? Ananias calls Saul by name and claims him as "my brother" (Acts 9:17). Can you imagine how this address must have struck Saul? He set out for Damascus in order to tear down men like Ananias, and now Ananias who stands in a position of power over the blind and weak Saul responds to those murderous threats with an offer of kinship.

Through Ananias's ministry, Saul immediately regains his sight, but let us not forget the three days he spent blinded and in total darkness. What happened during those three days? Saul was separated from the way he *saw* things previously. In those three days of blindness, his habitual and committed way of seeing was interrupted. He touched his own vulnerability and was left at the mercy of how others would see and therefore treat him. In that blindness, his sight was being refashioned: he would no longer see things the way he had before.

At the hands of the disciple Ananias, Saul undergoes a conversion to humility. Saul was blinded because he had been blind to any way but his own. Saul was dumbfounded because his way of hearing was polluted with the desire to condemn. Saul did not eat or drink because he had to purge himself of his old life if he was to live the life to which the Lord was calling him. This new life was one he had to accept as a gift.

"He got up and was baptized, and when he had eaten, he recovered his strength . . . and he began at once to proclaim Jesus in the synagogues" (Acts 9:18-19, 20, NABRE). With the old way renounced and a new way professed, a new man is born: Saul of Tarsus now lives in Christ.

If ever there were a conversion that we think of as immediate, it is that of Saul of Tarsus who becomes Paul the disciple and apostle of Christ. Yet, in our haste to see this conversion as oh so sudden, we miss not only the three days of blindness and weakness, but also the ministry of Ananias and especially the thorough transformation that is begun in Paul. There are stages here in Paul's conversion, and these stages are the beginning of a lasting change.

Paul is being transformed in the way he *sees*, which has to do with the renewal of his mind because it is about the way in which he views things and the lens by which he looks at the world and at others. In brief, he begins to see in the very light that first wounded him: the light of Christ.

Paul is being transformed in how he *hears*, which certainly has to do with his ears but even more profoundly with his heart. It is about how he is willing to listen to others and to take in their words without an agenda of his own. From his heart, the movement from rage to charity has begun.

And Paul is being transformed in what he *speaks*, which will now become ordered to the end of building up the communities of those who follow the Way. Where he once spread threats, he will now spread Good News. He will no longer proclaim his own power but Jesus as the Son of God (Acts 9:20). He will back up his words with his life.

chapter four

St. Paul: The Source of Goodness

The conversion of Paul is not for his own good alone; it is, in the end, for the good of others. Paul is not just changed from the old way of sin to the new way of God; he is also changed into a source of goodness. Just as his conversion concerned all of who he was in his mind, heart, and lips, his transformation is thorough. He himself is made into a wellspring of charity.

The Renewal of Paul's Mind

The proud man who looked upon the disciples with anger is no longer; in his place is a man who "will boast of the things that show my weakness" (2 Cor 11:30, NABRE). In humility, he is honest about being weak, but he does not just admit it—he boasts about it. That is an odd thing.

Paul goes on in the next paragraph of this letter to the Corinthians to give an account of his odd boasting:

> Therefore, that I might not become too elated, a thorn in the flesh was given to me, an angel of Satan, to beat me, to keep me from being too elated. Three times I begged the Lord about this, that it might leave me, but he said to me, "My grace is sufficient for you, for power is made perfect in weakness." I will rather boast most gladly of my weaknesses, in order that the power of Christ may dwell with me. Therefore, I am content with weaknesses, insults, hardships, persecutions, and constraints, for the sake of Christ; for when I am weak, then I am strong. (2 Cor 12:7b-10, NABRE)

Why might Paul become "too elated"? Maybe because he did quite a lot. He traveled more than 10,000 miles. He preached the gospel effectively. He was successful in his mission and bore its consequences in suffering. Paul had a lot of opportunities for pride, even and perhaps especially in his new life in Christ.

Against this pride, Paul suffers from what he calls a "thorn in the flesh." Paul is never clear about what this thorn is, though many speculate or make educated guesses. Perhaps it was some lingering temptation from which he could not separate himself, no matter how much he desired to do so. Some suspect that Paul suffered from a speech impediment, which was not only a challenge to his ministry but also embarrassing. Others think that severe headaches afflicted him, draining him of his energy and focus. Maybe a false teacher rivaled him and even forged Paul's name, making Paul's work all the more difficult and bothersome. These are all indeed possible, and perhaps even more than one of these burdened Paul. I want to consider, however, something that I think must have certainly weighed on Paul.

Do you think that Paul remembers who he was before his conversion? Of course he does. In fact, as we saw in the latter chapters of Acts, Paul openly confesses to the rage that consumed him. What kind of things did Paul do under the control of his zeal for persecuting disciples? He dragged people from their homes, he bound them in chains, he unleashed murderous threats, he oversaw executions, he ruined people's lives. Paul is a man with blood on his hands. And what do you think the effect of all that is in his mind, upon his memory? Did he not feel the guilt and the shame of who he had been and what he had done?

If this is the "thorn in the flesh" that afflicts him—his own mind, his own memory—then it is perfectly understandable that he would pray to the Lord to clear his memory and help him forget what he had done. If this is indeed what he asks, though, then the Lord does not erase his memory. Why not? Is the Lord punishing him by making him remember his sins? That is not in keeping with the Lord's character, as revealed in how the Lord consistently acts. Maybe, then, the Lord allows Paul to remember who he was so that Paul will always remember what *Christ has done for him.* Paul has been saved from being the man that he was. This salvation comes not by Paul's power but by Christ's, and it is Christ's power that motivates Paul's life now.

"My grace is sufficient for you," the Lord says to him, over and over again. If this is the Lord's response to the burden of Paul's memory, then what Christ is saying to Paul is something like this: "Believe in my love more than you believe in what you're ashamed of, what you regret about yourself, and what you wish you were not." Paul has been freed to see the world, other people, and indeed himself not according to his own deeds and misdeeds, but according to the power of Christ's love. In his love, Christ teaches Paul how to see.

The Renewal of Paul's Heart

We do our most important listening not with our ears but with our hearts—this is true of Paul no less than the rest of us. The way our eardrums receive soundwaves does not say anything about the kind of person someone is. The way one is willing to receive the words of another person does. In his old life, Saul of Tarsus was dead set on interpreting the prayers and teachings of the disciples of Jesus as condemnatory evidence. He listened for their sounds with enmity. That is not so much a matter of his ears but of his heart.

Ananias broke that vile spell when he called Paul his brother and claimed him for Christ Jesus. The antidote of Ananias's charity opened Paul's heart to a profound transformation. It is of and from this very heart—his own heart—that Paul writes to the church at Philippi:

> I give thanks to my God at every remembrance of you, praying always with joy in my every prayer for all of you, because of your partnership for the gospel from the first day until now. . . . It is right that I should think this way about all of you, because I hold you in my heart, you who are all partners with me in grace. . . . For God is my witness, how I long for all of you with the affection of Christ Jesus. And this is my prayer: that your love may increase ever more. (Phil 1:3-5, 7-9, NABRE)

Saul of Tarsus had no room in his heart; it was filled to the brim with anger. Paul the disciple, however, has practiced making room in his heart for the needs of others. In his own heart, he seeks after *their* good, *their* joy. He claims them as intimate to him.

This transformation is endlessly astounding. The very man who spent his entire self in persecuting these disciples—employing all his passion and strength, all his time and skill, all his knowledge and cunning—now suffers for them in his heart. It hurts to will the good of others. He makes himself dependent on their well-being. He makes his heart into a home—a place for them to dwell.

Paul's heart becomes a space for bringing people together—this same heart that, once dead in sin, was intent on driving them apart and breaking them down. He loves them and dedicates himself in prayer for them. He makes himself their servant.[1]

The Renewal of Paul's Tongue

Paul had a great deal he could have boasted about, including the generosity of his heart. The response of gratitude to the Lord for saving him from what he, in honesty, knew he had been along with the dedication to the needs of others, like those in Philippi, for whose well-being he took responsibility, guarded him from the pride that would be his undoing. We would not be wrong to say that for Paul, the difference between pride and humility was a matter of perspective. It is the difference borne of what he counts as most important and then, afterward, what is counted as of only relative importance.

If we were to think of Paul's biography and ask what was the most important experience of his life, some pretty appealing candidates would quickly emerge. *He* witnessed the angelic face of the first martyr. *He* was blinded by the light of the Lord and heard his voice. *He* was elevated in a mystical experience "up to the third heaven" (2 Cor 12:2-5, NABRE). Few are those who could claim a more impressive list of life experiences. And yet, Paul does not claim any of them as most important. Rather, he cites what he received from and was taught by the apostles who came before him as most important of all:

> I handed on to you as of first importance what I also received: that Christ died for our sins in accordance with the scriptures; that he was buried; that he was raised on the third day in accordance with the scriptures; that he appeared to Cephas, then to the Twelve. After that, he appeared to more than five hundred brothers at once, most

1. Pope Francis marvels at the beauty and health of Paul's heart, which he identifies as the heart of an evangelizer, in *Evangelii Gaudium: The Joy of the Gospel* (Washington, DC: United States Conference of Catholic Bishops, 2013), 281–82.

> of whom are still living, though some have fallen asleep. After that he appeared to James, then to all the apostles. Last of all, as to one born abnormally, he appeared me. For I am the least of the apostles, not fit to be called an apostle, because I persecuted the church of God. But by the grace of God I am what I am. (1 Cor 15:3-10, NABRE)

By his own words, Paul testifies to the most important thing: who *Christ* is, what *Christ* has done. Like all the rest of us, Paul *received* the gift of Christ, and like all but those apostles who came before him, Paul was reliant upon other Christians to communicate this gift to him. Paul had Stephen, Paul had Ananias, and Paul had Peter and the other apostles. What they passed on to him is of first importance; what he is, who he is, and everything about him is only important relative to that.

At the same time, Paul does not succumb to the false humility of counting himself as nothing. He does not deserve to be called an apostle, but he does not deny that he is an apostle. It is not something he has made of himself; rather, as he says, "by the grace of God I am what I am." It is Christ's identity and mission that is primary and Paul receives his own identity and mission from Christ. For him to claim that of himself is to speak truthfully, for it is to testify to the power of Christ. With his own lips Paul witnesses to the truth.

The Source of Goodness

Paul himself becomes an instrument of gratitude, lending a vision to others of the wonders the Lord works in the lives of those he redeems. Paul becomes a space for communion, praying and acting for the well-being of others. Paul becomes a living testament to what was handed on to him: the passion, death, and resurrection of the Lord. This whole man once set to tearing down the Church is now a whole man given over to the gospel.

The transformation of Paul began unnoticed in the blood of Stephen, turned dramatically with the Lord's encounter and the ministry of Ananias, and blossomed into what Paul became for the sake of others (1 Cor 9:21-23). For Paul, this is not an add-on to receiving the gospel; instead, offering this goodness to others is itself part of receiving the gospel as his own good. Paul is a witness to what is true of every Christian: in Christ, God does not give some*thing* but draws us into his *life*, and by practicing this life, others become beneficiaries of the same gift.

chapter five

Paul, Apostle of Christ

I took my teenage son and his friend to see *Paul, Apostle of Christ* shortly after the film was released in theaters. It seemed an appropriate thing to do during Holy Week. Besides, I thought there was something potentially powerful in watching a film about the origins of the Christian faith in the same theater where my son had watched the most recent *Star Wars* films and other things like that. He has loved those stories of great heroism, adventure, and matters of life or death. Maybe seeing this film in the same setting would reinforce for him that this story is about all those things and more. I think my son liked the film, and we talked about it in the days that followed. I liked the film, too, but I also found myself challenged and inspired. And it was actually several little things that did this to me.

On Mentoring

First, I was captivated by the mentoring that the film portrayed in the early Christian communities. In this particular narrative, it began with Paul who mentored Luke, strengthening the younger man amid his doubts and counseling him into the maturity of freedom, where one discerns patiently, takes responsibility, and acts. In turn, Luke mentors the community at Rome, especially in the persons of Priscilla and Aquila, who have taken the poor, the widows, and the orphans under their care. Luke is not only the go-between for Paul and the community from which he is absent, but also the community's source of nourishment, becoming for others what Paul is for him. While caring for and guiding the many who are gathered in their community, Priscilla and Aquila also mentor each other. They speak honestly, they listen to each other, they discern patiently, they are willing to accept the possibility of going different directions from one another according to the Lord's will for each of them, and they bless each other.

It was inspiring and challenging to witness all of this in the film, especially because I came away with the clear impression that growth in the gospel—in "the Way"—has always been like this and always must be. Those who have received and who have been strengthened must become the ones who give to those who came after them and strengthen them. Passing on the gospel is not merely a study of facts or the communication of principles—though it is that, too. Rather, it means becoming a witness to others and a source of life for others, out of love.

Paul himself, while passing on his story to Luke who is writing the Acts of the Apostles from his mentor's words, recalls the years of his own formation in "the Way." It was once new to him and he, who had not walked with the Lord as Peter and the others had, relied on them to teach him how to pray, how to speak, how to love. Mentoring goes all the way back to the beginning.

On the flip side of this, it was also evident that Luke was a comfort and blessing to Paul. In like fashion, Aquila and Priscilla were treasures to Luke, as they were to one another. The poor, the widows, and the orphans gave Aquila and Priscilla life. The ones who mentored received solace and joy from the ones for whom they cared.

On Costliness

The second thing that struck me is that the early Christians had "skin in the game." That particular phrase had been ringing in my ears because my kids were obsessed with the musical *Hamilton*, in which we hear: "When you got skin in the game, you stay in the game / But you don't get a win unless you play in the game." Alexander Hamilton would not have fit easily in the early Christian community of Rome, but his lyrics nevertheless apply to those early Christians. They had skin in the game and they endured the pains of love for it.

It is obvious how the Christian martyrs had skin in the game—those who were burned in the streets and forced into Nero's circuses clinging to nothing other than their faith and their poverty. But that wasn't the only thing that made an impression on me; I was also stirred by how much living "the Way" required all these Christians to have skin in the game. Living peaceably with others in the community and especially within the violence of Rome in the 60s (AD) was painful, costly, and not easily achieved. Returning violence for violence, hate for hate, evil for evil would have been easier. Absorbing the repercussions of all those things took a toll on Paul, Luke, and the others. They had to learn—through their bodies, their minds, their hearts—what it means for love to be "patient and kind" and all the rest. It was a lesson learned through their bodies. Peace is hard, and it is costly.

The same may be said of charity. Priscilla and Aquila above all witnessed to the costliness of assuming the needs and wounds of others with kindred affection. They subjected themselves to weeping for the sorrows of others, mourning for the loss of others, experiencing heartache for the absence of others, and they shared the burden of pain with others. Performing the works of mercy has never been easy, and it was even more difficult for those Christians living in Rome under Nero. They had skin in the game.

Something about the true depth of beauty in the gospel is made present here. It is a harsh beauty at times. What I saw in the film's portrayal of these early Christians is that the gospel they received and which freed them also cost them. Yes, it cost the martyrs who gave their lives as a final testimony, but not just them—it cost all of them. They all had to change, to grow, to struggle, to move through uncertainty, to become creative in their ways of loving in the most inhospitable of environments. Theirs was no mere intellectual faith, no faith of perpetual optimism, no faith of simply consolation. Theirs was instead the faith that this "Way" was the truth, that it was the only "Way" to live. It was a faith that acknowledged that what Christ did for all of them was the pattern for what they must do for others.

The gospel was not then and is not now just a message to be passed on, but a transformation to be undergone.

That transformation is so very human. The early Christians learned to absorb the cost of peace, they learned to absorb the cost of charity, they learned to absorb the cost of communion, and by absorbing that cost, they learned the beauty of the gospel in a way that surpassed understanding. The price of that gift was their willingness to have skin in the game.

On Affliction

The third and final thing that moved me in the film was the presentation of the "thorn" in Paul's side (2 Cor 12:7-9). As we discussed in the last chapter, there is no way to be certain what Paul means when he writes of this thorn, yet the filmmakers offered something stirring for our imaginations.

In the darkness of his cell, all alone in the watches of the night, Paul is afflicted with flashbacks to the violence he inflicted upon others during the years he was filled with zeal for persecuting Christians. He has blood on his hands. The devil stirs in the night to remind Paul of his sins and urges him to consider his sins as greater than the grace that has set him free.

In the first book of the Bible, the serpent is a tempter, but in the Bible's last book, the serpent is full grown and no longer merely a tempter. He is now an accuser. The dragon accuses the saints of their sins, reminding them of their unworthiness, tempting them to believe that their sins are greater than the grace they have received. Paul's memory is haunted by these accusations. It is a perpetual thorn in his flesh. And in that way, it is also ground zero for his faith in Christ. To trust in Christ is visceral, bodily, tied up in the darkest parts of his memory. All of his evangelical zeal springs from his bedrock belief that what Christ has done for him is true. He *did* live in sin, but *now* he lives in Christ.

Even Paul—especially Paul—never gets past this fundamental act of faith: believing that Christ heals *me*.[1]

1. A version of this chapter appeared as a review of the film in the *Church Life Journal*. Used here with permission. See Leonard J. DeLorenzo, "Skin in the Game," *Church Life Journal*, accessed June 24, 2019, https://churchlifejournal.nd.edu/articles/skin-in-the-game/.

chapter six

The Life of Paul and the Love of Jesus

"I appeal to you therefore, brethren, by the mercies of God, to present your bodies as a living sacrifice, holy and acceptable to God, which is your spiritual worship" (Rom 12:1, RSV).

Paul, the apostle of Christ, urges Christians to give unto the Lord as an act of worship the very best gift they can give him: the gift of themselves. "[P]resent your bodies as a living sacrifice," he instructs them, but he instructs only what he himself has already done. As we have seen, his conversion to Christ became complete in the transformation of his seeing, of his hearing, and of his speaking. On his last day, Paul would give all of this—his mind, heart, and tongue—as the final sacrifice to Christ when he gives his own life out of love for the Lord. He had practiced giving that gift day after day, for years. Paul practiced holding on to Christ more dearly than he held on to himself (see Acts 20:24), and by clinging to Christ he allowed himself to become a new man in Christ, "by the mercies of God." The entire ministry and witness of St. Paul was a commitment to hand on to others as of first importance the mystery of Jesus Christ (1 Cor 15:3). Paul delivered that gift with his own life.

The person and work of Jesus is primary. Who he is, is made manifest in what he does, and what he does reveals who he is. But that only begs the critical question: Who is Jesus? We learn who Jesus is through the ministry of the Church, including through the testimony of Scripture, just as Paul received the testimony to Christ from St. Stephen, Ananias, and ultimately Peter and the other apostles. Paul took his place as one called upon to pass on what he had received. We learn who Jesus is primarily through preaching and catechesis.

There is a second question, though, which is no less important even though it depends on the first one. The second question is this: Who is Jesus *for me*? In responding to this question, a disciple confesses that Christ, who is Lord of all, is Lord of my life too. Just like it is one thing to remember and tell others who your grandmother was and another thing to recount how your grandmother loved you, personally, so too it is one thing to testify to who Jesus is and another to testify to how Jesus has loved you. Paul preached Christ Jesus *and* gave an account of how Christ Jesus changed his life.

In a homily on the first few chapters of St. Paul's Letter to the Ephesians, Pope Francis recognized how that second question—Who is Jesus *for me*?—can be quite challenging and even a little embarrassing to answer. It is embarrassing because you have to dig into your heart and share something about yourself in order to answer it. St. Paul embarrassed himself over and over again in this way, testifying to who Jesus is for him. Paul wants those who learn from him to follow his example. Pope Francis explained:

> Paul wants Christians to feel what he himself felt. [In response] to the question that we can put to Paul—"Paul, who is Christ for you?"—he spoke about his own experience: "He loved me, and gave Himself for me" (Gal 2:20). But he was involved with Christ who paid for him. And Paul wants every Christian—in this case, the Christians of Ephesus—to have this experience, to enter into this experience, to the point that each one can say, "He loved me, and gave Himself for me," but to say it from their own personal experience.[1]

No one can give someone else that personal testimony—each disciple must give that testimony as his or her own gift as part of one's "living sacrifice, holy and acceptable to God." It is also not a gift that is just given once, but more often is a testimony that each disciple gives

1. Debora Donnini, "Pope at Mass: Who Is Jesus Christ for You?" October 25, 2018, https://www.vaticannews.va/en/pope-francis/mass-casa-santa-marta/2018-10/pope-francis-homily-daily-mass-knowing-jesus.html.

time and again, in different ways, throughout life. The crucial thing is to take the risk and begin to practice giving that testimony.

In the four chapters that follow, I will lead us in an exploration of the question "Who is Jesus?" I will attend to Scripture and the Tradition in doing so, inviting us into a deeper understanding of the person and work of Christ. While we engage in this scriptural, theological, and spiritual study, we should keep in mind that second question for which each of us takes personal responsibility: "Who is Jesus *for me*?" I will close each of the next four chapters with a prayer or testimony from a saint speaking from his or her own life of Jesus's love; in listening to them, may we open ourselves to the grace of adding our testimony to their chorus.

chapter seven

Who Is Jesus? The Son of the Father Drawn Near to Us

Everything about the life of St. Paul leads us to ask the question "Who is Jesus?" This is the central question of each of the four gospels and indeed the question at the heart of the faith of the Church. It is not, however, a question for which the Church herself or any member of the Church conjures up an answer on their own. Rather, the mystery of Jesus's identity is a matter of revelation: God provides the answer. In faith, our duty and our delight is to contemplate the answer we receive.

The most complete response that St. Paul offers to the question of who Jesus is comes in the great hymn he composed in his letter to the Philippians. If we are to contemplate Jesus as he is, and not as we might otherwise think him to be, then we must come to behold him as the one,

> [w]ho, though he was in the form of God,
> did not regard equality with God something to be grasped.
> Rather, he emptied himself,
> taking the form of a slave,
> coming in human likeness;
> and found human in appearance,
> he humbled himself,
> becoming obedient to death,
> even death on a cross.
> Because of this, God greatly exalted him
> and bestowed on him the name
> that is above every name,
> that at the name of Jesus
> every knee should bend,
> of those in heaven and on earth and under the earth,

and every tongue confess that
Jesus Christ is Lord,
to the glory of God the Father. (Phil 2:6-11, NABRE)

What we see when we look at Jesus is the one who took the form of a slave, who humbled himself, and who endured death in obedience. This is what appears to our senses and what was seen by all who gazed upon him. But the eyes of faith see further—in faith, we see exactly who it is that took on this fate: it is the one who shared equality with God, who was in the form of God. To put this another, less poetic way: the one who was above the highest things descends down below the lowest things. This is who Christ Jesus is and what Christ Jesus does.

Despite what we might think, the glory of God is not separate from the lowliness of Jesus in humility and death. Instead, his lowliness reveals his lordship and redounds to the glory of God the Father. To see Jesus as he is means seeing him as *the Son of the Father drawn near to us.*

St. Paul expresses this mystery with unparalleled eloquence, respecting the tension of the holy mystery. Yet, on its own, this might sound like a puzzle to be solved. I wrote above that no one conjures up a response to the question of Jesus, but rather that it is a matter of revelation: God provides the answer. What St. Paul bestows to the Church with this hymn in the Letter to the Philippians (which is very much worth memorizing, by the way) is an invaluable piece of preaching, a kind of summary of the mystery of the person of Christ. This is a summary of what has been revealed, which means we can see this mystery performed in the life of Jesus. He is this mystery.

What I will do, therefore, is guide us in considering two moments in the life of Christ with the hymn of St. Paul in mind. We want to learn to see better and to contemplate in faith how this one person of Jesus is the Son of the Father and the one who draws near to us even to the point of death. Paul's hymn is true only because the action of God has revealed Jesus to be who Paul later said he is. The two events to which we will turn our attention are the baptism of Jesus and the transfiguration of Jesus.

The Baptism of Jesus

It seems pretty obvious that the baptism of Jesus has to do with who Jesus is. In no uncertain terms, St. Luke tells us that upon Jesus's baptism, "heaven was opened and the holy Spirit descended upon him in bodily form like a dove. And a voice came from heaven, 'You are my beloved Son; with you I am well pleased" (Luke 3:21-22, NABRE).

This verse is of incomparable importance, but focusing on this verse alone without considering the entire event is like remembering a famous movie quote and forgetting everything else about the scene. In a film, it is the whole scene that makes the particular quote powerful or memorable in the first place, whereas here it is the whole event that gives the context for just how remarkable this pronouncement of Jesus's identity is. Yes, it is the voice from heaven alone that can and does proclaim Jesus as "my beloved Son," but just what this beloved Son is doing requires more from our imaginations.

It is of course John the Baptist and not Jesus who is doing the baptizing in Luke 3. Of John, St. Luke writes, "He went throughout [the] whole region of the Jordan, proclaiming a baptism of repentance for the forgiveness of sins" (Luke 3:3, NABRE). So what did all the people who presented themselves to John for baptism have in common? All of them were sinners. Baptism is for sinners.

Though this particular scene is not described for us, we should imagine that these people are standing on the banks of the River Jordan, awaiting their turn to go down in the water under John's hands. A whole line of sinners, just waiting. And into that line walks this man Jesus. He waits his turn, such that right before St. Luke writes of the voice from heaven, he states, "After all the people had been baptized and Jesus also had been baptized" (Luke 3:21, NABRE). It almost sounds as if Jesus was baptized last—like he waited until the end.

This Jesus who is the Father's beloved Son, with whom the Father is well pleased, is the only one who is *not* a sinner. He does not need the baptism that others need; he is not in need of repentance. And yet, he waits with the sinners on the banks of the Jordan, and then he goes down into the water under John's hands just like all the sinners. If we did not know better, we would assume that he was just like them—that he was just one more sinner in need of forgiveness. Could anything be more humiliating than being confused with those who are less than yourself, who have problems you do not have, who are sick with a sickness not your own, a sickness for which they and not you are responsible? This is precisely what the Father's beloved Son has allowed himself to become. He who is without sin goes down with the sinners, in the sinners' place, to pray in solidarity with them and offer himself for them.[1] In doing this, Jesus fulfills the prophecy of the prophet Isaiah:

> "My righteous servant makes the many righteous,
> It is their punishment that he bears;
> Assuredly, I will give him the many as his portion,
> He shall receive the multitude as his spoil.
> For he exposed himself to death
> And was numbered among the sinners,
> Whereas he bore the guilt of the many
> And made intercession for sinners." (Isa 53:11-12, JPS)[2]

In Paul's language, he who "was in the form of God . . . emptied himself." This strange movement of Jesus does not end when he emerges from the waters of the Jordan. Where he goes right after his baptism further deepens the mystery.

1. Pope Benedict XVI meditates on the mystery of Jesus's baptism and his acceptance of the plight of the sinners in the following manner: "The act of descending into the waters of this Baptism implies a confession of guilt and a plea for forgiveness in order to make a new beginning. In a world marked by sin, then, this Yes to the entire will of God also expresses solidarity with men, who have incurred guilt but yearn for righteousness. . . . Jesus loaded the burden of all mankind's guilt upon his shoulders; he bore it down into the depths of the Jordan. He inaugurated his public activity by stepping into the place of sinners. His inaugural gesture is an anticipation of the Cross. He is, as it were, the true Jonah who said to the crew of the ship, 'Take me and throw me into the sea,' (Jon 1:12). . . . The Baptism is an acceptance of death for the sins of humanity, and the voice that calls out 'This is my beloved Son' over the baptismal waters is an anticipatory reference to the Resurrection" (Benedict XVI, *Jesus of Nazareth, Part I: From the Baptism in the Jordan to the Transfiguration* [New York: Doubleday, 2007], 17–18). Pope Benedict's chapter on the baptism of Jesus is replete with biblical and patristic references, and would serve as an excellent resource for readers who wish to study the mystery of Jesus's baptism in greater depth.

2. For more on this, see my "Hastening to Heal: To Read, Pray, and Move in the Order of Grace," in *Dante, Mercy and the Beauty of the Human Person*, ed. Leonard J. DeLorenzo and Vittorio Montemaggi (Eugene, OR: Wipf and Stock, 2017), especially 108–9.

In order to grasp this, we must remember where the River Jordan is located. When the Israelites left Egypt, they crossed through the Red Sea and into the desert, where they wandered for forty years. Their pilgrimage came to an end when they left the desert by crossing another body of water—the River Jordan—and entered into the land the Lord had promised to them. The River Jordan is the eastern border of that Promised Land.

Now think about where Jesus started as he made his way toward the River Jordan—he began west of the Jordan, in the Promised Land. But where did he go after he went into those waters? St. Luke tells us: "Filled with the holy Spirit, Jesus returned from the Jordan and was led by the Spirit into the desert" (Luke 4:1, NABRE). The people of Israel who were freed from slavery wandered for forty years through the desert of temptation toward the River Jordan and then crossed over into the Promised Land. Jesus goes the other direction: he begins in the Promised Land, passes through the same waters, and proceeds into the desert where Israel wandered in temptation. How long did Jesus spend in that desert? "[F]orty days." Why? "[T]o be tempted by the devil." And what occurred during that time? "He ate nothing during those days, and when they were over he was hungry" (Luke 4:2, NABRE).

Let's rephrase all of this using Paul's language from Philippians 2: He who was at home in the Promised Land did not deem that home "something to be grasped," but rather "emptied himself," being confused with sinners, journeying back into the desert of their waywardness, and "found human in appearance, he humbled himself," becoming obedient through temptation . . . and he was hungry.

But why didn't he eat anything? Surely, the desert is a generally inhospitable place that offers little, but the text doesn't say that "he found nothing to eat," but rather "[h]e ate nothing" (Luke 4:2). This is the active voice—what is passive is the state in which the action of not eating left him: "he was hungry." Surely something edible could be found in the desert over forty days, so why not eat? Because eating of what the desert provides—what is found there—is to enter into the economy of the desert wilderness. To agree to the terms of the desert is to become one who agrees to the sly beguilement (cf. Gen 3:1) of its "winding ways," which obscure, confound, and contort the "straight highway" of the Father's love secured in the Spirit (see Luke 3:4-5; cf. Isa 40:3-4). To consume in this wilderness is to become tangled in its web of disobedience, its bramble of deception, thus morphing desire into a fickle thing. And so, in order to bend this thicket of misdirected desires into a "straight highway" of the Lord, "[h]e ate nothing" (Luke 4:2).[3]

In all of this, what Jesus does reveals who Jesus is. He is the Son of the Father who goes to the place of temptation where sinners dwell. He goes freely.

The Transfiguration of Jesus

If we read the account of the transfiguration of Jesus alongside the baptism of Jesus, we will discern the same movement and the same revelation. The obvious connection occurs when the voice from on high says: "This is my chosen Son; listen to him" (Luke 9:35, NABRE; cf. 3:22). What was said and heard at Jesus's baptism is said and heard atop Mount Tabor.

Though the declaration from heaven is the same, the theatrics are comparatively more spectacular on the mountain than at the river. Jesus's face is changed in appearance and his clothes become a radiant white (9:29). Moses and Elijah appear and they speak with Jesus. A cloud, not unlike those of Old Testament theophanies, descends upon the mountain (cf. Exod 24:15; 33:9; 40:34). To our amusement, Peter is sort of swept up in the moment and seems utterly dumbfounded. He is having the mountaintop experience that will be the cautionary example for every "retreat high" thereafter. He just wants to stay right there: "Master, it is good that we are here; let us make three tents, one for you, one for Moses, and one for Elijah," to which St. Luke quickly adds, "but he did not know what he was saying" (Luke 9:33, NABRE). We like to think that Peter was wrong in saying this, as if he is playing the part of the bewildered buffoon for us. But what Peter says is not wrong: he wants to dwell where they are. He is right to want to dwell in the glory of the Son, who dwells in glory with the Father. It is just that Peter does not yet understand what dwelling with Jesus means.

3. For more on Jesus in the desert, see my article from which this particular paragraph is taken: Leonard J. DeLorenzo, "Being Hungry Is What Happens to Us," *Church Life Journal*, accessed June 24, 2019, https://churchlifejournal.nd.edu/articles/being-hungry-is-what-happens-to-us/. Furthermore, it is no mere coincidence that Luke places the genealogy of Jesus between the baptism and the temptation of Jesus. By this genealogy, Jesus is connected to and assumes the whole history of Israel, and even back before the founding of Israel to "Adam, the son of God" (Luke 3:23-38).

It is right after Peter's request that the voice from heaven identifies Jesus as the beloved Son. When the disciples look up afterward, they see only Jesus, for he is God dwelling in their midst. Even as Peter and the other disciples look at Jesus, his identity remains a mystery to them. They see him and yet they do not see him fully for who he is. It is significant, then, that the very next verse describes the movement of Jesus and his disciples: they come down the mountain (Luke 9:37; cf. Mark 9:9; Matt 17:9). Peter sought dwelling above but he ends up descending with Jesus, according to Jesus's own action.

As Jesus returns to the "crowd" down below, the very first request he heeds is for healing by exorcism. By drawing near to the possessed boy and speaking words of rebuke to the one who plagues him, Jesus cleanses the boy of this unclean spirit. Jesus, who was transfigured atop the mountain, has descended to drive out what opposes God and harms us. That unclean spirit is the spirit of a world closed to the Father's love.

Peter saw all of this. Peter saw Jesus in radiating glory above, and Peter saw Jesus come down the mountain and plunge himself into the crowd where an unclean spirit waits. Peter wanted to dwell in Jesus's glory, but he did not understand what he said. Peter, in following Jesus down the mountain, saw that the glory of God is revealed in Jesus.

Appealing again to Paul's hymn to the Philippians, we can say that gazing upon Jesus, Peter saw him who, though he is the beloved Son of God, did not remain up above in light; rather, "he emptied himself," descending the mountain, his divine radiance hidden, "coming in human likeness; and found human in appearance." He went into the crowd and "healed the boy, and returned him to his father. And all were astonished by the majesty of God" (Luke 9:42-43, NABRE).

It is easier and more likely to read the transfiguration account as just being what happens atop Mount Tabor, but that leaves us in the same position as Peter—not understanding what we see. Peter wanted to dwell with Jesus, but dwelling with Jesus means following Jesus, and Jesus goes down the mountain toward *us*, to heal *us*, and to return *us* to *his* Father. This Jesus who went from the Promised Land into Israel's desert of temptation is the same one who comes down from glory into a world possessed of an unclean spirit.[4]

4. Portions of this section come from my *Work of Love: A Theological Reconstruction of the Communion of Saints* (Notre Dame, IN: University of Notre Dame Press, 2017), 191–95.

So who is Jesus? Jesus is the Son of God who comes to us—sinners—in our mess.

A Daily Prayer to Jesus

As I mentioned above, I will close each of these four chapters dedicated to "Who is Jesus?" with the prayer a saint prayed to Jesus. In each of these prayers, we can hear each saint saying something in response to the question of "Who is Jesus for me?":

> O Jesus,
> I promise to submit myself to all that you allow to happen to me.
> Only make me know your will.
> My most sweet Jesus,
> infinitely merciful God,
> most tender Father of souls and especially the weak,
> the most wretched,
> the sickest whom you carry with special tenderness in your divine arms,
> I come to you to request by the love and merits of your Sacred Heart
> the grace of understanding and always doing your holy will,
> the grace of trusting in you,
> the grace of resting securely for time and for eternity
> in your loving, divine arms.
>
> –St. Gianna Beretta Molla[5]

5. Pietro Molla and Elio Guerriero, *Saint Gianna Molla: Wife, Mother, Doctor*, trans. James Colbert (San Francisco: Ignatius, 2004) 136.

chapter eight

Who Is Jesus? I AM

Prelude to the Name

What's in a name? This is not Shakespeare; it's Scripture. Well, it's not exactly a line from Scripture, though it is a central question for salvation in Scripture. The question is not just about any name; it is about the name of God. What's in *that* name?

To take this question seriously, we should begin with that event in the history of Israel where God gives over his name. This happens, of course, with Moses out in the wilderness, in a burning bush, while the Israelites are still in slavery in Egypt. This event is given to us in the third chapter of the Book of Exodus. But the introduction of God actually begins just a little earlier in Exodus, at the end of chapter 2.

By the end of chapter 2, quite a lot has already happened. It has now been about four hundred years since the entire house of Jacob—Israel—came down to Egypt. It was through Jacob's son Joseph that Egypt prospered during a worldwide famine and fed the other nations, thus increasing Egypt's wealth and the power of its pharaoh. But Jacob and Joseph are long dead, as are all the other sons of Jacob. The pharaoh that is now in power "did not know Joseph" (Exod 1:8, JPS) and so he does not know that his kingdom's power grew from the gift of the Israelites. All the pharaoh sees when he looks at the Israelites—who have grown exponentially in number—is a workforce and a potential threat. Pharaoh's entire agenda relative to the Israelites is to keep them pinned down and thus render them harmless to his own power. He orders that the male children of the Israelites be killed at birth. In this setting, Moses is born, but hidden, then raised by Egyptians in the pharaoh's household (and ironically cared for by his own mother). As Moses grows, he has standing with Pharaoh but he also identifies with his own people. He once saw an Egyptian beating a Hebrew, so he defended the Hebrew by killing the Egyptian. Then he fled to the countryside, where he lived for years. He married Zipporah out there and they had a son. And that brings us to the final verses of chapter 2, where we read:

> A long time after, the king of Egypt died. The Israelites were groaning under the bondage and cried out; and their cry for help from the bondage rose up to God. God heard their moaning, and God remembered His covenant with Abraham and Isaac and Jacob. God looked upon the Israelites, and God took notice of them. (Exod 2:23-25, JPS)

In this passage, we discover something about God for the first time in the Book of Exodus. The Israelites are crying out and their cries are "going up." And what does God do? God hears, God takes notice, and God remembers by identifying this people according to their ancestors.

So what? What does it mean for God to take notice? That is what we are about to find out. As the next chapter begins, Moses is tending his father-in-law's flock and approaching the mountain of Horeb. It is upon this mountain that Moses sees a bush aflame but not consumed. And here is what happens:

> God called out to him out of the bush. "Moses! Moses! . . . I am," He said, "the God of your father, the God of Abraham, the God of Isaac, and the God of Jacob." . . .
>
> And the Lord continued, "I have marked well the plight of My people in Egypt and have heeded their outcry because of their taskmasters; yes, I am mindful of their sufferings. I have come to rescue them from the Egyptians and to bring them out of that land" . . .
>
> Moses said to God, "When I come to the Israelites and say to them, 'The God of your father has sent me to you,' and they ask me, 'What is His name?' what shall I say to them?"
>
> And God said to Moses, "*Ehyeh-Asher-Ehyeh*." (Exod 3:4-6, 7-8, 13-14, JPS)

Though the Hebrew here is transliterated, I have intentionally left it untranslated because we need to ask our crucial question: What's in *this* name?

The Revelation of the Name

If we were to ask just about any English speaker who has even a passing familiarity with the Bible how this name that God gave to Moses should be translated, the person would almost certainly respond with "I Am Who (I) Am" or simply, "I AM." And that would be correct. That is a faithful translation of this given name, which the tetragram YHWH then comes to mark.

What we hear when we translate this name as "I Am Who Am" is just how substantive this God is. This is the God *who is*. Full stop. This is like the most concrete of all concrete existence. It is not to be surpassed: God is. Maybe we can say that this is like the noun quality of the name. The super-noun quality. The super-proper noun.

But we also lose something pretty important in English when we accept this as the exclusive translation of the name. There is more to this name in the Hebrew, yet we do not hear it because we do not know we should. That is because in addition to this "noun" sense, which rightly conveys substance and being, there is also something like a "verb" sense in the Hebrew name. Maybe a super-verb sense. The verb sense would offer another equally accurate translation of the name: "I Will Be What I Will Be."

So what did Moses hear? Moses asked for the Lord's name, but has the Lord really given a name? Has he told Moses who he is? The answer is yes and no, because at the very same time, the Lord gives a name and tells Moses to wait for the Lord's name. On the one hand, this name means "I Am What I Am" and, on the other hand, it means "If you want to know who I am, watch what I do . . . what I do will tell you who I am."

If we observe and revere this name rightly, we discover we need to get away from a certain way of thinking about God. We cannot think of God as *something* or even *someone* who then happens to do certain *things*. Rather, we must see that we only come to know who God is through what God does. In other words, God reveals his name in his deeds. God shows us who he is.

In the Book of Exodus, then, who does God reveal himself to be? We can actually let the Israelites tell it, from the other side of the Red Sea. Having been loosened from the bonds of slavery through the ten plagues and given a clear path through the waters that then swallowed up their persecutors, we read:

> Moses and the people of Israel sang this song unto the Lord:
> I will sing to the Lord, for he has triumphed gloriously;
> the horse and his rider he has thrown into the sea.
> The Lord is my strength and my song,
> and he has become my salvation;
> This is my God, and I will praise him. (Exod 15:1-2, RSV)

So who is the Lord God? What is his name? Right here, the Israelites proclaim that they know. They have seen his work, they have known his deeds, and they have reaped the benefits. So who is he? They say, "He is my strength. He is my song. He is *my* salvation."

Moses was instructed to tell the Israelites that the Lord's name is "I Am Who I Am" and "I Will Be What I Will Be." The Israelites have come to know him because they have seen him and they are now testifying to him. He is their salvation. That's his name.

The Power of Presence

If we make space in our minds to hold onto the revelation of the name in the Book of Exodus when we read the gospels, we will discover Jesus anew. We can even limit ourselves just to one gospel—the Gospel of John—to see how the name of God from Exodus is brought forth in the person of Jesus.

When the disciples went out on the sea by themselves and a storm hit, while they were three or four miles from shore, they saw Jesus walking on the water coming toward them. They were afraid. And Jesus said: "'It is I. Do not be afraid.' Then they were glad to take him into the boat, and immediately the boat was at the land to which they were going" (John 6:20-21, RSV; cf. Mark 6:50). What is here translated as "It is I" may also be translated as "I am." As the disciples look upon the one who has power over the elements, they hear this same one pronounce the name of God: "I am."

In his long discourse with the disciples in John 8, Jesus tells his disciples, "You belong to what is below, I belong to what is above. You belong to this world, but I do not belong to this world. That is why I told you that you will die in your sins. For if you do not believe that I AM, you will die in your sins" (8:23-24). The disciples immediately ask him the critical question: "Who are you?" Jesus again responds with the name of God: "When you lift up the Son of Man, then you will realize that I AM" (8:28). And again, as this discourse draws to a close before a new episode begins, Jesus completes his address, now offered to the Jews, by saying, "Amen, amen, I say to you, before Abraham came to be, I AM" (8:58; NABRE). On the water, Jesus had shown himself in his power before uttering the divine name, and now he has claimed this divine name as his own in response to the question "Who are you?"

One final episode in the Gospel of John brings us to the night of Jesus's arrest, when Judas and the soldiers come to him in the garden (see John 18:1-8). To them, Jesus asks, "Whom are you looking for?" They answer, "Jesus the Nazorean." And Jesus says to them, "I AM." And immediately these men are thrown to the ground by the force of the name. He asks them again whom they seek, and again they say, "Jesus the Nazorean," and he answers them, "I told you that I AM" (NABRE). Judas and the soldiers have come seeking a mere man, and what they encounter is the power of God.

What these three episodes reveal—alongside all the other "I am" sayings in the gospels—is that Jesus is one with the God of Israel. The one who has acted for Israel throughout salvation history is acting now. Jesus is the action of God.

The Name of Jesus

The question of "Who is Jesus?" is inseparable from the question of God's name, and vice versa. That is why, in light of the gospel, there is even more for us to grasp from the burning bush, and the deeds recounted in Exodus, and the acclamations of the ancient Israelites. What is here for us is wonderfully expressed in the words of Joseph Ratzinger (later Pope Benedict XVI) who wrote:

> The name of Jesus brings the mysterious name at the burning bush to its fulfillment; now we can see that God had not said all that he had to say but had interrupted his discourse for a time. This is because the name "Jesus" in its Hebrew form includes the word "Yahweh" and adds a further element to it: God "saves."

> "I am who I am"—thanks to Jesus, this now means: "I am the one who saves you." His Being is salvation.[1]

Remember that the first thing we heard about God in the Book of Exodus was that God heard the cry of the people Israel, and God remembered them, and God took notice of them. And then God showed what it means for God to take notice: it does not mean to respond with an explanation—like, "Here's why you're in slavery" or "Here's why there's evil"—but rather with an action. God responds by drawing near. God responds by liberating. God responds by giving his name through what he does. Their cries "went up" and God "came down."

What Ratzinger is marveling at is that this very movement of God is not complete in the Book of Exodus. That movement is complete in the person of Jesus, who, as we read at the beginning of St. John's gospel, was with God on high and was God on high, but then came down: "And the Word became flesh and dwelt among us" (1:14, RSV).

Ratzinger is also sort of delighting in the literal name of Jesus, which literally means "God saves." Jesus is God's saving action: he is the name of God; he gives God's name to us.

To tie this together, then, I need to make one last connection, which is this: What was true of the Israelites on the other side of the Red Sea is also true of us if we are to call the name "Jesus." The Israelites knew God's name because they recognized him as their salvation, their Savior. Their answer to the question "Who is God?" was "The one who has saved me! The one who has liberated me! My strength! My song!"

What does that mean for the name of Jesus? It means that to know God's name in full is to recognize Jesus as *my* salvation. It means seeing his deeds, accepting his deeds, and being grateful.

"Who are you?" the disciples asked, to which Jesus's whole life says, "I am your salvation."

1. Joseph Ratzinger, *The God of Jesus Christ: Meditations on the Triune God*, trans. Brian McNeil, 2nd ed. (San Francisco: Ignatius Press, 2018), 34.

A Prayer to Love the Lord

I love you, O my God,
and my only desire is to love you
until the last breath of my life.

I love you,
O my infinitely lovable God,
and I would rather die loving you,
than live without loving you.

I love you, Lord,
and the only grace I ask
is to love you eternally. . . .

My God, if my tongue cannot say
in every moment that I love you,
I want my heart to repeat it to you
as often as I draw breath.

Amen.

–St. John Vianney[2]

2. John Vianney, "Prayer of St. John Vianney," quoted in CCC 2658.

chapter nine

Who Is Jesus? The Power and Wisdom of God

The Name above Every Other Name

Jesus claims as his own the name that the God of Israel gave to Moses. The pledge that "I Will Be What I Will Be" is fulfilled in the Son of the Father who says, "I AM." So here is an easy follow-up question: Is this name that Jesus claims power or weakness? Obviously, power! . . . Right?

Think about what people with power are like and what people with power typically do. People with power are in control. They get their way. They win. They are the kind of people about whom it is said that if you cannot beat them, you better join them. Powerful people can direct other people, and they usually do. Powerful people also want to hold on to power or, even better, increase their power if at all possible.

Perhaps we have similar notions in mind when we hear St. Paul call Jesus Christ "the power of God and the wisdom of God" (1 Cor 1:24, RSV). It is tempting to hold on to just that line and presume to know what it means because of a preexisting understanding of what power is. There seem to be endless examples of power in the world, with the list we just rehearsed above standing as a mere representation. But St. Paul's declaration gets a little peculiar in the very next verse, when he says that "[t]he foolishness of God is wiser than men, and the weakness of God is stronger than men" (1 Cor 1:25, RSV). How and why did foolishness suddenly become wisdom and weakness become power?

Power Made Strange

Jesus does not fulfill an expectation of power according to "conventional wisdom." Rather, he is the revelation of the power and wisdom of God. He shows what true power is according to God's way of reckoning. Jesus is not what we expect.

I propose we lay aside our expectations so we can gaze with fresh eyes on Jesus. Let's just trust what St. Paul says—that Jesus is "the power of God and the wisdom of God"—without presuming to know in advance what power and wisdom are. Let's see if we can be flexible enough to allow Jesus to disturb the ways we might tidily separate wisdom from foolishness and power from weakness. And let's do this by focusing on four different gospel episodes to see how, in Jesus, power is made strange. With each episode, let's try to answer this question: If Jesus is the power of God, what does that power look like here?

Episode 1: The Death of Lazarus

Jesus was close to Mary and Martha, and their brother Lazarus. When Lazarus was ill, the sisters sent word to Jesus. He did not come right away. In fact, he waited until Lazarus had died before he started moving toward the house. When Martha heard Jesus was coming, she ran out to meet him. A little later, Mary ran out to meet him. And this is the key passage for us:

> Then Mary, when she came where Jesus was and saw him, fell at his feet, saying to him, "Lord, if you had been here, my brother would not have died." When Jesus saw her weeping, and the Jews who came with her also weeping, he was deeply moved in spirit and troubled; and he said, "Where have you laid him?" They said to him, "Lord, come and see." Jesus wept. (John 11:32-35, RSV)[1]

This should strike us as bizarre. Jesus is troubled, even though just moments ago he had declared to Martha, "I am the resurrection and the life; he who believes in me, though he die, yet shall he live, and

1. For a reflection on this particular question of Jesus—"Where have you laid him?"—see my *A God Who Questions* (Huntington, IN: Our Sunday Visitor, 2019), 75–78.

whoever lives and believes in me shall never die" (John 11:25-26, RSV). He *is* the power of new life that conquers death, and yet what he does here seems like weakness: Jesus weeps.

Episode 2: Washing the Disciples' Feet

All through the Gospel of John there is a tight tension of anticipation and fulfillment. One prominent signal of this tension is with the repeated mention of Jesus's appointed "hour." His "hour" is mentioned seventeen times. On the night before he died, as he gathered with his disciples in the Upper Room, "Jesus knew that his hour had come" (13:1, RSV). With all the notes of anticipation from the beginning of his ministry, it is now clear that this is what he has been waiting for.

In this apical moment, here is what he did:

> Jesus, knowing that the Father had given all things into his hands, and that he had come from God and was going to God, rose from supper, laid aside his garments, and tied a towel around himself. Then he poured water into a basin, and began to wash the disciples' feet, and to wipe them with the towel that was tied around him. (John 13:3-5, RSV)

Again, this is bizarre. Jesus possess all things from the Father, and he knows it. Now he is at the moment that his whole life has been building toward, and with all that he is and all that he has, he displays his power by doing what? By washing feet. We are looking for a display of power and what do we see? Jesus serves.

Episode 3: The Agony in the Garden

For the remainder of this final night before his arrest, when Jesus can still move where he wills, he does what he did over and over again: he goes off to pray. It was, as St. Luke so aptly puts it, "his custom" (Luke 22:39, RSV). Because Judas and the crowd come to seize him immediately afterward, what happens on the Mount of Olives could be considered his last free act (though of course, in a far more significant way, the entire passion is itself Christ's free act). In this garden, he freely dedicates himself to his mission, and it sounded and looked like this:

> "Father, if you are willing, remove this chalice from me; nevertheless not my will, but yours, be done." And there appeared to him an angel from heaven, strengthening him. And being in agony he prayed more earnestly; and his sweat became like great drops of blood falling down upon the ground. (Luke 22:42-44, RSV)

Jesus had just told his disciples that "my Father appointed a kingdom for me" (Luke 22:29, RSV), and here he is, calling upon that same Father, weakened and sweating in agony. It was "his custom" to go off and pray, it is by his power that he came to this place, and it is by his own free will that he seeks the Father's will. This is the beginning of his last act—his totally free act—and what do we see of him? Jesus suffers.

Episode 4: The Crucifixion

Kings are rulers: when they speak, other people heed what they say. Their words make things happen; people move because of what they utter. It is hard to imagine a form of power higher than regal power. It is a kind of power that is unrivaled: the power of the realm is invested in the king.

Jesus's accusers charge him with claiming to be a king (Luke 23:2-3). They have not been moved by his words, so they render him silent and move him as they wish. And when they made a parody of his enthronement by raising him on a cross, St. Luke tells us:

> [T]he people stood by, watching; but the rulers scoffed at him, saying, "He saved others; let him save himself, if he is the Christ of God, his Chosen One!" The soldiers also mocked him, coming up and offering him vinegar, and saying, "If you are the King of the Jews, save yourself!" There was also an inscription over him, "This is the King of the Jews." (Luke 23:35-38, RSV)

This is the ultimate denial of Christ's power. He is rendered powerless and ridiculed for his helplessness. It appears to all that he cannot make things happen, that he cannot move other people, that no one is subject to him because he has been made subject to them. This is the one to whom a kingdom has been appointed? We come in search of one invested with the power of the realm and what do we find? Jesus is mocked.

If Jesus is one with the God of Israel, what is the God of Israel doing in each of these episodes? He weeps; he serves; he suffers; and he is mocked. Is it really true that Jesus is the power of God if this is what happens to him? Yes.

The Correction of Power

Power in Jesus is not what we would otherwise expect. More often than not, it is not the kind of power we want. It would not be an overstatement to say that all of us are corrupted by delusions of grandeur and by desires for kinds of power—sometimes very subtle—that would lift us up above others. This was precisely what James and John, the sons of Zebedee, had in mind when they came to Jesus with a request: "And they said to him, 'Grant us to sit, one at your right hand and one at your left, in your glory'" (Mark 10:37). When he heard this request, Jesus replied, "You do not know what you are asking" (10:38, RSV).

James and John wanted to be lifted up by sharing in Jesus's power. They thought they knew what power was, but they had no idea what Jesus's power really is. It is not just them, though, since the other ten were furious with them because, it seems, James and John wanted to be elevated over them (10:41). Even the Twelve who gather around Jesus had a lot of worldly ideas about power. It was to all of them that Jesus said:

> "You know that those who are supposed to rule over the Gentiles lord it over them, and their great men exercise authority over them. But it shall not be among you; but whoever would be great among you must be your servant, and whoever would be first among you must be slave of all. For the Son of man also came not to be served but to serve, and to give his life as a ransom for many." (Mark 10:42-45, RSV)

Jesus tells his disciples what the "power of God" is by these words, and then later he reveals the "power of God" in what he does: weeping, serving, suffering, and being mocked. Wisdom comes from learning to see these things as the marks of divine power.

When St. Paul prayed that the thorn in his flesh might be removed, the Lord responded to him by saying, "My grace is sufficient for you, for my power is made perfect in weakness" (2 Cor 12:9, RSV). How in the world can power be made perfect in weakness? It is so because Jesus claims as his own the power to *not* play the world's games of power. He is free of that trap. In the world, it always goes the same way: those with power cling to it and seek to exert their power over others. The power of God is the power to be free of that game. God is powerful enough to weep, serve, suffer, and be mocked in order to save those he loves.

We will remember from Exodus that God instructs Moses to tell the Israelites, "What I do will show you who I am." In his passion and death, Jesus says, "I am the one who is *for you,* no matter the cost." In Jesus, God has given everything to the point of weakness. That is the power of God.

A Prayer before the Eucharist

O boundless charity!
Just as you gave us yourself,
wholly God and wholly man,
so you left us all of yourself as food
so that while we are pilgrims in this life
we might not collapse in our weariness
but be strengthened by you, heavenly food.

O mercenary people!
And what has your God left you?
He has left you himself,
wholly God and wholly man,
hidden under the whiteness of bread.

O fire of love!
Was it not enough to gift us
with creation in your image and likeness,
and to create us anew to grace in your Son's blood,
without giving us yourself as food,
the whole of divine being, the whole of God?

What drove you?
Nothing but your charity,
mad with love as you are!

Amen.

—St. Catherine of Siena[2]

2. Benedict J. Groeschel, ed., *Praying in the Presence of Our Lord: Prayers for Eucharistic Adoration* (Huntington, IN: Our Sunday Visitor, 1999), 44.

chapter ten

Who Is Jesus? The Gift of Beatitude

Jesus is the power and the wisdom of God, but this is not power as we would otherwise expect, nor does he seem wise by the world's standards. In Christ, the power of God is made perfect in weakness, which looks pretty strange. Jesus is the full manifestation of divine power, in whom God has given everything to the point of weakness, which looks a lot like the opposite of how power typically appears. As we saw, the power of God looks like weeping, serving, suffering, and being mocked.

If we imagined the opposite of those four marks of divine power in Christ, we would probably end up with a far better set of descriptions concerning what most people would expect from power. When we went through those four episodes to see power made strange in the last chapter, I arranged those episodes chronologically as Jesus approaches and enters into his passion. To think about the opposite of each of those marks, though, I am going to slightly rearrange them for reasons that will become clear before long.

With the Agony in the Garden (Luke 22:39-66), we saw that Jesus suffers. The opposite of suffering would be doing what you prefer, following your whims and wishes, and enjoying comfort. In a word, we might say that the opposite of suffering is to indulge.

With the washing of the disciples' feet (John 13:1-14), we saw that Jesus serves. In the language of Philippians 2, he was "taking the form of a slave." The opposite of serving would be to command, to consume, and to use others. In a word, we might say that the opposite of serving is to lord over.

With the death of Lazarus (John 11:28-35), we saw that Jesus weeps. To avoid weeping, one would remain unbothered, concerned only with one's own happiness, and set on pleasure. In a word, the opposite of weeping is to laugh.

With the crucifixion (Luke 23:33-38), we saw that Jesus was mocked. One who avoids being in a position to be mocked might ridicule others, laugh at others, and exalt oneself above others. In a word, the opposite of being mocked is to be praised.

These four pairs of opposites might seem random, until we are given the chance to see them in a new way. This new way of seeing is offered in Jesus's own preaching. These pairs of suffering—indulging, serving—lording over, weeping—laughing, and being mocked—being praised provide the structure for the heart of Jesus's Sermon on the Plain: the Beatitudes.[1]

As we find the Beatitudes in the Gospel of Luke, Jesus preaches them according to a set of blessings and then a set of curses. Here is the first part, the blessings:

> "Blessed are you poor, for yours is the kingdom of God.
> "Blessed are you that hunger now, for you shall be satisfied.
> "Blessed are you that weep now, for you shall laugh.
> "Blessed are you when men hate you, and when they exclude you and revile you, and cast out your name as evil, on account of the Son of man!" (Luke 6:20-22, RSV)

The blessings fall upon those who are poor, hungry, weeping, and reviled. Seen from one angle, we could say that in his suffering, serving, weeping, and being mocked, Jesus shares the plight of those he blesses. Seen from another angle, though, we could say that the poor, hungry, sorrowful, and excluded are drawn into the life of Christ. Those who are blessed are on the side of the power of God.

The second part of the Beatitudes is like an echo of the first, but an echo in which everything is switched around. Instead of blessings, there are curses:

1. The full list of eight beatitudes is, of course, in Matthew's Sermon on the Mount (5:3-11). I am appealing here to Luke's version precisely because it provides the parallels of opposites that contrast the power of God to the power of the world.

> "Woe to you that are rich, for you have received your consolation.
> "Woe to you that are full now, for you shall hunger.
> "Woe to you that laugh now, for you shall mourn and weep.
> "Woe to you, when all men speak well of you, for so their fathers did to the false prophets." (Luke 6:24-26, RSV)

The curses fall on those who are rich, full, laughing, and praised. It turns out that these are not just on the opposite side of the poor, hungry, sorrowful, and excluded, but indeed on the opposite side of Christ who suffers, serves, weeps, and is mocked. Even more, these seem much more like the marks of those who persecuted Christ than anything else. If those who are blessed align with the power of God, those who are cursed align with the power of the world.

The Beatitudes thus present two opposing images of power. One side presents power as power is consistently presented in the world, according to might and violence and exploitation. The other side—the side of blessing—is taken up into the revelation of the power of God.

To respond to the question of "Who is Jesus?" is not just a matter of words, but also a matter of how you live. To live in the name of Jesus means practicing the power of God, by God's wisdom. If you are not poor, you throw your lot in with those who are. If you are not hungry, you give of your fill to those who are. If you are not sorrowful, you share in the sorrow of those who are. And if you are not the object of ridicule, you join yourself with those who are. The power of God is siding with the lowly, in the name of Jesus Christ.

By his own words, Jesus assures us that those who heed the lowly will come to know him, and those who neglect the lowly will be separated from him: "as you did it to one of the least of these my brethren, you did it to me" and "as you did it not to one of the least of these, you did it not to me" (Matt 25:40, 45, RSV). Jesus instructs those who seek him—those who want to know who he is—to live into him by practicing the works of mercy. This means that by feeding the hungry, giving drink to the thirsty, clothing the naked, sheltering the homeless, visiting the sick, visiting the imprisoned, and burying the dead, we come to know more of who Jesus is. Likewise, by instructing the ignorant, counseling the doubtful, admonishing sinners, bearing wrongs patiently, forgiving offenses, comforting the afflicted, and praying for the living and the dead, we are drawn into the life of the one who has drawn near to us in our need.

In these four chapters of contemplating the central question of "Who is Jesus?" we have discovered the following: Jesus is the Son of the Father who comes to us as we are (even in our mess). Jesus is one with the God of Israel; he reveals the name of God. In Jesus, God has given everything to the point of becoming weak. And Jesus is the way, the truth, and the life whom we profess both by what we say and by how we live. Rather than doing away with the deeply personal question that the Church echoes down through the ages on behalf of the Lord, all of this only serves to deliver to each of us and all of us together the single question on which the faith of the Church depends: "But who do you say that I am?" (Mark 8:29, RSV).

A Prayer to Live in Christ

Lord, make me an instrument of your peace.
Where there is hatred, let me bring love.
Where there is offense, let me bring pardon.
Where there is discord, let me bring union.
Where there is error, let me bring truth.
Where there is doubt, let me bring faith.
Where there is despair, let me bring hope.
Where there is darkness, let me bring your light.
Where there is sadness, let me bring joy.

O Master, let me not seek as much
to be consoled as to console,
to be understood as to understand,
to be loved as to love,
for it is in giving that one receives,
it is in self-forgetting that one finds,
it is in pardoning that one is pardoned,
it is in dying that one is raised to eternal life.

Amen.

—"Peace Prayer," attributed to St. Francis of Assisi

chapter eleven

Advent: Prepare the Way of the Lord

If the Lord were coming, what would you do? Would you pray and ready your heart? Would you examine your conscience and mend your ways? Would you seek out others to proclaim the Good News? Would you shift your focus to those in need?

The problem, of course, is that no one knows when the Lord is coming. Anyone who claims to know is either delusional or lying. Jesus himself tells his disciples, "But of that day and hour no one knows, not even the angels of heaven, nor the Son, but the Father only" (Matt 24:36, RSV). The coming of the Lord will be the end and fulfillment of history, and this event is hidden within the mystery of God's salvific will.

This does not, however, mean that because no one can know the day or the hour, that Christians should remain unprepared. Quite to the contrary, Christians are called to continual readiness. Wouldn't that mean, depending on what you answered above, that the practices of the Christian life should be filled with prayer, examination of conscience and repentance, proclamation, and contemplating the needs of others and acting on their needs? These practices of readiness resonate with the parable of the Wise and Foolish Maidens that Jesus tells his disciples right after telling them that no one knows the day or the hour. The ones who were wise stayed ready, while the ones who were foolish waited until they knew the Lord was coming to begin their preparations. It was too late for the foolish ones, for while they went off and tried to quickly prepare themselves, "the bridegroom came, and those who were ready went in with him to the marriage feast; and the door was shut" (Matt 25:10, RSV). Remaining ready is no small matter—everything might hang in the balance.

The Church lives between memory and hope: the memory of Christ who has come and the hope of Christ who will come again. Even while Christ is made present in and through the Church, the life of the Church is always preparation for the final union with Christ. In the Church's liturgical life, Advent is the season of practicing perpetual watchfulness. Advent is not just one cordoned-off season, but a practice for life. As one preacher put it, "Advent is a time of being deeply shaken, so that man will wake up to himself."[1] The point, then, is to remain awake and vigilant, to increase in hope.

To hope for the Lord who will shake the earth at the end, it is imperative to remember the Lord who has already shaken the world in Jesus Christ. If we look to the Gospel, we will see all manner of reactions to the coming of the Lord, but some of those reactions are left to our imaginations, especially in parts of Scripture that we might otherwise pass over too quickly. One such part is a short passage that seems intended to simply set the scene for the important stuff to come. But if we slow down and ponder this passage with a little guidance, we will see how much the issue of preparing the way for the Lord is pulsing through every word. This passage comes at the very beginning of Luke 3, following the infancy narratives that closed chapter 2, and inaugurates the years of Jesus's active ministry. This is how Luke 3 begins:

> In the fifteenth year of the reign of Tibe'ri-us Caesar, Pontius Pilate being governor of Judea, and Herod being tetrarch of Galilee, and his brother Philip tetrarch of the region of Iturae'a and Trachoni'tis, and Lysa'ni-as tetrarch of Abile'ne, in the high-priesthood of Annas and Ca'iphas, the word of God came to John the son of Zechari'ah in the wilderness. (3:1-2, RSV)

It is unlikely that anyone would cite this as their favorite Scripture passage. This is just a list of names connected to places most people have never heard of. Clearly, it seems, the only purpose is to get to that

1. Alfred Delp, *Advent of the Heart: Seasonal Sermons and Prison Writings, 1941–1944* (San Francisco: Ignatius, 2006), 23.

name at the end—John—whose words and actions announcing the coming of the Lord in the verses to follow are what's really important. That might be true if the only thing that mattered were the coming of the Lord and not the issue of readiness to meet him. These names are indicators of readiness—or lack thereof.

To help us meditate on this more fully, I turn to a sermon by a priest who was ordained in 1937 in Germany. The beginning of his priesthood—and, actually, the entirety of his priesthood—was lived out in the time of the Third Reich's dominance. His name is Alfred Delp and, as a preacher, he presented Advent as a way of life. Especially in a time and place that was maximally inhospitable to the Word of God, he preached brilliant and challenging sermons in Advent "so that man will wake up to himself." Fr. Delp was eventually arrested and even put into solitary confinement, but he kept writing sermons on little slips of scrap paper that were smuggled out of the prison in his laundry. He wrote in handcuffs. He wrote throughout periods of intense sleep deprivation. He kept preaching, especially on Advent, because readiness mattered and the truth was too valuable. He wrote and preached until the Nazis executed him on February 2, 1945.

On the Fourth Sunday of Advent in 1941, before he was arrested, he preached on the figure of John the Baptist and, in the process, broke open this passage from the beginning of Luke 3. In doing so, he focused on each of the figures recounted in those two verses, identifying what kind of person each one was and what each person really wanted. Here is what Fr. Delp had to say:

> Tiberius Caesar . . . This was the Roman Emperor. This was the co-regent and heir of Augustus. This was the man who, to secure his own power, granted his predecessor more and more divine honors, because he knew that reverence for an emperor who is dead implies reverence for the emperor who is alive. . . .
>
> Pontius Pilate. This was a man who wanted the world . . . This was the man who ordered the emperor's image set up in the sacred space; and this was the man who had only one priority in his life: to remain a friend of Caesar. . . .
>
> Herod. This was the son of a profligate father, the son of a man with nine wives, whose father wasted all his energy on his passions . . . Herod was a sly, self-indulgent hedonist. He knew only one thing: how to follow his impulses. . . .

> Philip (Herod's brother) was an innocuous type, harmless, not dangerous, but hooked on foreign traditions. He betrayed his people through foreign rights, foreign morals, and foreign customs. Nothing could be expected from him. . . .
>
> Lysanias. He was a harmless and unremarkable man, who presented no danger, but could not be expected to protect human rights, his people, or the civil order. . . .
>
> Annas. He was high priest for nine years and, afterward, he bought the office year after year for his family of five sons. . . .
>
> Caiaphas (Annas's son-in-law). This backstabbing, gruesome, hard-hearted fellow who had discovered one thing: religion as a means to power . . .
>
> Think of it: When was there a more hopeless hour?[2]

From these names of figures who seem, at first glance, to be merely fill-ins before we get to the stuff that really matters, we are given, with Delp's help, a vivid picture of the time and place in which John the Baptist proclaimed the coming of the Lord. To recap: Caesar wants to makes himself into a god, Pilate is consumed by ambition, Herod does whatever he pleases, Philip is addicted to exotic and new things, Lysanias is weak and unreliable, Annas buys what he wants, and Caiaphas uses religion to secure his own power. These are the lords of this time and place; everyone in this region is subject to this swirl of passions.

If there is one rule that these figures hold in common, it is this: Increase your own power and prestige if possible, but whatever happens do not lose what you have. In their own way, all of these individuals are fundamentally committed to protecting their station, their authority, their influence and ease of life. This is the setting in which "the word of God came to John the son of Zechariah," but notice where John is: he is not in the middle of this matrix of power; instead he is off in the wilderness. He is in an arid place of desire and longing.

What does this lonely man, this insignificant man, this man off the grid and out of the way of the powers of his day, preach to the crowds? He echoes the words of the prophet Isaiah, who prophesied about the coming of the Lord:

2. Delp, *Advent of the Heart*, 128–30.

> "The voice of one crying in the wilderness:
> Prepare the way of the Lord,
> make his paths straight.
> Every valley shall be filled,
> and every mountain and hill shall be brought low,
> and the crooked shall be made straight,
> and the rough ways shall be made smooth;
> and all flesh shall see the salvation of God."
> (Luke 3:4-6, RSV; cf. Isa 40:3-5)

After everything we have just discovered about that litany of power figures that open this chapter in Luke's gospel, do you see how stunning the proclamation of John really is? The high things—the mountains—are not just abstract images; the towering mountains are named Caesar, Pilate, Herod, Philip, Lysanias, Annas, and Caiaphas. These are the ones whose power overshadows the plains and valleys of the land and its people. John the Baptist is proclaiming that the time of the great reversal is at hand: the high things will be made low, and the low things will be raised up. The Lord is coming, and for him all the paths will be cleared and the rough things smoothed out. The ones who lord over others with their passions twist everything to their own purposes, but the Lord of all is about to straighten things out. No wonder John was executed by the powers of his day.

We should pay attention not only to the message of John the Baptist, though, but also to what he does. The crowds are flocking to John, listening to his message, begging him to teach them, and giving themselves over to the baptism he offers. To put it succinctly: John is becoming powerful. He is becoming important. He is growing in influence. But what does he do?

John walks away and gives his place of prominence to the one coming after him. John chooses to lose. "I baptize you with water," he says, "but he who is mightier than I is coming, the thong of whose sandals I am not worthy to untie; he will baptize you with the Holy Spirit and with fire" (Luke 3:16). In the Gospel of John, John the Baptist says that with the coming of the Lord, his joy is full and that now "[h]e must increase, but I must decrease" (John 3:30, RSV). This is precisely what none of the powerful figures of his day would ever dare to do: unlike all of them, John makes room.

Between John and all those other figures, we see the decisive difference that preparing for the Lord makes. To prepare for the Lord means to be ready to give Jesus the center of your life. It looks and sounds like a whole bunch of "no's": "no" to acting like a god, "no" to being consumed by ambition, "no" to doing whatever you want, "no" to being distracted by shiny new things, "no" to shirking responsibilities, "no" to using your wealth to get your way, and even "no" to practicing religion as a means to power. But all of these "no's" are really just preparation for one gigantic "YES." The "yes," in the end, is the "yes" of John the Baptist: the "yes" that gives the Lord, who is the center of history, the central place in your own life.

The upshot of all of this is that Advent is a dangerous time. Advent is a time of reckoning for the powers of this world. And for much the same reason, Advent is a time of hope for those who are lowly and all those who, alongside the lowly, make themselves meek in a posture of waiting for the Lord.

chapter twelve

Advent: Waiting for the Lord

Who waits for the Lord? Certainly not those figures who hoarded power in the time of John the Baptist. Their ironclad rule of "don't lose" would never permit them to welcome another who would claim lordship over them. To wait for him would mean being willing to change, to become obedient, and to learn to rejoice in what the Lord rejoices in. Those power players were dead set against being shaken like that.

So if these are not the kind of people who wait for the Lord, then who is? To whom is the coming of the Lord good news? Not the high and mighty, but the down and out. It is the meek and lowly who await the Lord.

Let's remember that when John the Baptist announced the imminent coming of the Lord, he proclaimed words from the book of the prophet Isaiah. It was Isaiah who heard a voice ring out—the voice of God—to say that the high things would be made low, the low things raised up, and the crooked things made straight. Those who heard John's proclamation would know whose words John was repeating, and they would also know the setting in which Isaiah himself proclaimed that message. When Isaiah prophesied, Israel was in exile, under the power of the Babylonian empire. To give a sense of scale, it would be like if Haiti were conquered by the United States, and the Haitians removed from their land and exiled in the US.

What does it mean to live under an unimaginably strong foreign power like that? For Israel, it meant they did not enjoy the freedom to practice their religion, for the Babylonian's state religion, which was tied into their political structure, was the only one allowed. The Israelites could not speak as they might want to, and they did not have the freedom to develop and express their own culture. Instead, the ways and customs of the Babylonians were thrust upon them. Frankly, it was just easier to go along with the Babylonians than to resist. Resistance, it seemed, was futile. Under the weight of the Babylonian empire, the Israelites were poor and in slavery. They had been removed from their land and stripped of their possessions. What had been theirs now belonged to their conquerors. They were close to hopelessness.

In that very condition, what did God tell his prophet Isaiah to proclaim? We can summarize the proclamation from Isaiah 40 like this:

First, God tells his people that the power of their conquerors cannot and will not last forever. "Comfort, oh comfort My people, says your God. Speak tenderly to Jerusalem, and declare to her that her term of service is over. . . . All flesh is grass, all its goodness like flowers of the field: Grass withers, flowers fade when the breath of the Lord blows on them" (Isa 40:1-2, 6-7, JPS; cf. 15-17). Babylon is in full bloom, but what appears now so spectacular and everlasting will wither and perish. Babylon's power will pass away, so those under its rule can take comfort.

Second, God tells his people that they are known by God himself.

> Like a shepherd [the Lord] pastures His flock: He gathers the lambs in His arms and carries them in His bosom; gently He drives the mother sheep. . . . Why do you say, O Jacob, Why declare, O Israel, "My way is hid from the Lord, my cause is ignored by my God?" Do you not know? Have you not heard? The Lord is God from of old, Creator of the earth from end to end, He never grows faint or weary, His wisdom cannot be fathomed. (Isa 40:11, 27-28, JPS)

Even in this place where all seems lost and Israel has in fact lost itself, buried under these foreign customs and forgetting its very identity, the Lord God knows his people and never loses sight of them.

Third and finally, God is coming. "Ascend a lofty mountain, O herald of joy to Zion; raise your voice with power, O herald of joy to Jerusalem—raise it, have no fear; announce to the cities of Judah: Behold your God! Behold, the Lord God comes in might, and his arm wins triumph for Him; see, His reward is with Him, His recompense before Him" (Isa 40:9-10, JPS). Into the predicament that Israel cannot escape, the Lord God is coming to liberate the Israelites. The Lord God will draw near, he will lift them up, and he will restore them to all they have lost. He is coming.

In the time of great exile in which Isaiah prophesies, Israel has sinned and Israel is being crushed. Precisely at this time Israel's *only* hope is in the Lord, who alone can both forgive sins and raise up the lowly under the great powers of the world. Israel must therefore prepare and wait for the Lord, who is coming.

When John the Baptist preaches, this very prophecy is being spoken again, though its impact will go further. John's proclamation is for Israel again, who is now being crushed by Rome, but it is also for all, including the Gentiles. John the Baptist is proclaiming that the power held by the powerful is coming to an end, that the Lord knows his own by name, and that the Lord is coming. John is proclaiming that salvation is coming from the one born of Mary.

Mary is not from the center of things—Rome, or even Jerusalem—but from a far-off village in Galilee. She is not a man of standing, but a woman of low degree. She is not an adult but a young person. She is not rich but poor. She is not prominent but humble. The Word of the Lord came to her and she has borne the Savior.

Thinking of the ancient Israelites in captivity, or the people on the bottom whom John proclaims will be lifted up, and Mary the lowly handmaiden, we should ask again: Who waits for the Lord? Who needs him? Who longs for him? Whose hope is in him alone?

The ones who wait for the Lord are more often the poor, the sick, the lonely, and the victimized. It is more often those weighed down by their own sins and the sins of others. It is more often those not in the center of things, but off in the margins. It is more often those who have not been comforted, but those who long for comfort.

For those with the time, the peace of mind, and the relative comfort to do so, the practice of Advent asks us to call to mind those who need the Lord. As we discussed with the Beatitudes, for those who are not poor, hungry, sorrowful, or ridiculed, the way to be on the side of the Lord's blessings is to join yourself with those who are. So, too, with this Advent practice regarding the poor, the sick, the lonely, and the victimized. The practice of Advent has to do with renouncing being for ourselves (a whole bunch of "no's!") and professing being for others ("YES!"). It is an echo of the baptismal promises, where after the way of Satan has been renounced, the way of the Triune God is professed.

Advent is a season of practicing the Christian life of waiting for the Lord. The four candles of the Advent wreath can become a reminder of how we are to wait for the Lord: with others. Each candle can become a reminder of the poor, the sick, the lonely, and the victimized. Prayers in Advent can be offered for and with them. And this Advent practice is a practice for how to live in between the memory of Christ who has come and the hope of Christ who will come again.

chapter thirteen

Where We've Been, Where We're Going

God's plan is to share his life. To become a Christian is to be initiated into that life, offered to us in Christ. In Christ we become who we were created to be.

The first part of this book has been about power: the power of the life of God and the false power that opposes God. We recalled how in the baptismal rite, we renounce the power of this world—the power of Satan—and profess belief in the Triune God. We are immersed into the life we profess in the waters of baptism, and are thus drawn into the life of the Father, Son, and Holy Spirit. By sharing in that divine life, we are endowed with the power to become a source of goodness, which is the character of the Christian that the sacrament of confirmation seals upon us. We practice becoming what we are called to be in "the Way" of Christianity, which, as demonstrated already in the earliest Christian community, is an habitual formation in prayer, the breaking of the bread, the teaching of the apostles, and sharing all things in common, including serving the needs of the neediest.

In the conversion of St. Paul, we saw how the encounter with Jesus broke Paul from the power of the world, a power in which he had been deeply immersed. The way he saw, the way he listened, and the way he spoke were all transformed. That transformation went so deep that Paul became a source of goodness for the very same people whose lives he was once committed to ruining. By what he proclaimed and who he became, Paul hands on to us—"as of first importance"—the person and works of Jesus Christ. Everything about Paul shows us that the point of everything is to discover who Jesus is—the one who gives life.

Asking "Who is Jesus?" opened us to contemplating the mystery of the Triune God, in whose name we as Christians are baptized. Jesus is the Son of the Father drawn near to us. Jesus is the one who claims and reveals the name of God: "I AM." Jesus is the power and wisdom of God, which is not at all what we would normally expect power and wisdom to be. And Jesus is the way, the truth, and the life of beatitude—of everlasting joy—who draws us into communion with each other.

The Christian life, therefore, is a time of waiting and preparing, of remembering and hoping, for Christ who has come to give the life of God to us and for Christ who will come again to bring that good work begun in us to its completion in him. In the Church, we prepare the way for the Lord by readying ourselves to give him the center of our lives, as John the Baptist did. To wait for the Lord means waiting not for a private benefit but for what is good for our neighbors also. To wait for the Lord means exercising the power to join the weak in their weakness, as God has joined us in ours.

Being drawn ever more deeply into the life of Christ is to become nothing less than everything we were created to be: it is to receive in full the life God desires to give us. But who and what we were created to be is not forced upon us; rather, it requires our response. We have been wounded in sin and, in the Church, we are undergoing healing through the grace of Christ in the Spirit. In the end, that healing will lead us to the freedom of the saints. The second half of the first part of this book focuses on this journey: from who we are created to be all the way to who we are to become in Christ, as members of his body.

Over the course of the following chapters, we will move between the Book of Genesis and the gospels. We will rediscover who we were always created to be, what sin is and what it does to us, how the recovery from sin takes place through the Spirit, and how we grow in virtue to cooperate in becoming who Christ frees us to be. In the process, we will see the gifts of the Holy Spirit in a deeper, more beautiful way. We will meditate on the meaning of the body and of the sexes. We will take a long time considering chastity, but not in the way chastity is typically considered. We will heed the Blessed Mother to learn about the conditions of discipleship. We will enrich our appreciation for the mystery of the sacraments as initiating us into, healing us as, and bestowing upon us a mission as the Body of Christ.

As was the case with St. Paul, so it will be with us: we must allow our minds, hearts, and words to be renewed by Christ. We must open our imaginations, pushing past our settled certainties and our deficiencies in wonder, to marvel afresh at the beauty of the life God desires to give us. We must allow ourselves to be challenged by the call to be thoroughly transformed into a source of goodness for others, for the love of God in the world.

chapter fourteen

Who We Are Created to Be

The Way Things Are

The things we take for granted can be the most important things of all. Even if most people never vocally articulate it, everyone relies on a set of basic assumptions about who and what a human being is, who God is, and what the world itself is. These are the kinds of foundational beliefs that influence everything else: how we live, what we consider "good," and how we judge our lives.

We might think that just about everyone has the same basic ideas about what, for example, it means to be a human being or what the world essentially is, but this is far from the case. If you stop to think about it, you might be surprised at the sort of foundational beliefs we tend to fall back on.

Consider, for example, what I saw printed in large block letters on a tote bag for sale in the children's section of a local bookstore: "Life isn't about finding yourself. Life is about creating yourself."[1] Or consider what the student of a colleague of mine said about how she and other young adults have come to think about the world and their place in it: "Because we view humanity—and thus its institutions—as corrupt and selfish, the only person we can rely upon is our self. The only way to avoid failure, being let down, and ultimately succumbing to the chaotic world around us, therefore, is to have the means (financial security) to

1. This quote is sometimes attributed to George Bernard Shaw, but it is not clear that it actually originates with him. Regardless, you can easily find this quote on banners, throw pillows, bookmarks, posters, and picture frames, in addition to the tote bag I saw, which happened to be in a bookstore on the campus of a major Catholic university, by the way.

rely only upon ourselves."[2] What view of the human person, God, and the world goes along with statements of belief such as these?

None of this is new. We could look at ancient Greek myths, ancient Roman myths, or other myths of the ancient world to see how foundational beliefs were enshrined in their respective cultures. We might consider one of the greatest civilizations in the sixth and seventh centuries BC—the Babylonian Empire—which had a well-developed creation myth known as the *Enuma Elish*. According to the Babylonian worldview, the earth was made from the body of a dragon split in two, human beings have dragons' blood flowing through their bodies, and the king of the Babylonians is the emissary of the creating deity who has to impose order by force, especially in terms of subduing foreign nations. Think about what this myth asserts. A dragon is a violent, covetous creature, and if the world is made of a dragon's body, then the world is a sinister and threatening place. Or you can flip this around and say that the Babylonians' fundamental view of the world is that it is a sinister and threatening place, and they passed down this fundamental understanding from generation to generation by imaging the world as a dragon's body. To say that humans have dragons' blood is to say that humans are *naturally* and *inherently* greedy, vengeful, and rivalrous. And that bit about the king doing his divinely ordained duty by subduing other nations really puts a fine point on everything, since the conquering of smaller nations is not only approved but mandated.

The Babylonian creation myth is more than just one more example among many, because in 587 BC, the Babylonians invaded and conquered Israel—specifically the southern kingdom of Judah. The majority of Israelites were taken into captivity in Babylon where they were forcefully subjected to a foreign culture and religion, while those who were left behind in Judah were ruled by an occupying force. The worldview of the Babylonians surrounded the Israelites: it was the basic assumption of the culture in which they were forced to live. And it was while the Israelites were in captivity in Babylon that the first creation account in the Book of Genesis was authored. Genesis 1 is, in part, a counter-claim to the Babylonians' totalizing vision of the world.

2. Quoted in Patrick Deneen, *Why Liberalism Failed* (New Haven, CT: Yale University Press, 2018), 12.

The Creator God of Genesis 1 is definitely not the creator the Babylonians imagined and worshipped, who creates and rules through conflict.[3] The world is not sinister but ordered and life-giving. Human beings are not inherently sinister but made in the image and likeness of their life-giving God. Human beings are given the divine mandate to "[b]e fruitful and multiply" (Gen 1:28, RSV). Humans are charged with the task of claiming dominion over the world not through conquest by might, but rather by offering the whole world back to God as an act of worship on the seventh day: the Sabbath. Between Israel and Babylon there is far more than two different stories; what separates Israel from Babylon is a totally different way of seeing everything and of living in the world.

We could spend ages exploring the significance of the first creation account in Genesis 1—of how its structure expresses its content, of how God is presented as a priest and monarch at once, of how the Word is the source of all life, of how creation itself is configured to the properties of the Temple, of how the account itself is a testament to God's liberating action for Israel, and so on. For our purposes, though, I want to narrow our focus specifically to the creation of the human being. I want to ask "What is the human being?" or, to put it another way, "Who are we created to be?" To explore this question, we will shift our gaze to the complementary but distinct creation account presented in Genesis 2, which zooms in from the cosmic dimensions of the first account to a frame that principally concerns the creation of this one distinctive creature: the human being.

The Creation of the Human Being

In the second creation account, the focus is on the human being from the very start:

> When the Lord God made earth and heaven—when no shrub of the field was yet on earth and no grasses of the field had yet sprouted, because the Lord God had not sent rain upon the earth and there was no man to till the soil, but a flow would well up from the ground

3. The first creation account actually runs to the first half of the fourth verse of Genesis 2, but I will keep writing Genesis 1 for the sake of ease.

> and water the whole surface of the earth—the Lord God formed man from the dust of the earth. He blew into his nostrils the breath of life, and man became a living being. (Gen 2:4b-7, JPS)

The first duty for reading Scripture—after preparing yourself to read humbly and patiently—is to pay close attention to what the text actually says.[4] So what does this text say that the human being is? In posing this question, I am not asking us to make an act of interpretation or to extrapolate; I really mean for us to make sure we see what the text says.

On the basis of this text, we may say the human being is intentionally formed "earth stuff" that is given breath. The human being lives only through the union of these two. The human being is in fact a living union.

Even as we say this, though, there is more work to do in terms of actually seeing what the text says. In at least one important respect, reading this text in translation makes it very difficult, if not impossible, to see everything we should see here. That is because we do not see anything particularly interesting in the words "the Lord God formed man from the dust of the earth," but if we were reading it in Hebrew, we would. What we would see in Hebrew is that the word translated here as "man" would be *'adam*, while the word "earth" would be *'adamah*. The *'adam* is not yet a proper name but instead a word of relation: the *'adam* is the one who is from the *'adamah*. If we wanted to capture this more literally in English, we would perhaps do well to say the "earth creature" is intentionally formed from the "earth."[5] And if we allow the refrain from Genesis 1 to echo here—"and God saw that it was good"—then we can remember that the earth God has created is "good" and therefore everything that comes from the earth is also "good." The human being is in *harmony* with the earth.

As for the breath of life that is breathed into the nostrils of this intentionally formed "earth creature," there is not so much something hidden in translation as there is something we should pause for a

4. This corresponds to the literal sense of Scripture, although I am not going to get into the senses of Scripture here. For some guidance on the senses of Scripture, see CCC 115–19.

5. We could also think about the etymological connection between "human" and "humus."

moment to notice. This breath is given directly to the creature from the life of the Creator: it is the Creator's breath that fills the creature. It is hardly possible to imagine a more intimate action or more intimate gift than this. The Creator gives his own breath for the creature to breathe as his own. The human being is in *harmony* with the Lord God.

The union of the intentionally formed earth stuff and the breath intimately given is what makes man "a living being." It is not difficult to think of the intentionally formed earth stuff as the body and the breath intimately given as the soul, so that the image of the human being with which this second creation account begins is of the human being as the living union of body and soul. St. Irenaeus of Lyons—a second-century Church Father—would repeatedly speak of the human being as "the whole man," by which he meant not just the body, not just the soul, but indeed the union of the body and the soul. Without this union, there is no human being. The creature who is in harmony with the earth and in harmony with the Lord God is, himself, a creature that only exists as a harmony: the *harmony* of body and soul.

It is evident by now what I am drawing out from the beginning of the second creation narrative—a reading devoid of any overdone act of interpretation. On the basis of the text itself, the overwhelming impression of how the human being is created and what the human being is created to be is that the human being is a creature of *harmony.* This is a foundational claim.

Harmony by Another Name

Alongside this opening passage of Genesis 2, I want us to look at the closing passage of the same chapter. What can we see when we put this later passage next to the first one?

> So the Lord God cast a deep sleep upon the man; and, while he slept, He took one of his ribs and closed up the flesh at that spot. And the Lord God fashioned the rib that He had taken from the man into a woman; and He brought her to the man. Then the man said, "This one at last is bone of my bones and flesh of my flesh. This one shall be called Woman, for from man was she taken." Hence a man leaves his father and mother and clings to his wife, so that they become one flesh. (Gen 2:21-24, JPS)

Remembering what we discerned in our reading of the earlier passage, let's point out two things right from the outset. First, the body of the man was itself created from the good earth (*'adam* from *'adamah*) and here, the body of the woman is taken from the body of the man. Both bodies are made of the same "good stuff," so to speak. Second, if we recall how intimate and direct the action of creation was in the first passage, we can see here again that this creature is likewise the direct creation of God: beheld and intended in equal measure. If we step back for a moment, we can say that all human beings are directly willed and created by God, even as we each come from other human beings.

There is a third important observation that would be very apparent to us in the Hebrew, though even in English we can see some indication of the significance. When the *'adam* says of the companion the Lord God has created that "[t]his one shall be called Woman, for from man was she taken," the word translated as "man" is not actually the word *'adam* in Hebrew, as it was in the previous verse (2:22). Instead, here in verse 23, where the "man" speaks, the word he uses to refer to himself is *'ish*. This is important because the word translated here as "Woman" is the word *'ishshah*. These are still not proper names, but perhaps something even more powerful: they are relational names. Just as *'adam* is related with *'adamah*, so are *'ish* and *'ishshah* relational names to one another. Even more, the "man"—previously *'adam*—recognizes and identifies the "Woman" in relation to himself, and himself (*'ish*) in relation to the Woman (*'ishshah*). We can see a similar resemblance in the words "man" and "woman" in English, but since the word "man" in verses 22 and verses 23 appear the same to us in English, we miss the way in which "man" renames himself in relation to *'ishshah*. To take a step back again, we can already anticipate the upshot of this: the two sexes refer to and imply each other, and they do so naturally, according to the dignity of how human beings are created.

We all know what lurks in the verses following this very passage—the beginning of Genesis 3 and the story of the Fall. We know that "original sin" is on the way. But lest we run ahead to the impending tragedy too quickly, we ought to remain here at the end of chapter 2 for a while longer to marvel at the fact that more original than original sin is something we may call "original solidarity." The man relates himself to the woman, and the woman is related in her very being to the man, and the first recorded words of the human being in this creation account are words of rejoicing at one another's creation and of the gift of their union. This is the true and created condition of human beings—it is indeed "good news."

It is especially important that union of man and woman is singular and lasting, as the penultimate verse of chapter 2 declares: "Hence a man leaves his father and mother and clings to his wife, so that they become one flesh." Man and woman can give and receive security in one another. Come what may, this bond is stability, and this stability is the basis of all human community. We ought to consider just how important this was especially in the ancient world, despite all the suspicions we may have gathered from modern opinions about this being some kind of limitation on "freedom" in terms of autonomy and self-determination. This security was *especially* important for women in the ancient world, who would be singularly vulnerable when pregnant or with a young child. In Israel's creation account, the order of the world as God has created it dictates that what is right, just, natural, and good is that the man remains faithful to and attached to the woman, and that the security of this bond endures when circumstances change.

In sum, we can see that the "union" or "harmony" of man and woman—*'ish* and *'ishshah*—recalls and refers back to the *harmony* of the human being with the earth, of the human being with God, and of the human being as a whole creature. Harmony reigns as the rule of life in each human being and as the basis of our social order. We are created in the condition of original solidarity—what we call original sin is indeed a fall from that original condition. Harmony is the overwhelming message of the creation narrative.

And as with all foundational claims, we would do well to ponder what this Judeo-Christian worldview means for how we are to live, what we consider "good," and how we judge our lives.

chapter fifteen

Male and Female God Created Them

God intentionally and carefully forms human beings from the earth and intimately breathes into them the breath of life. God's creation is thoroughly marked by harmony: the harmony between human beings and the earth, between human beings and their Creator, between the human being in body and soul, and between one human being and the next, specifically as man and woman. The distinction and complementarity of those two sexes is itself intended, beautiful, and meaningful. The meaning of the two sexes is borne out in their mission, and their mission expresses the dignity of who we are created to be.

When we read that "God created man in His image, in the image of God He created him; male and female He created them" (Gen 1:27, JPS), we discover that these two sexes are good, natural, and intended, as part of God's creation.[1] There is *one* image of God yet *two* ways of being that one image—namely, as male and female.

One of the most important ways of understanding what something is requires you to recognize what that thing is created to do. What is a toaster? That thing that is intended to toast bread. What is a garden

1. I am quite conscious of continuing to use the word "sex" instead of "gender" because of the associations with "gender" that have accrued to that word and concept in recent decades. For an incredibly instructive and illuminating lesson on the history of the construction of gender and the importance of "bodiliness" related to biological sex, see Abigail Favale, "The Eclipse of Sex by the Rise of Gender," *Church Life Journal*, March 1, 2019, https://churchlifejournal.nd.edu/articles/the-eclipse-of-sex-by-the-rise-of-gender/.

hose? That thing that is intended to carry water from a spicket to the garden. What is the human being, created male and female? The ones who are intended to be procreative and unitive. That is, of course, language typically associated with marriage because the sacrament of matrimony uplifts and blesses the sacred mission and character of human beings as realized through the love of one particular man and one particular woman. What is made particular in a single marriage is the common mission and character of human beings as we are created to be. If we are ordered to procreation, that has to do with the power and mission to give life; if we are ordered to union, that has to do with the gift and mission of intimacy. These two created ends of the human being as created male and female teach us the meaning of human flourishing and indeed Christian maturity.

Procreation: Power and Responsibility

What does it mean to give life? It means two complementary things. First, to give or create life means to cause someone to come into existence. This is the power of procreation—the power to cooperate with the incredible act of causing "to be" someone who "has not been." This is, of course, a power properly belonging only to God (see Rom 4:17) but which human beings share in their created capacity to procreate. Second, to give life also means to pass on what is most beautiful, what is most grand, what is true to the next generation. This is the responsibility of procreation—it is an act of blessing those who come after you with what is good for them.

Every generation is invested with this mission and responsibility. In other words, every generation *engenders* the next generation.[2] Man and woman together are given this specific mission and responsibility, so that every marriage carries in itself the mission and responsibility of an entire generation. What is universal to every generation is specific to each particular marriage of man and woman. But even further, growth in Christian maturity is growth toward becoming capable of

2. Though I am intentionally using the language of "sexes" rather than "genders" throughout, we can see here how the very notion of human "gender" has to do with this mission and responsibility to pass on life. It is, in other words, a relational, social, and indeed intergenerational concept rather than an individualistic one.

and accountable for participating in this mission according to one's own state of life. It is the mission expressed in the power to create and the responsibility to nurture.

The power and responsibility of procreation brings us human beings to share in God's own character. To be made in the "image of God" means to partake in the mission and responsibility that God freely enacts in his free act of creation. Two passages from the *Catechism of the Catholic Church* express this mystery in lucid and compelling fashion:

> Each of the two sexes is an image of the power and tenderness of God, with equal dignity though in a different way. The *union of man and woman* in marriage is a way of imitating in the flesh the Creator's generosity and fecundity. (CCC 2335, italics in text)

> Called to give life, spouses share in the creative power and fatherhood of God. Married couples should regard it as their proper mission to transmit human life and to educate their children; they should realize that they are thereby *cooperating with* the love of *God the Creator* and are, in a certain sense, its interpreters. (CCC 2367, italics in text)

Human beings are thus created male and female not merely to do certain things, but indeed to share God's life by participating in the giving and nurturing of new life in every generation.

Union: Transparency and Intimacy

In the last chapter, we recognized the intimate union of man and woman in creation. It is a union that is bodily and expressive. The first words of man are words spoken in praise and delight of the woman whom God has created and indeed at the gift of human communion that God has brought into existence. When the man speaks of the woman, he speaks of her in relation to himself and of himself in relation to her. By name, by origin, by desire, and by word, the union of man and woman as the foundation of the human communion is harmonious and indeed intimate.

What we did not look at in the last chapter was the very last verse of Genesis 2, which is the completion of the second creation account. This was an intentional omission because I wanted to save that verse until now when we will begin to bridge the creation account of Genesis 2 to the account of the Fall in Genesis 3. Here are the two verses that make that bridge:

> The two of them were naked, the man and his wife, yet they felt no shame. (Gen 2:25, JPS)

> Now the serpent was the shrewdest of all the wild beasts that the Lord God had made. He said to the woman, "Did God really say: You shall not eat of any tree of the garden?" (Gen 3:1, JPS)

When we hear that the two of them were naked without shame, we might think of them bearing their bodies to one another without bashfulness and without lust. We would not be wrong to think that. But that does not seem to have anything to do with the verse that follows, at the beginning of Genesis 3, which quite clearly opens another chapter in the narrative. The problem, though, is that we do not hear everything we should hear because, again, something significant is lost in translation. What is lost is that the word translated into English as "naked" in 2:25 is the Hebrew word *'arummim*, while the word translated into English as "shrewd" (or as intensified, "shrewdest") is the Hebrew word *'arum*. Because this etymological connection is missing in English, we are not likely to hear that "to be naked" is the opposite of "to be shrewd," because *'arummim* means to be "without *'arum*" in the same way that "guileless" means to be "without guile."

What does it mean to be "shrewd" or "full of guile" or "cunning"? Without overlaying a definition to the text, we can simply pay attention to the question the serpent asks at the conclusion of Genesis 3:1. In particular, we should compare this question to the actual command that God gave to man about eating from the trees.

> Here is what God said when he commanded the man: "Of every tree of the garden you are free to eat; but as for the tree of knowledge of good and bad, you must not eat of it; for as soon as you eat of it, you shall die." (Gen 2:16-17, JPS)

> And here, again, is the question the serpent asked the woman: "Did God really say: You shall not eat of any tree of the garden?" (Gen 3:1, JPS)

You can hear the difference in that command and that question in any language! The tone of the Lord God's commandment is overwhelmingly positive: *everything* is given to his creature, but for this one thing that is prohibited. The serpent's question is cast in a wholly negative tone. There is a hidden message in the serpent's question: the serpent is suggesting that this entire garden is one gigantic prohibition because, in the end, God is keeping everything from you. The serpent does not come right out and say that; instead, he plants the seed of that idea. This is indeed what we would call a "loaded question."

If a man is at dinner with his in-laws and they ask, "So, Billy, have you made anything of yourself yet?" what is clearly implied is that Billy has not, to date, amounted to anything. If a boyfriend asks his girlfriend, "Do you love Oscar more than me?" the boyfriend has already suggested that his girlfriend does, in some way and to some degree, love Oscar. If a friend says to you, "Does your teacher always point out how stupid you are?" after that teacher strongly critiqued and corrected an essay you wrote, all of a sudden the possibility that the teacher thinks you are stupid arises, even if you do not believe that to be true. The kinds of questions that get asked and the way in which questions are asked can say quite a lot about the person asking the question.[3]

Loaded questions veil ulterior motives and hidden agendas. A question like this is not honest because the questioner has something else in mind but is not telling the other person about it. The serpent is not really looking for information; he is setting the terms of the encounter. This all points to what it means to be "shrewd" or "full of guile" or "cunning." The serpent is crafty, he is hiding things, and he is engaging in an act of manipulation.

With this in mind, we may now ask what it means to be "naked without shame." It means everything that is the opposite of what the serpent is exhibiting. Being naked without shame means being honest about your intentions. It is about saying what you mean and meaning what you say. It has to do with being transparent to each other, clear and up front about your motives. It is the sign and precondition of intimacy. And it

3. For a scriptural study of the meaning and hidden meaning of questions in Scripture, see my *A God Who Questions* (Huntington, IN: Our Sunday Visitor, 2019), perhaps especially the epilogue.

is the condition of being free from the self-consciousness about or the fear of being seen as you are, and seeing the other person as he or she is.

The natural, created condition of the man and woman, as created, is to bear themselves to each other: honestly, openly, and genuinely. Genesis 3 begins by introducing a new way of being—one that is duplicitous, manipulative, or, in a word, "shrewd." With no more than a moment's reflection, we can name which of these two ways is more common in the world today. The way of shrewdness is obviously more common, almost as if it were written right into the rules of the world. In a world where there is this kind of duplicity or even the worry about such duplicity, it becomes incredibly difficult to be transparent—almost unbearably difficult. When you are transparent to others, you risk being taken advantage of. You may be seen or treated as gullible. Besides, there is also the challenge of really knowing what you think and mean so that your speech may be true, the challenge of hearing others well, the challenge of using words or expressions that always seem limited, and the challenge of each of us carrying around our own baggage from previous wounds or habits or poor choices.

The unitive gift and mission of the creation of man and woman—as particularly evident in matrimony—is to practice a way of relationship marked by openness, transparency, honesty, and mutuality, without the hidden motives, manipulation, or duplicity. Just as human beings who are created male and female in their procreative character express together the generative mission of human society, so too do we express and practice the renewal of human relationship in terms of trust and honesty, reconciliation and mutuality. The old way of the world—the way of the serpent—always comes down to domination and deceit, whereas the unitive character of our creation is a call to practice transparency. Transparency is the heart of intimacy.

In God's providence, he created human beings male and female as the two ways of sharing in God's own image. This image is fulfilled in the complementarity of the two sexes, especially in terms of the twin mission of procreation and union. God, who gives and nurtures life, calls us to give and nurture life. God, whose Word is truth and who reveals himself in his actions, calls us to transparency and intimacy, allowing us to be truly present in how we relate to each other. The dignity of our creation as male and female is inviolable and inalterable, though sin severs us from our calling and makes us less than we are created to be. Nevertheless, God persists and grace abounds. But before we consider how God heals and strengthens us, we must look more closely at what precisely is sin and its effects.

chapter sixteen

Sin and Its Effects

He Said, She Said

God gave a command, the man and woman trespassed against this command: that seems pretty straightforward. Already, though, we have seen that with the serpent's question at the beginning of Genesis 3, there is something unnatural going on. The original condition of nakedness without shame was about transparency and intimacy, but the first question of the serpent is loaded with suspicion and unclear motives. At the very least, it is not a straight line from commandment to disobedience, and perhaps there is even more going on here than we initially think.

Having already looked at the serpent's question alongside the original commandment, we should now look at the woman's initial response to the serpent's question.

> Here, again, is God's commandment: "Of every tree of the garden you are free to eat; but as for the tree of knowledge of good and bad, you must not eat of it; for as soon as you eat of it, you shall die." (Gen 2:16-17, JPS)

> And here is the woman's response to the serpent's question: "We may eat of the fruit of the other trees of the garden. It is only about fruit of the tree in the middle of the garden that God said: 'You shall not eat of it or touch it, lest you die.'" (Gen 3:2-3, JPS)

There is one obvious difference between the original commandment and the woman's response, which is this: God says that they shall not eat of the fruit, but she says that God says they shall not eat of it *or touch it*. She adds something to the commandment. What are we to make of that?

To try to grasp what is going on here and whether or not this small emendation is important, let's ask another question: Where was the woman when God gave that original commandment? There are, I suppose, two possibilities, with the first being that she had not yet been created, since her creation is narrated later, and therefore the man was responsible for passing on the commandment to her for her own good. In other words, he was responsible for a crucial act of communication. If he communicated the commandment with this addition, maybe he did not trust her fully or think she could be strong enough to hold to the commandment. And so, like a parent who tells a child to not even touch a cigarette in the hopes that the child will not smoke one, or like an older sibling who tells her younger sister to not even look in her closest because she doesn't want her to steal her clothes, the man adds on this rule about not even touching the fruit. If the woman received the commandment through an act of human communication, perhaps the man hedged the commandment for her sake.

The second possibility would be that she was there with the man when God issued the commandment, since it was one undivided humanity that received this word from the Lord. Out of this one earth creature—*'adam*—the two came to be in a second act of creation. If we think of it in those terms, what does this addition signify? Perhaps it is a sign of the failure or weakness of memory. How do you remember driving directions if someone gives them to you just once? You repeat them to yourself until they are committed to memory, and you keep repeating those directions to yourself even after you think you know them by heart so you don't forget something small and miss a turn en route. Or, alternatively, if someone entrusts you with a sensitive message that must not be written down but only verbally passed on to someone else, your duty is to rehearse that message over and over again so you get it just right when the time comes to share this message. This is how memory works. For memory to be strong, it must be exercised. If you do not exercise memory, it weakens.[1] In this case, this little addition would already be a sign of the failure of rehearsal. The commandment

1. This is a major theme of C. S. Lewis's *The Silver Chair*.

has not been taken as something of the utmost importance because it has not been rehearsed to the point of unerring fidelity.

We do not need to choose between these two possibilities. In fact, the ancient Jewish rabbis regularly meditated on both possibilities as they pored over this text, considering both possibilities worthy of further thought. The text is not so crass as to say "and this is because the man did not communicate the commandment well to her" or "and this is because she was slack in her memory." Instead, Scripture invites us to be troubled by that little detail and to ponder over it. We do well to recognize, therefore, the importance of both *communication* and *memory*.

There is one other thing I find myself thinking about when it comes to the woman's initial response to the serpent, which has to do with her identification of "the tree in the middle of the garden." To be precise, there is not just one tree in the middle of the garden: there are two (see Gen 2:9). In her response, she has narrowed her attention to one without mentioning the other one. From that other one—the tree of life—they were permitted to eat fruit. This leads me to imagine the way in which something that is forbidden suddenly—in our mind's eye—becomes the center of everything else. If you are invited to make yourself at home in someone's room and that person gives you permission to touch or look at anything you want, except the journal sitting on the nightstand, isn't it strange that the journal probably becomes the center of your attention? Even if you do not look at it, you are especially mindful of that journal, above everything else in the room. It is, in that way, in the middle of everything. Why do we shower the prohibited thing with our attention? This is part of the mystery of human freedom.

The Proposal

Some Jewish rabbis would view that added bit about touching the tree as the serpent's opening. As one early rabbi wrote, the serpent "touched the tree with his hands and his feet, and shook it until its fruits dropped to the ground," thus shattering the credibility of the entire commandment in the woman's mind.[2] Although this action is

2. Quoted in *The Jewish Study Bible* (Oxford: Oxford University Press, 2004), 16–17.

left to our imaginations, the words of the serpent are plainly written. In response to the woman, the serpent says, "You are not going to die, but God knows that as soon as you eat of it your eyes will be opened and you will be like divine beings who know good and bad" (Gen 3:4-5, JPS). That hidden agenda in the serpent's opening question is becoming more and more apparent. Think about what the serpent is implying: "God is your rival! God is withholding power from you! God doesn't want you to be like him because he wants to be the boss! This whole garden is a prison where he is controlling you! Break out, choose for yourself! You do you!"

The Deliberation

The temptation is not just about a piece of fruit. It is about reimagining God, reinterpreting the meaning of this garden, and asserting your own autonomy. The woman takes the bait. In the very next verse we read what happens:

> When the woman saw that the tree was good for eating and a delight to the eyes, and that the tree was desirable as a source of wisdom, she took of its fruit and ate. She also gave some to her husband, and he ate. (Gen 3:6, JPS)

When the woman judges this fruit to be tasty, beautiful, and useful for wisdom, what standard is she using to make that judgment?[3] It is tasty according to what, beautiful according to what, useful according to what? Consider that the only criterion the man and the woman had for judging anything in the garden was that it was all given as a gift from God, and by God's word one thing was prohibited. God was the standard by which they were to judge. So what is this new standard? Scripture does not say, and that is precisely the point. The point is

3. These three forms of fallen desire are present in the three temptations of Christ in the desert (see Luke 4:1-13). These three are also explicitly named in the First Letter of John: "For all that is in the world, the lust of the flesh and the lust of the eyes and the pride of life, is not of the Father but is of the world" (1 John 2:16, RSV). The three evangelical counsels—poverty, chastity, and obedience—are set to curing desire from these corruptions.

that she has made up her own standards. Isn't that quite an elegant statement about what gives rise to sin? It is us making up our own order and justifications.

By the way, what was the man doing this whole time? He was just standing there, not doing anything. He just takes and eats what is given to him, without saying a word. He consummates the sin (joining her in this act) rather than struggling at all. At least she deliberated. What he certainly does not do is sacrifice for her to bring her back from this transgression. He chooses to join her in it, rather than help redeem her from it (and here, we get a glimpse of what Christ will do in contrast to what the first man did not do).

The Fallout

As soon as they eat of the fruit, everything changes for them:

> Then the eyes of both of them were opened and they perceived that they were naked; and they sewed together fig leaves and made themselves loincloths. (Gen 3:7, JPS)

What they suddenly realize is that their motives are visible: they see what they personally have done, what the other one has done, and that by eating the fruit, they have given in to the desire to displace God as the one who gives order to the world. Remember, they were created to be *naked*—that is, transparent in their motives so their deeds show their intentions and their intentions are expressed through their deeds. But now they quiver, unwilling to allow their true intentions to be seen and so they begin to cover themselves up, both from God and from each other. Fig leaves make for uncomfortable, irritating clothing, and yet they use fig leaves to cover their most intimate parts. They are now guarded against the intimacy that was natural to them by virtue of their creation.

If we read the next six verses—Genesis 3:8-13—we begin to recognize the effects of sin. Because of their sin, they hide themselves behind the trees. These trees were all given to them as gifts from their Creator, but now they are using what God has created to shield themselves from God's gaze. Moreover, rather than confess their transgression in honesty—speaking truthfully and humbly—they choose to use their words to blame. Who do they blame? Each of them blames someone else and God at the same time. The man says, "The woman You put at my side—she gave me of the tree and I ate" (Gen 3:12, JPS). The woman, for her part, says, "The serpent duped me, and I ate" (Gen 3:13, JPS). The man says it is the woman's fault . . . the woman God created. The woman says it is the serpent's fault . . . the serpent of God's creation. Neither says, "Through my fault, through my fault, through my most grievous fault." Instead, they blame. We have come a long way from those joyful words of praise that burst forth from the man when the woman was created, when he claimed her as his own companion and gave himself to her.

All of this is the inauguration of a new way of living in the world, a fallen way of living. In place of transparency, they hide themselves and their motives. In place of intimacy, there is shame. In place of honesty, they blame. In place of truthful communication, deception reigns. In place of trust of God, they are suspicious. In place of love for each other, they compete with each other and spite each other, seeking to save themselves at the other's expense. This whole narrative shows sin as one slow-motion tragedy, with the effects of sin being the ways in which we have become accustomed to living in the world. Genesis 3 is not about what happened way back when; it is about the kind of world we have created for ourselves. It is also, therefore, about what any possible redeemer would have to reckon with and what we need to be healed from.

The Good News in the Bad

Genesis 3 seems like a real downer, as if there is only tragedy and no beauty. But that is not true. As is God's custom, right when things are bleakest God works to bring about salvation. We could note several things in this regard about Genesis 3, but I will mention only one. Look back over the passage and ask yourself: What is God's first action—his first words—once the man and the woman have fallen into sin?

With the man and the woman hiding themselves behind the trees, "The Lord God called out to the man and said to him, 'Where are you?'" (Gen 3:9, JPS). They are hiding but God seeks them. They are lost but God finds them. They have cut off communication from God but God addresses them. God does not ask "Where are you?" because he is looking for information or because he does not know. God asks "Where are you?" because they are lost to themselves. They do not know where they are. They do not know who they are. This is what our sin does to us. But while we hide in our sin, God addresses us and those words are the beginning of mercy. They are mercy because they give us a new chance to respond, and by responding to God we allow ourselves to begin to be found. We run away but God draws near and speaks to us. This approach and this word of mercy will become complete in the Incarnation, when the Word is made flesh and dwells among us.

chapter seventeen

The Gifts of the Holy Spirit and the Strength of Virtue

The Air We Breathe

In Eden, the man and the woman are tempted to claim the power to animate themselves rather than allowing the Lord to fill them. In the end, do they seem very powerful? They are hiding. They indulge in a pattern of blaming. They are consumed by rivalry. It is one thing to know the difference between good and evil, and quite another thing, it turns out, to know what evil is by participating in it. Their participation in evil—in willfully opposing God—has spoiled them and now the garden that had been a paradise to them feels like a prison. They are trapped in the consequences of choosing their own way, and they feel weak, not powerful.

As created, the human being lived by God's own breath; it was God who breathed the breath of life into this creature and he became a living being (see Gen 2:7). The breath of God animates the man and the woman. To live in the garden as paradise is to breathe the Lord's breath as we breathe oxygen. By their actions, however, they attempt to breathe some other way. They do not want the Lord's breath to animate them; they want to animate themselves. They fill their lungs with jealousy, envy, ambition, and lust.

We might think of a couple examples of breathing something other than oxygen to get a sense of the weakness that comes from ceasing to live by the Lord's breath. If you breathe helium from a balloon, it is fun at first, as your voice elevates to a high pitch. If you keep sucking in helium, you get light-headed. Take in more and more helium—which feels like oxygen but is not—then you will damage your brain cells. We need oxygen to live and function, and though helium feels like oxygen, it cannot give us what we need.

As another example, we might imagine mountain climbers ascending Mount Everest. It is just over 29,000 feet to the summit of Everest. After 26,247 feet, however, there is not enough oxygen in the air to sustain the human body. The area above that altitude is known as the "death zone" because if someone remains there too long without supplemental oxygen from a tank, their body will begin to shut down. It is only a matter of time before they perish. The human body is absolutely dependent on oxygen.

We should keep this in mind when we look back again at Genesis 2 and the creation of the human being. The breath that God gives to the intentionally formed earth creature is precisely what that creature needs in order to move from an inanimate sculpture to a "living being." Without that breath, this living being will perish. Helium is no substitute. Deprived of the breath that God gives, the human being enters the "death zone," where he or she may continue functioning for a little while but, sure enough, is dying.

Where do Adam and Eve end up? Outside the garden. They are banished. Why—is it a punishment? It is easy to see it that way, as if they do not deserve to live in this paradise any longer. But that can become a rather narrow interpretation of this narrative, since we have already seen that the disastrous consequences of their fallen freedom were not imposed on them from the outside but rather followed from their own disobedience. They have chosen to breathe something other than God's own breath, to live for themselves deprived of God's animating Spirit. They have become ill, with symptoms like chronic blame, persistent distrust, and acute transparency sensitivity. They are dying.

Seen from this perspective, then, the banishment from the garden is not just a punishment but indeed an act of mercy. God will not allow them to continue without obstruction to live in the way they have chosen to live, as if it were natural. The garden is no paradise for them because they do not know how to enjoy it; they have made the very air they breathe toxic to themselves because they are not living in harmony with their Creator. The Lord God banished them from the garden so they would not live like that forever—in sin and disobedience, into the certain death of their self-induced isolation (see Gen 3:22-23).

The Breath of (New) Life

The Holy Spirit is the breath of life. In the third part of the Creed we profess belief in "the Holy Spirit, the Lord, the giver of life." The Holy Spirit "proceeds" or is "spirated" from the Father and the Son. The Holy Spirit is the divine life of the eternal bond of Father and Son, which is breathed out and given to us as our life. Spiritually, our respiration depends on this breath of God.

At the conclusion of the Creed—under the belief in the Holy Spirit—we profess belief in what the Spirit brings about and makes possible. These include the holy Catholic Church, the communion of saints (in the Apostles' Creed), the forgiveness of sins, the resurrection of the body, and life everlasting. How you ever considered what the opposite of each of these things is?

"Church" is, in Greek, *ecclesia,* which means that which is "called out." It is both holy (that is, set apart) and universal (as in, all of it, everywhere). The opposite of that is to be disregarded, discarded, and divided.

The "communion of saints" is the fellowship of holy persons, who share together the holy things. They are bonded together in charity. The opposite of that is utter isolation, radical individualism, and loneliness.

The "forgiveness of sins" is both a state and activity. Under belief in the Holy Spirit, Christians profess belief that sins have been forgiven and that we are given the power to forgive sins ourselves. In the end, all the wounds of sin will be healed and forgiveness will reign as a perpetual state. The opposite of that is entrenched enmity, bitter hostility, and unending grudges.

The "resurrection of the body" is the remembrance of all that each of us has been. It is to be remembered in two senses: to be pulled back together again (think of everything that goes into our lives that is pulled apart in death, all that is lost) and to be recalled and known for who we are. The opposite of that is to disintegrate and be forgotten.

Finally, "life everlasting" is what it sounds like. This life in the Spirit of being set apart and revered, bonded with others, forgiven, and remembered is not ephemeral, but lasting. This is the permanent state of peace. The opposite of that is unending death: just total loss.

To consider the opposite of all these things is to imagine "life" without the gift of the Holy Spirit, which, in the end, is no life at all. In other words, all of these things are marks and effects of life in the

Spirit. Recall what the first section of the *Catechism of the Catholic Church* proclaims: "God, infinitely perfect and blessed in himself, in a plan of sheer goodness freely created man to make him share in his own blessed life" (1). The Holy Spirit is the communication of God's life to us. The Spirit brings us into life in Christ.

In Genesis 2:7, God breathes this life into his creature, who becomes a living human being. God gives life to what is not yet living. But what about when that creature refuses to breathe in harmony with that God-given life, rejecting the breath he or she needs to live? What does God do then? We do not have to conjure up an answer to this question on our own, as if we were merely speculating. Rather, we can see what God does in the person of Jesus.

When Jesus is buried in the tomb, his disciples bear the marks of death. They scattered when they denied and abandoned him, who held them together. They hide. They lose courage. They are imprisoned in fear. And so, as we read in the Gospel of John:

> On the evening of that day, the first day of the week, the doors being shut where the disciples were, for fear of the Jews, Jesus came and stood among them and said to them, "Peace be with you." When he had said this, he showed them his hands and his side. Then the disciples were glad when they saw the Lord. Jesus said to them again, "Peace be with you. As the Father has sent me, even so I send you." And when he had said this, he breathed on them, and said to them, "Receive the Holy Spirit. If you forgive the sins of any, they are forgiven; if you retain the sins of any, they are retained." (20:19-23, RSV)

Upon this lifeless community and these fearful people overwhelmed by their grief, shame, and sorrow, the Lord himself breathes his breath so they may "[r]eceive the Holy Spirit." The Lord gives life to those who have rejected his life by breathing back into them the gift of the Holy Spirit. And with that gift comes the plentitude of the Spirit's own gifts, by which disciples share in the power and strength of Christ's own life.

The Gifts of the Holy Spirit

It is far too common to consider the gifts of the Holy Spirit as a mere list of various things that must be memorized and regurgitated for a test rather than as ways of coming to share in the life of Christ, with all his power and strength. Just like imagining the opposite of those marks of the Spirit in the third part of the Creed can help us see that the Spirit's presence really is a gift, so too can the condition of the fallen Adam and Eve help us to appreciate how the gifts of the Holy Spirit are more than trivial add-ons to already perfectly respectable lives. Indeed, these gifts give life and with that life comes vital power.

The seven gifts of the Holy Spirit are as follows:

1. Wisdom: the gift and the power to judge and direct things in accordance with divine truth. Remember, the temptation of the serpent is to create our own standards and thus fall out of harmony with the wisdom of God.
2. Understanding: the gift and the power to see what is really going on, to get to the heart of the matter, and to move past mere appearances. Remember, the serpent is shrewd and hides the real agenda from us.
3. Counsel: the gift and the power to appeal to God for direction and guidance for specific decisions and fundamental commitments. Remember, the serpent inclines us to depend on ourselves alone, to do our own thing.
4. Fortitude: the gift and the power to remain firm in mind, heart, and will in doing the good and avoiding evil, especially when doing the good is costly and requires sacrifice. Remember, it was the weakness of memory and communication that was the opening for the serpent, and then the man refused to make a sacrifice to aid his helpmate in being redeemed from the transgression.
5. Knowledge: the gift and the power to judge correctly about matters of faith and justice, recognizing when to apply mercy and how to uplift dignity in the world. Remember, the serpent misrepresented the fruit when he said that eating it would not bring about death; it was not an outright lie, but rather a shifting of meaning so that immediate physical death became the focus rather than the looming threat of spiritual death.
6. Piety: the gift and the power to love God with a childlike love, and thereafter the right appreciation and reverence for one another, as neighbors. Remember, the serpent seeks to change the

meaning of God's gifts—the trees, the fruit, the garden—so that we see everything in terms of rivalry and competition.

7. Fear of the Lord: the gift and the power of remaining in utmost reverence for the Lord so as to always avoid separating from him, come what may. Remember, the serpent presents God as a jailer and turns the healthy fear of the Lord into an unreasonable fear of being taken advantage of by the One who has given us life.[1]

The effects of sin begin with the diminishment of life and lead eventually to death. The gifts of the Holy Spirit revive and embolden us—we whom the Lord has redeemed. Into the "death zone" of sin, the Lord breathes onto his disciples and they receive the gift of new life.

Being Made Whole

The Israelites had been led out of slavery into paradise: the Promised Land, where they were free to be God's people. But Israel was not faithful, it did not heed the commands of the Lord, and it chased after foreign ways. The ancient Israelites were exiled from their Promised Land, first by the Assyrians and then, as we discussed in chapter 14, by the Babylonians. The Babylonian exile, in particular, left Israel as nearly nothing. If it had been a blossoming tree, it was reduced to nothing more than a stump. When Israel was in precisely that condition, the prophet Isaiah prophesied these words on behalf of the Lord:

> But a shoot shall sprout from the stump of Jesse,
> and from his roots a bud shall blossom.
> The spirit of the LORD shall rest upon him:
> a spirit of wisdom and of understanding,
> A spirit of counsel and of strength [fortitude],
> a spirit of knowledge and of fear of the LORD,
> and his delight shall be the fear of the LORD. (Isa 11:1-3, NABRE)

1. As a good, free, helpful follow-up resource to the gifts of the Holy Spirit, I would recommend "The Seven Gifts of the Holy Spirit," *Catholic Answers*, accessed July 17, 2019, https://www.catholic.com/magazine/print-edition/the-seven-gifts-of-the-holy-spirit.

This passage forms part of the biblical basis for the gifts of the Holy Spirit, but why exactly is this particular prophesy made in this way and at that particular time? Jesse is, of course, the father of David, and David is the king of Israel, the first of the united monarchy in Israel. Under his reign, the twelve tribes are one kingdom. David is the head or the image of the whole: the whole of Israel, as one kingdom. David is the image of wholeness and of health, the image of the healthy and thriving life of Israel.

But Israel has been reduced to a stump: Jesse's son, once the sovereign king, has nearly wasted away. The whole is nearly nothing. The Assyrians and then the Babylonians have dismembered the kingdom. The Israelites have been exiled from their land. They have seemingly lost their identity. They have become slaves of a foreign power, imprisoned in hostility. In a real way, this is the consequence of Israel's infidelity to the Lord—Israel has not clung to the Lord who gives it life and so it has become lifeless. Israel tried to animate itself in other ways, to disastrous effect.

The shoot that will sprout from the stump—the new bud that will blossom—is fresh hope for the reconstituted, new and enduring life of Israel. The prophet Isaiah proclaims that a "new David" will come from the same roots as the first David. This is hope for Israel *after* the exile, *after* it has been pulled apart. The gifts that are then listed are the forms of strength that will be given to all of Israel through this new king. He will be the one with this strength, and because he is the head and image of the whole, the rest of the nation will share in his vital life.

Jesus is the new David; he is the promised king. When he finds his disciples cowering in the locked room, drained of hope and lacking in zeal, he breathes on them. His apostles are the twelve tribes of Israel, and under him what has been pulled apart is made whole again. His kingdom will have no end. Those whom Christ claims as his own are made one in him, and together we are given the gifts of his life, his strength, by the Spirit that is his own. Jesus Christ does what the Creator did when he formed the earth creature and made it into a living being: he gives the gift of his own breath.

The gifts of the Holy Spirit build up each disciple and build up the whole Church.

The Strength of Virtue

The Lord breathed new life into St. Paul and St. Paul built up the Church. At the beginning of Paul's conversion narrative, we read that as he set out for Damascus in his mission to destroy "the Way," Paul was "still *breathing* murderous threats against the disciples" (Acts 9:1, NABRE, italics added). From what we have been exploring in this chapter, we can now say that Paul is described as attempting to live in a way opposed to God's way. He is animated not by the Spirit of life but is filling his lungs with what harms him. This way of breathing is toxic, it is burdensome, and it leads to death.

Paul is broken from this old way so that new life may be breathed into him. He no longer breathes murderous threats but begins to breathe God's own Spirit. This is no mere resuscitation, as if the conversion were the end of the change. No, Paul's change is so profound it is nothing short of a complete transformation. The breath that now animates him transforms everything about him: the way he sees, the way he hears, the way he speaks. His lives anew in Christ. As he himself writes, "Therefore, if any one is in Christ, he is a new creation; the old has passed away, behold, the new has come" (2 Cor 5:17, RSV).

Paul becomes a source of goodness. He builds up what he once sought to tear down. He does not just breathe the life of Spirit; he becomes a source of that life for others. He was not merely resuscitated; he lives anew. But none of this happens without his own cooperation, his own work. The life that the Lord gives him is truly the Lord's gift to give, but receiving and growing with that life requires Paul's own consent and his own willingness to love.

To put this briefly, Paul is at once the beneficiary of grace and a man who matures in virtue. Virtues are perfected abilities, whereby our own humanity becomes responsive to and cooperative with the action of God. We were created in harmony with our Creator, in harmony with each other, and in harmony with the earth from which we were formed. In sin, we rebel against that harmony. By the strength of virtue, we slowly become fit again to allowing our lives to harmonize with the Spirit who fills us and gives us life.

In the chapters to follow, I am going to focus on a single virtue concerned with the ability—the power—to give one's whole attention to another person in intimacy. We saw how in the garden, this intimacy was forfeited in the Fall. By the strength of the virtue of chastity, though, this power is restored and perfected. It makes us especially open to the gifts of the Spirit and to the life for which God frees us.

Chastity is often considered in a rather narrow way, as if it has to do exclusively with sex, or specifically with avoiding sex. While this issue is certainly worthy of serious attention, the virtue of chastity is much richer and indeed more beautiful than we tend to think. As we consider this virtue, we will focus on those three dimensions that were crucial to Paul's own transformation: the chastity of the ears, the chastity of the eyes, and the chastity of the tongue. In each and in all, we will deal with chastity as *power*—namely, the power of attentiveness, of presence, of generosity.

Chastity has to do with what we listen to, and how. Chastity has to do with what we look at, and how. Chastity has to do with what we say, and how. In sum, chastity has to do with what we do with our bodies, and what we don't do with our bodies. It all has to do with how we allow the Spirit of the Lord to animate us.

Before we move to the project of growing in the virtue of attentiveness, let us call on the Spirit of God to bring us new life, today and always:

Come, Holy Spirit,
fill the hearts of your faithful
and kindle in them the fire of your love.
Send forth your Spirit
and they shall be created.
And you shall renew the face of the earth.

O, God, who by the light of the Holy Spirit,
did instruct the hearts of the faithful,
grant that by the same Holy Spirit
we may be truly wise and ever enjoy his consolations,
Through Christ our Lord.

Amen.

chapter eighteen

Chastity of the Ears: Inclining Our Hearts

"If you feel yourself drifting, set your feet."

This is what the professional counselor said to a roomful of young adults in a workshop about learning how to listen better. You would not normally consider your feet when thinking about listening. Your feet cannot hear. They do not nod in assent. Your feet are rarely seen while in conversation, especially when you are seated at table. So why did this counselor advise them to focus on their feet? Because listening begins from the ground up, and it involves your whole body.

Whether you are sitting in a lecture hall or sitting across from someone at dinner, there comes a point at which your mind will start to wander and it becomes difficult to pay attention. You may miss a sentence or two, or even zone out for several minutes at a time. "If you feel yourself drifting, set your feet." Two feet firmly planted on the ground lead you to straighten your posture, sit upright, and focus your attention in the direction your feet are pointing. If you want to invest your attention on the lecturer or your dinner date, it starts with your feet.

When standing in conversation, the direction of people's feet indicates the quality of their attention. As a general rule, people point their feet—especially their lead foot (usually the right foot)—in the direction where they are giving their attention. Even though people might be making eye contact, if their feet are pointing away from their conversation partner, they are checking out of the conversation. Feet don't lie.[1]

1. A great deal has been written about the importance of feet for attentiveness. For just a couple of examples in the popular realm, see Carol Kinsey Goman, "A

Of course, there is more that goes into good and attentive listening than just the feet, but by bringing up the importance of feet here, we identify a crucial truth about the art of listening: listening is about much more than the sounds you happen to hear; it is about what you do with your body.

I think about things like this when I read St. Paul's words to the Philippians, specifically when he tells them, "I hold you in my heart" (Phil 1:7, RSV). We remember that these are the same Christians whose prayers and discourse Paul once heard with great enmity, seeking to tear them down in persecution. The change in Paul began when the Lord silenced Paul's companions so that Paul could only listen to the Lord's voice. The change in Paul did not end there. He also had to mature into the kind of person who listened to others with care and compassion. What did it cost Paul to make a space in his heart for all these people? How much practice went into learning to listen to their joys and sorrows, their wishes and well-being? How much patience did Paul exercise? How much time must he have spent listening to the Philippians in person or thinking of them in absence? The transformation of his heart did not happen through grace alone, nor through desire alone. His heart was transformed in response to grace, through repeated practices of paying attention even to those whom he once disparaged in anger. The disciplining of his body was the pathway to his heart, so his heart could become the seat of his listening.

The chastity of the ears is a full-body endeavor that changes the quality of a person's heart.

Toward a More Perfect Union

Like a golfer who may need to watch film of his swing to recognize a flaw or a ballerina who must practice in front a mirror to evaluate her technique, those who wish to practice better listening benefit from intentional exercises to assess and improve the quality of their

---

Body Language Secret: Look Below the Belt," *Forbes*, July 15, 2010, 2010/07/15/body-language-feet-leadership-managing-legs; and Hanan Parvez, "What Do the Seated Legs and Feet Gestures Reveal," accessed July 22, 2019, https://www.psychmechanics.com/2015/05/body-language-seated-leg-and-feet.html.

attention. The following three exercises—designed for pairs—are a good place to start.[2]

For the first exercise, one person is the designated speaker and the other the designated listener. The topic can be anything, like telling the other person about a trip you have taken. The speaker should talk on the topic for about two minutes. While that person is talking, the other person—the listener—is only going to use her body, not mind, to show signs of paying attention. In other words, the listener has to appear to be paying attention, but try to not actually pay attention to what the other person is saying. Then, after a minute, the listener does the opposite: now she will listen attentively only with her ears but not with her body. Using her body, she acts as if she is not paying attention, even though she is trying to listen. The two people can switch roles for a second round, so the listener becomes the speaker and the speaker becomes the listener.

What people find in this exercise is that, when you are the speaker, it is hard to keep talking or feel like you are being listened to when the other person is doing other things with her body. When the other person is trying to appear to be listening with her body but also trying to not listen with her mind, it can feel deceptive for both people. Even when you are speaking and a lot of the nonverbal clues suggest that the other person is paying attention, you can usually still detect when someone is not really listening.

When you are the listener, it proves rather difficult to *not* listen with your ears and mind when you are trying to appear to be paying attention with your body. Conversely, even though you are working very hard to listen with your ears and your mind, if you are doing other things with your body, it is a struggle to actually listen. Bodily action, posture, and expression in a listener makes a huge difference not only in one's ability to listen, but also in a speaker's confidence and comfort when trying to share something with someone else.

For the second exercise, which is still between two people, each partner again takes a turn speaking and a turn listening. The subject of what each person will speak could, once again, be any number of

2. I am indebted to Stacey Noem for these three exercises, which she shared as part of a workshop for the Catholic Formation Group at our parish that prepared early teens for the sacrament of confirmation.

things, like talking about the best gift you have ever received. Each person will speak for a minute or two about this best gift, telling the other person all about it and why he or she liked it so much, maybe even describing the gift in detail. While one person is speaking, the other person will just listen, absorbing as much of the information as possible, but without making any verbal or nonverbal affirmations. This means the listener is just listening while keeping physically still and remaining expressionless.

With this exercise, people find that talking to someone who does not give any feedback whatsoever is kind of creepy and makes it difficult to continue talking with the person without becoming self-conscious or nervous. On the flip side, listening in this way can be very trying, in a physical sense. If you are really listening, you find yourself wanting to offer some verbal affirmations, nods of the head, or facial expressions. Of course, all those verbal and nonverbal responses can be taken too far and become distractions and impediments to good conversation themselves, but the complete absence of these things tends to smother conversations in a prevailing sense of awkwardness.

For the third exercise, then, each person practices active listening. Again, each person will take a turn as speaker and as listener, and the topic can be something like telling the other person about a hobby or game you really enjoy. In this exercise, the listener should pay attention using his ears and mind *and* body. Facial expressions, bodily gestures, and verbal feedback are all allowed and encouraged.

By this point, the listeners might be so sensitive about giving the right kind of verbal and nonverbal feedback to the person speaking that they overdo it. This is productive because it highlights just how much of an art and practiced skill attentive listening is. When you listen to another person speak as an attentive listener, you pay attention to the whole person: what the speaker says but also how the speaker reacts to your feedback. Are your verbal responses helping the other person to speak more confidently and comfortably, or does the speaker lose momentum when you offer that kind of feedback? Are you showing the person that you are listening by what you say and do, or does the speaker seem unsure about whether you are really listening? The best way to get better at listening is in the context of conversations, but it is also helpful to assess from time to time what you do and do not do when you are in the role of listener. Where are your feet pointing?

How is your eye contact? Do you remember what the speaker said afterward?

The union of ears and mind with body is critical for good, attentive listening, and good attentive listening changes the person who listens. When you listen attentively, you give over to someone else the most precious thing you have—your attention—and this makes space in yourself for what someone else has to say, and even for who someone else is. The discipline of attentive listening is a discipline of harmony, in yourself and with others.

Models of Attentiveness

Who is the best listener you know? Is there someone or maybe a couple of people who, when you are talking with them, give you the feeling of being really listened to? What do those individuals do? How do they act, what kinds of things do they say, what are they doing with their bodies? It is worth spending some time thinking about these things in order to learn more about the art of listening and the gift of attention.

One of the best listeners I know is Kaitlyn Patterson. She is a good listener all the time, but I have really noticed how well she listens when we are walking together, side by side. This became apparent to me the very first time I walked somewhere with her, which was about a dozen years ago. I noticed that when I was speaking, Kaitlyn turned her shoulders toward me while walking. She did the same thing when she had to tell me something important or there was something that required just a little more emphasis. I don't think I have ever noticed this in anybody else, or if I have, I do not remember it as well as I remember it with Kaitlyn. She has impressed her quality of attention on me through that simple but intentional bodily practice.

Another excellent listener is my college friend Michael Sena. I happened to eat a lot of meals with Mike because he lived in my dorm and our class schedules aligned. But I ate a lot of meals with a lot of different people in college, so why do I remember these meals with Mike? Because there was never any doubt that Mike listened to what I said. When I told Mike something—whether that was sharing a story or talking about something from class—the same thing would happen pretty much every time. When I stopped speaking, there would be at least five seconds of silence. I have to admit, this was a little unsettling for me at first because I am so used to conversations moving along very quickly, even to the point where the person "listening" sometimes begins speaking before the other person has finished. That is the way I "listen" most of the time. Mike, though, had acquired the discipline of listening all the way through to the end of what the other person said. You know someone has *not* listened to *everything* you have said if he or she starts speaking immediately, because it takes a little bit of time—even just a few seconds—to register everything. I grew to not only appreciate but even admire the way in which Mike listened, so much so that I hold it up as a practice worthy of emulation.

Kaitlyn's and Mike's practices might strike us as peculiar because most of us have become quite comfortable in scattering our attention. The turn of the shoulders and the pause before responding are small, intentional counter-practices to the seemingly unstoppable drift toward inattentiveness in our world. How common has it become for most people to be in one place with one group of people and yet, with their attention, run off toward other places and other people? Yes, smartphones and other devices have aided this drift toward attention-less living, but the technologies that distract and disintegrate us are symptoms of a deeper ailment. We have become resistant to the practices of presence. And so, if attentiveness is to be reclaimed at the heart of the virtue of chastity, then practices like Kaitlyn's and Mike's must become more common.

Who's Listening

They who listen lean in. They point their feet, turn their shoulders, set their eyes, open their ears. They observe the pause, they weigh and consider what they have heard, they respond in kind. They are here—really here—right now. It would be virtually impossible to overemphasize the importance of all this, since all throughout Scripture this attentive "leaning in" appears as a fundamental spiritual posture and disposition. In biblical parlance, "leaning in" appears as "inclining your ear," "inclining your heart," or even "inclining the ear of your heart."

The primary instruction the Lord gives his people is to pay attention to him. "Hear, O Israel, the Lord is your God, the Lord alone" is the beginning of the daily Jewish prayer, the Shema, which God enjoins on the people through Moses (see Deut 6:4). The first and most important duty, from day to day, is to listen to the Lord, and this listening involves every part of yourself.

In his farewell speech to the Israelites, Joshua echoes this instruction, saying, "Incline your hearts to the LORD, the God of Israel" (Josh 24:23, RSV). The Lord speaks directly to his people in Proverbs and the Psalms, telling them, "Incline your ear, and hear my words" (Prov 22:17, NABRE; cf. 5.1) and "incline your ears to the words of my mouth!" (Ps 78:1, RSV). When St. Benedict of Nursia wrote the Rule for his monastery, he put this primary biblical instruction up front as the starting point for the community that was being formed to follow the Lord: "Listen carefully, my child, to your master's words, and incline the ear of your heart" (see Prov 4:20).[3]

While it might not surprise anyone that paying attention to God is essential for the spiritual life, what might be surprising is that our attentiveness to God is in response to God's attentiveness to us. God is attentive first, and in being attentive to God we imitate him and grow toward him. How is God attentive? By inclining himself to us; God leans in. Here are just some of the prayers we find throughout Scripture begging God to heed us, as God always does:

> The psalmist prays, "Incline your ear to me; hear my words" (Ps 17:6, RSV; cf. 86:1).
>
> The prophet Isaiah prays, "Incline your ear, O Lord, and hear" (Isa 37:17, RSV).
>
> The prophet Daniel prays, "O my God, incline your ear and hear" (Dan 9:18, RSV).
>
> King Solomon prays, "May He incline our hearts to Him. . . . And may these words of mine, which I have offered in supplication before the Lord, be close to the Lord our God day and night" (1 Kgs 8:58-59, JPS).

The joy of salvation comes, first of all, from the Lord *listening* to the words and cries, the needs and desires of his people. The liberation God gives comes through God paying attention to and inclining

3. Benedict of Nursia, *The Rule of St. Benedict*, ed. Timothy Fry (New York: Vintage, 1998), 3, Prologue.

himself toward us: pointing his feet, turning his shoulders, listening to everything all the way through the pause. And his attentiveness gives his people joy, as the psalmist proclaims:

> I waited, waited for the LORD;
> who bent down and heard my cry. (Ps 40:1, NAB)

And again:

> I love the LORD, because he has heard my voice and my supplications.
> Because he inclined his ear to me, therefore I will call on him as long as I live. (Ps 116:1-2, RSV)

When St. Paul held the Philippians in his heart, rejoicing at every remembrance of them, he had learned how to share in the Lord's gift of attending to his people. In Paul, then, the Philippians knew the saving power of the Lord who inclines the ear of his heart to us. To incline our ears is about more than the sounds we hear: it is about what we do with our bodies, and what we do with our bodies changes our hearts. Developing the skill of attention from our ears through our bodies to our hearts enriches us in prayer, in relationship, and in compassion. Learning how to listen makes us more like God.

chapter nineteen

Chastity of the Tongue: Harnessing the Power of Words

"Death and life are in the power of the tongue" (Prov 18:21, NABRE).[1]

That seems a bit excessive, doesn't it? Since when could words give life or bring about death? Since the beginning, actually.

Without God's act of creation there is formlessness, darkness, and chaos. But when God creates, there is form, light, and order. What is the difference between these two states? God's word.

"Then God said: Let there be light, and there was light" (Gen 1:3, NABRE). The first thing God creates is light, but the agent of creation is God's word: "God said." Life comes from the power of that word.

It doesn't stop there. "God said" appears again in verses 6, 9, 11, 14, 20, 22, 24, 26, and 29 of Genesis 1. That means there are ten instances of "God said" in the first creation account, whereby the creation of the entire cosmos, of every plant and animal, and of human beings themselves, is the gift of God's word. Those ten words form a Decalogue, which is of course also known as the Ten Commandments—the ten divine words of the law. Creation comes from God's word and life is ordered by God's word. God's word is life: behold, the power of the tongue.

When God created humans, "God said: Let us make human beings in our image, after our likeness" (Gen 1:26, NABRE). By God's word,

1. I am grateful and indebted to Michael Palmer, who led an excellent workshop on the power of words for the young people preparing for confirmation at our parish, in our Catholic Formation Group. This chapter draws from Michael's presentation.

God creates human beings to share in God's own power. That power includes the power of speech, by which we, like God, are endowed with the power to give life or to bring about death—to bless and to curse.

When and how is death introduced? When the serpent initiates the abuse of language, and human beings follow right along. From the tongue of the serpent came the words: "Did God really say . . . ?" (Gen 3:1, NABRE). Words, previously used to bring form to formlessness, light to darkness, and order to chaos, are now used to deceive, manipulate, and sow suspicion. The serpent did not invent the power of words; what the serpent did was initiate the misuse of words.

By the end of time, that serpent will be all grown up, appearing in the Book of Revelation as a dragon (that's a big serpent). What does the dragon do? He accuses. Like a prosecuting attorney, he accuses the human beings of their sins, arguing for our condemnation by the force of his words. The way of words that the serpent initiates thus spans from deception to condemnation, and condemnation is the final death. The one who undoes the dragon's power is the Word, who was there in the beginning before the serpent; who suffered, died, and was buried; who endured all the consequences of our misuse of words, and then rose on the third day to ascend to the Father. It is Christ, the Lamb, who washes the saints in his blood: the blood of the Word made flesh (see especially Rev 12).[2]

So maybe the line from Proverbs is not so excessive after all: "Death and life *are* in the power of the tongue."

2. That whole drama is already present *in nuce* in the Book of Genesis. The initial misuse of words in Genesis 3 opens up a wide and sprawling tragedy about the downfall of human community. Yes, that happens in Genesis 3 with the exile from the garden, but the death-dealing from wicked tongues continues. Cain slays and slanders his brother, then disclaims responsibility for him. The wickedness of men brings on the flood, from which only Noah and his kin are saved—then the Lord speaks his word to Noah: a covenant. Even still, the wickedness of men reemerged and persisted, rising up in the lust for power as people from all over the world, speaking the same language, conspired to build a tower to their own greatness, to "make a name for ourselves" (Gen 11:4, NABRE). So the Lord confused their speech, so they could not rise up in their lust for power, continuing to do what the first couple had done in the garden by speaking out and separating from the Lord.

The Worlds Our Words Create

We create with our words. We create a reality for ourselves and for other people by the way we speak, by what we speak about, and by the intention we invest in our speech. We who have lived to see the power of propaganda in the rise of totalitarian states and the dizzying dissemination of fake news through various media know only too well how reality becomes warped through the malfeasance of those with the power to control speech. But this malfeasance occurs in more local and intimate settings too.

Spouses deceive each other by their words and intentions, and families fall apart. Colleagues try to one-up each other by playing all the slippery games of office politics, and careers if not companies are ruined. Friends gossip, corroding friendships from the inside. We create with our words, and much of what we create leads to disorder and decay because too few of us use words carefully and honestly.

Jesus had little patience for the abuse of language. He saw right through the lies and deceptions, and he reckoned with the fact that oftentimes the sweetest sounding language carries within it the most poisonous venom. "You brood of vipers," Jesus said to the Pharisees, who were setting traps by what sounded like virtuous speech:

> "[H]ow can you say good things when you are evil? For from the fullness of the heart the mouth speaks. A good person brings forth good out of a store of goodness, but an evil person brings forth evil out of a store of evil. I tell you, on the day of judgment people will render an account for every careless word they speak. By your words you will be acquitted, and by your words you will be condemned." (Matt 12:34-37, NABRE)

The words the Pharisees speak are "careless," and this affects everything. In Greek the word translated as "careless" is *argos*, which can also mean "idle" or "barren." The Pharisees' words are empty and they bear no fruit. They do not give life; rather, they spread meaninglessness and rot.

Right before he calls the Pharisees a "brood of vipers," Jesus said that they must "[e]ither declare the tree good and its fruit is good, or declare the tree rotten and its fruit is rotten" (Matt 12:33, NABRE). He means that the Pharisees need to say what they mean, to mean what they say, and to accept the consequences. They call Jesus demonic when he drives out demons, because they are quite comfortable judging others by their words but completely resistant to being judged themselves. They presume to have the power to say what is real and what is false, yet at the bottom of that presumption is their claim to being above judgment themselves. By their words, they create a reality in which everybody else must abide, but Jesus calls them out. He says their speech is fruitless because their hearts are filled with venom: they seek to build themselves up by tearing down others. Death is in the power of their tongues.

One of the things that comes from an honest reading of the gospels is the discovery that the Pharisees are not outliers in this regard. It is oh so tempting and all too comforting to see the Pharisees as dense and even idiotic hardliners who just don't get it. But think again about all the ways in which we create realities for ourselves and each other, whether in geopolitics, on social media, or in the confines of our homes, classrooms, offices, and communities. Being careful with words is often inconvenient, even costly. To say what you mean, mean what you say, and accept the consequences is often burdensome. It might mean someone else's foreign policy priorities are achieved rather than yours, that your spouse is right rather than you, and that your students or teachers or colleagues or friends actually ought to get their way, be praised, or set the agenda . . . and not you.

To be honest, it is much more enticing to use words loosely, even idly, in order to present a "truth" you prefer, to shade the truth toward your advantage, or even to bend the truth completely in order to avoid what you want to avoid. Moreover, it is also really tempting to just be cruel with words: disregarding others' needs or feelings, saying what you want how you want instead. You might even call someone demonic.

The Bridle, the Rudder, and the Well-Trained Tongue

The Pharisees speak as the serpent speaks, which is not of God. They are responsible for spreading decay by their words. When the dragon accuses them, God will hold them accountable. Needless to say, it is important to part ways with the Pharisees, especially the Pharisee within—that tendency in each of us to want to re-create the world in our image.

The apostle James, who spent a great deal of time in the company of the Lord, both recognized this problem and hinted at the solution. As he writes,

> If we put bits into the mouths of horses to make them obey us, we also guide their whole bodies. It is the same with ships: even though they are so large and driven by fierce winds, they are steered by a very small rudder whenever the pilot's inclination wishes. In the same way the tongue is a small member and yet has great pretensions. . . . With it we bless the Lord and Father, and with it we curse human beings who are made in the likeness of God. From the same mouth come blessing and cursing. This need not be so. (Jas 3:3-5, 9-10, NABRE)

Jesus called out the Pharisees for their fruitless words that emerged from wicked hearts, but it is not easy to change your own heart. So what can you do? You can practice controlling your words, speaking fewer words, and employing words more carefully.

As James notes, it seems like such a small thing, but he knows not only from his love of the Lord but likely also from his own experience that what comes forth from our mouths can have massive consequences. Such a little thing as a bit in the mouth of a horse can direct its whole body, and a rudder that is but a tiny fraction compared to the size of an entire ship can steer the whole thing even in a storm. Just so, becoming a more conscious charioteer of your tongue and captain of your own words can guide the whole of you in the direction of care, consideration, and blessing. By our tongues we can speak blessings and curses, so it's essential to practice speaking blessings. This is how the Lord himself speaks, creating by his word and then blessing what he creates: "God saw that it was good" (Gen 1:4; 1:10; 1:12; 1:18; 1:21; 1:25; 1:31, NABRE).

How do you create life with your own words? By complimenting, by encouraging, by offering prayers. By being honest, by being thoughtful, by being economical with your words. Words can communicate blessing.

How do you kill with words? By gossiping, by ridiculing, by profaning. By using a demeaning tone of voice, by manipulating, by lying. Words can communicate curses.

How do you correct for your own and others' misuse of words? By apologizing, by confessing, by trying again. By explaining, by forgiving, by setting the record straight. Words can help heal the wounds they have created.

How can flattery be sinister and critique be constructive? In part, by the intention given to each. We know that we can flatter in order to avoid honesty, curry favor with someone, or even to indulge in soft mockery. At the same time, we also know that honest critique, offered with kindness, can become, for ourselves and others, an occasion for growth. Sometimes it is what we say that matters, sometimes it is why we say what we say that matters, and sometimes it is just how we say the things we say that matters.

St. James calls upon his fellow Christians to practice chastity of the tongue, taking control of what and how they speak. It is a discipline learned over time, through hardship and training just like all disciplines. To acquire this virtue requires effort and commitment, but also support and guidance. We learn how to speak from others and we each need others to help us speak well. This also means, therefore, that if we are to become sources of goodness, then we must take seriously our responsibility to help others learn how to speak well. Following St. James, St. Paul says that Christians ought to sound different from pagans—meaning that the way we speak when we mature in the Christian life ought to be recognizable by its clarity, tone, and charity (see Eph 4:17-32).

In the end, what Isaiah prophesied about the Christ who was to come should, through Christ, be fulfilled in those who are his disciples. Like him, we should be able to proclaim, "The Lord GOD has given me a well-trained tongue, / That I might know how to speak to the weary / a word that will rouse them" (Isa 50:4, NAB).

That is the power to give life.

chapter twenty

Chastity of the Eyes: Risking the Joy of Encounter

"You were not created to look into a screen.
You were created to look into one another's eyes."

My friend Joe Campo says this to the young men he is raising. He has raised a lot of young men, only two of which are his biological children. Joe is the head of the St. Francis House in Brooklyn, New York, where young men in need live together under Joe's roof and in his care. They are young men without fathers and without a stable home, so Joe becomes a father to them and gives them a place to live together. They have dinner together every night, sitting together and talking for two hours or more. They look at each other as they practice seeing eye to eye.

Over the three decades that Joe has directed this home, the call and mission has remained mostly unchanged: to help young men reach Christian maturity. What has changed, though, are some of the conditions in which this mission is pursued. In the 1980s, 1990s, and early 2000s, the greatest threat to the stability of their home was typically drugs and alcohol. Now, as Joe attests, the greatest threat is pornography. It seeps in through the smallest of openings: the opening of the pocket-sized screens that every young man—even the poorest—carries with him day in and day out.

"You were not created to look into a screen. You were created to look into one another's eyes."

Pornography gives the viewer the sensation of looking at another person intimately and personally, but only through the medium of the screen. The screen is the barrier to presence. What these young people get used to are the quick rewards that sometimes go along with gazing at another person—excitement, passion, connection—but without any of the work, any of the messiness, or any of the actual reality of being in another person's presence. All that practice of seeing eye-to-eye at the dinner table is undercut by the counter-practice of one-way gazing through the screen. What Joe has seen firsthand is that it is not only what you look at that changes you, but also the way in which you grow accustomed to looking that matters.

More than what someone looks at, pornography is a way of seeing. The habitual practice of a way of seeing changes the way we see everything else. The greatest threat in pornography addiction, therefore, is that users develop a pornographic vision of the world. This does not mean they see nudity and sex everywhere; rather, it means they become accustomed to being detached from what they look at, desensitized to the actual reality of those who surround them, and stimulated only by what amuses or surprises.

This not only stops people from looking into others' eyes; they also forget they are supposed to.

It is all too easy to think that chastity of the eyes is about avoiding pornography. Of course, indulging in pornography is definitely an unchaste practice. But chastity is not merely reducible to what is to be avoided. In fact, what is avoided is the flip side of growing in strength and power. That is why Joe Campo is right on target with what he tells his young men, because chastity is about being able to look into another person's eyes.

Through Our Eyes

Who has the authority to shape the way you see things? We might think that we are each in control of how we see the world, but we deceive ourselves. What we look at shapes us. What we have some measure of control over is choosing what to look at. In choosing what to regularly look at, we grant the authority for shaping the way we see things.

We know this from some fairly obvious examples. If one person habitually follows an ostensibly "liberal" political site, while another follows an equally "conservative" one, those two people are very likely to look at the exact same political event in radically different ways. One person who has been taught to associate Christmas with abandonment and another who has always been shown festive companionship at Christmas will see Christmas very differently, like the Grinch and Cindy Lou Who. And a person who spends his or her time looking at other people's bodies through screens for pleasure and a person who regularly looks other people in the eye during conversations at dinner every night will steadily learn to see people differently.

In the Garden of Eden, it was not the sight of each other's bodies that was the source of the problem for the man and the woman who had just eaten the forbidden fruit. The problem was that they were afraid to be transparent to each other because they were ashamed. They hid behind trees because they did not want to be seen by a God whom they had come to view as a rival. Nothing about the garden changed; they changed. The way they saw things changed.

When Paul encountered that blinding light on the road to Damascus, he was broken from the way he had been seeing things. While he had seen things through a lens of anger, colored with rage, that vision was now being interrupted. On the other side of his blindness, he began learning to see in the light of Christ, who had mercy on him. He had to practice seeing that way, day in and day out. Seeing that way changed him, and it changed the way he saw other people. He no longer saw Christians as enemies, but rather as kin, beginning with Ananias who called him "brother."

While it is true that we inherit ways of seeing the world, especially from parents and a community, and our particular culture, it is equally true that we develop, refine, confirm, and/or recast how we see through what we regularly gaze at. The eyes are the windows to the soul not merely in terms of showing others what is on the inside, but also in terms of allowing what is on the outside to shape who we are inside. What we see regularly changes how we see. Our eyes are precious. We must entrust them with care.

In his Sermon on the Mount, Jesus preaches on the eyes right in between preaching on the importance of what we treasure and the fact that we can only serve one, not two masters. In other words, he places the eyes between what we value and who we worship:

> The eye is the lamp of the body. So, if your eye is sound, your whole body will be full of light; but if your eye is not sound, your whole

> body will be full of darkness. If then the light in you is darkness, how great is the darkness! (Matt 6:22-23, RSV)

The symptoms of an unsound eye are covetousness, greed, and envy (see Deut 15:1-11; Sir 14:8-10), while those with healthy eyes respond to the needs of others with charity (see Tob 4:7-11). These are completely different ways of seeing the world: one way through possessiveness and the other through compassion and solidarity. Rather than just singular choices in specific situations, Jesus is saying that the way one sees and responds to those around him or her indicates the kind of person one is. It is a matter of seeing, and *you* are the one seeing.

When you practice looking at another person—or the representation of another person—as an object for you to do with as you please, whether that be to reprove, judge, derive pleasure from, or disregard, you become the kind of person who sees others that way. When, by contrast, you practice looking at other people as people like yourself, who have their own needs and wishes and desires, their own faults and stories and complexities, then you become the kind of person who sees others that way. At the risk of making this all too clear-cut, we might say that, in the end, there are only two ways of seeing: one that is dehumanizing and one that is humanizing. To dehumanize means to see others as estranged from us, but to humanize is to see ourselves in relationship to others. As Pope Francis has written, "Every human being is the object of God's infinite tenderness, and he himself is present in their lives."[1]

Chastity of the eyes is therefore a matter of learning to see others how God sees each of us.

Learning to See Again

"Do not be conformed to this world," St. Paul writes to the Romans, "but be transformed by the renewal of your mind, that you may prove what is the will of God, what is good and acceptable and perfect" (Rom 12:2, RSV). This is easier said than done, of course. Without intention and effort, the default way of being shaped will be according to whatever "the

1. Francis, *Evangelii Gaudium: The Joy of the Gospel* (Washington, DC: United States Conference of Catholic Bishops, 2013), 274.

world" happens to approve of at any given time. So how do we build up the virtue of chastity for our eyes?

First, we should pay attention to what we gaze at. It would be helpful to dedicate a week or two to keeping a daily journal of how you spend your time and where you give your attention. Oftentimes, we are unaware just how much time we invest in certain apps, or websites, or media sources. At the beginning of the journal, in big and bold letters, write the question: "Who has the authority to shape the way I see things?" You could even write this on the top of every journal page, because the point is to use that question to judge whether those things that we lend our eyes to are worthy of the authority we give them.

Second, we can listen to Joe Campo. As a regular practice, engage in face-to-face conversation, where you can look into another person's eyes. From experience, I know how developing new "regular practices" usually goes: I start with intention and I end with a thud. A regular practice needs planned, scheduled, written-in-ink commitments. Joe is able to make the rule of his household the daily dinner conversation. While that dinner table environment might be desirable (and it is usually held up as the ideal), the really important thing is the regular, predictable, and scheduled rhythm that Joe and the young men in the St. Francis House follow. We can make our own plans for developing this habit of speaking face-to-face and seeing eye-to-eye, but the key is to actually make a plan and then follow through.

Third, we can regularly spend time in Eucharistic Adoration. We might not initially think of adoration as a practice in how to see, but isn't it true that the Lord dwells among us in unguarded intimacy in the exposed Host? St. Maximillian Kolbe practiced Eucharistic Adoration nearly daily for years and years, and then when he was condemned to the concentration camp at Auschwitz, he continued seeing the world in light of what he had learned to see in the Lord's presence. No one was ever under more pressure to "be conformed to this world" than Maximillian and other prisoners at Auschwitz, and yet that regular practice of gazing upon the Lord saved him, and through him others were saved. That might sound like a dramatic example because it is, but the truth holds. We are formed by what we constantly gaze at, and who is more deserving of the authority to shape the way we see things than our Lord and our God?

chapter twenty-one

The First and Perfect Disciple

On a scale of 1 to 10—with 1 being totally passive and 10 being absolutely active—where would you rank Mary's performance in the Annunciation narrative? On the one hand, the angel takes the initiative, does most of the talking, and seems to decide when the encounter begins and ends. Mary didn't come up with this plan, she doesn't negotiate any of the terms, and something is done to her. Even more, she is told, "The Holy Spirit will come upon you, and the power of the Most High will overshadow you" (Luke 1:35, RSV). Sure seems like sheer passivity. On the other hand, she does say "Yes," so maybe there are some traces of activity here, though perhaps not as much as one would like.

In truth, no matter where you'd place Mary between 1 and 10, you'd be wrong. You'd be wrong because the light of Christian discipleship does not bend to that spectrum and Mary herself is the revelation of a Christian disciple in all her brilliance.

Is there passivity? Yes, and it's total. Is there activity? Yes, and it's total too. Mary is a paradox because she embodies what we might call "willed passivity" or "active obedience," which disposes her to harmony with divine freedom rather than what we otherwise want to see, which is something like "freedom" as autonomy, maybe even rebellion. But especially in the Gospel of Luke, the explicit definition of a disciple is the one "who hears the word of God and acts on it" (see Luke 8:21; 11:28), and before Luke ever writes these words, he paints a portrait of the complete disciple in Jesus's mother. Later he shows how the transformation into discipleship follows the pattern first established in her.

How do we learn what true freedom is in Mary, the first and perfect Christian disciple? By paying attention to how she listened and how she acted, focusing mostly on the Annunciation narrative. I would need quite a number of words to provide a truly satisfactory account of the astonishing amount of activity hidden under Mary's disciplined passivity when the angel brought the Word of God to her. Rather than trying to squeeze all those words in here, I only want to point in the direction of where the full demonstration of her freedom lies. The virginal conception of Jesus is indeed the work of the Holy Spirit, with which Mary herself works in harmony. Though not reducible to these terms, we may certainly be mindful of the relationship between the gifts of the Holy Spirit and the growth in virtue that we explored in the previous four chapters when we set our sights now on Mary, seeking to learn from her what a disciple is.[1]

Hearing the Word of God, in Silence

Mary is the one who "hears the word of God and acts on it," completely and fully. Discipleship is first disciplined receiving and then bold acting. The first side happens with patience, the second with haste. Imagine an archer's bow that is drawn back slowly and carefully, only to be released suddenly with great force and purpose—that is a fairly apt image of Mary of Nazareth, disciple.

At first blush, we might consider hearing to be a wholly passive endeavor. If you clap your hands and I hear it, something just happened to me—I didn't *do* anything. But if you tell me how you're feeling, do I automatically *hear* you? Like, really hear you? Though it's a bit cliché, my wife certainly knows the difference between sound passing into my ears and me really hearing what she's saying. Mary hears the way a lover hears: with effort, care, openness, and a will to wait upon full understanding. She exhibits all the virtue of one who listens well. Be-

1. This chapter heavily relies on two articles I provided to two different publications. The first article is "Mary's Freedom: The Hidden Power of the First Disciple," *FemCatholic* (blog), February 1, 2018, http://www.femcatholic.com/marys-freedom-power-of-the-first-disciple/; and the second is "The First Disciple," *America* 219, no. 8 (October 15, 2018): 36–41. For a more complete exegesis of the Annunciation narrative and the marks of Marian discipleship, see my *What Matters Most: Empowering Young Catholics for Life's Big Decisions* (Notre Dame, IN: Ave Maria Press, 2018), especially 11–27.

ginning with her very first action in the Gospel of Luke, Mary shows herself to be one who is free to wait and strong enough to continually resist the temptation to rush to judgment. In the Annunciation narrative, the angel speaks in three parts, with three responses from Mary following each. The final response is the most famous, but the first response sets the tone, even though it is a response given in total silence. When the angel hails her, Mary is "greatly troubled at the saying and considered what sort of greeting this might be" (1:29, RSV). We can see the significance of this if we do what Luke the evangelist is begging us to do: read Mary's narrative alongside the one that comes immediately before it, which is the angel's announcement to Zechariah. In that narrative, Zechariah's first response—also in silence—is that "fear fell upon him" (1:12, RSV). With each of them Luke wants us to note their respective dispositions: Zechariah immediately becomes a slave to fear, while Mary is free to encounter this strange new thing.

This contrast between the two of them continues when they each speak to ask a question. These sound like basically the same question, but the form of the question changes everything. Zechariah asks, "How shall *I* know this?" (1:18) while Mary asks, "How can *this* be?" (1:34, RSV, italics added). Zechariah wants to pull the situation on to his terms; he wants to control what's going on; he basically says "prove it to me." Mary gives the benefit of the doubt; she is willing to trust; she stretches herself toward what is happening, even though it is unsettling. For Zechariah, he is the center of gravity; for Mary, she allows the word being spoken to hold the center.

It is pretty typical for people to be confused as to why Zechariah ends up getting punished while Mary is exalted. The reason lies in their respective approaches to the angel's announcement. Zechariah is not able to listen—he can't *really* hear—and so he is incapable of speaking well. The angel strikes him mute so the only thing he can do is the very thing he needs to learn how to do: *listen*. When he speaks again after the birth of his son, his words are full of praise. He's begun to *hear* the Word of God.

Mary doesn't just start off hearing in a trusting and open way, she actually never stops. Throughout the infancy narratives in the first two chapters of Luke's gospel, that deep listening becomes her defining characteristic. Luke calls it "pondering," which means letting the word enter into the depths of her heart, where it will make impressions like lunar craters.[2] She ponders what the shepherds tell her about the angelic announcement they've heard (2:19). The priest Simeon tells her that her heart will be pierced for her child (2:35). She ponders what her son says about staying in the temple to do his Father's will (2:51). She ponders everything about this boy: the Word who took flesh in her.

Hearing the Word of God, in Scripture

The sound of the Word does not just pass into Mary's ears; she welcomes him into her heart. She *hears* in a way that no one overcome with fear, or under the control of their own impulses, or lusting for control would ever be able to. She is free to receive.

But what exactly does she receive in hearing? What she hears is related to how she hears, and how she hears is connected to whom she hears.

The last thing the angel tells Mary is that her cousin Elizabeth is pregnant. It might seem like a little newsflash from the village over the hill, but to one whose memory is configured to Scripture—the living memory of Israel—Elizabeth's pregnancy is a potent sign.

In the opening verses of his gospel, Luke the evangelist introduces Zechariah and his wife, Elizabeth, divulging some rather personal information: "[T]hey had no child, because Elizabeth was barren and both were advanced in years" (1:7, RSV). It is not usually a wise practice to comment on someone's advanced age in public, and I cannot imagine calling attention to the fact that "this woman, right here: she's barren." Luke does—and for good reason. Both Elizabeth's age and her infertility make her resemble Abraham's wife, Sarah.

If we thought that Luke failed in upholding proper decorum, the author of Genesis commits an even more egregious lapse. In Genesis 18, we are told that "Abraham and Sarah were old, advanced in years; Sarah had stopped having the periods of women" (18:11, JPS). That is pretty vivid. Those who know Genesis, though, know that this detail is highly

2. I am indebted to Colleen Halpin. who introduced me to this image of lunar craters in relation to Mary's pondering in her beautiful essay "The Pondering Heart: Notre Dame's Special Consecration to Our Lady," *Church Life Journal*, October 7, 2017, https://churchlife.nd.edu/2017/10/07/the-pondering-heart-notre-dames-special-consecration-to-our-lady/.

significant. Why? Because the Lord's covenantal promise to Abraham is that his descendants will be exceedingly numerous.

As Abraham laments their failure to conceive and cries aloud to God, the Lord doubles down on his promise. Now in their advanced age, it seems that all hope is lost—except for the one hope that matters: hope in the Lord God, the giver of life. The amplification of God's promise and the desolation of Abraham and Sarah's infertility culminates in one critical question: "Is anything too wondrous for the Lord?" (Gen 18:14, JPS). The answer: No, nothing is too wondrous. God gives life.

So when Mary learns that Elizabeth—who is old and barren—has conceived a child, she hears "Sarah." How does she hear that? Through a memory alive with Scripture. Whose voice does she hear? She hears God's voice—the one who was working then has announced that he is working now in her midst, and her own call is from him. "[F]or with God nothing will be impossible" (Luke 1:37, RSV). What she hears is the God of Israel asking for her trust. And she says, "Yes."

Acting on the Word of God, in Mercy

Mary is poised in silence and receives the Word of God through a scriptural memory. In receiving the word, she also remains a disciplined student of the way God moves.

The angel Gabriel describes Mary's child in terms of power. He is a king, the son of the Most High, who will have an unending kingdom (Luke 1:32-35). And yet, when Mary herself speaks in the *Magnificat* (Luke 1:46-55), she proclaims the power of her son not as the world conceives of power but rather as the undoing of false, earthly power. In receiving the Word of God, she acts according to the true measure of divine power: mercy.

The power of divine mercy reveals itself as the willingness to suffer the consequences of a power-hungry world rather than play its game. Her *Magnificat* proclaims the power of the God of Israel as the one who hears the cry of the poor and hastens to respond, in person. Abiding within the movement of mercy is how one interprets and begins to respond to the Word of God.

Once Mary *hears* God well and as she *heeds* God's ways, she immediately *acts* in haste. What is the importance of haste? Well, have you ever wondered what to do in a particular situation when suddenly you just know what the right thing is? What might happen if you don't do that thing right away, especially if it is a costly thing to do like forgiving someone, or sacrificing something, or making a big change in your life? What might happen is that, if you dally, you will steadily become less certain of the action. It isn't that you necessarily second-guess yourself, but more that you start finding reasons to *not* do that one thing, especially if it's a hard thing to do. Justifications start creeping in for doing something else, or for doing nothing at all. Doctors are unwise if they operate before they know what's wrong with their patient, and unwise again if they don't do what needs to be done after making the diagnosis. Mary's no coward; she acts in haste.

We see this first, of course, when she rushes off to the hill country to her cousin Elizabeth right after the angel departs from her. We are told she went "in haste" (Luke 1:39, RSV). She is ready to respond to the Word of God, held back by nothing. Again, she's free.

Acting on the Word of God, in Sacrifice

How free is she? Well, if we step outside of Luke's gospel for a moment and move into John's, we are given an image of just how much freedom Mary exercises when she has everything to lose. Unique to John's gospel, those who are closest to Jesus are next to him while he is on the cross (in the Synoptic Gospels, they are all off at some distance). At the foot of the cross is a small company that includes the beloved disciple and Jesus's mother. Upon that cross is the child Mary was promised, the one whom she received when she trusted in God's word, the one for whom she had sacrificed control of her life. *He* is the one she was promised. And what does he say to her? He tells her to take another as her son. In this most urgent moment, when the temptation to grasp her son is greatest, she exercises the power to let him go and to receive the one he gives her. If we haven't prayed about Mary's sacrifice on Calvary, then we've missed something.

In *hearing* the Word of God, Mary displayed the freedom *from* fear, presumption, and pride. In *acting* on the Word, Mary displays the freedom *for* making a sacrifice, taking responsibility, and bearing the cost of love. When she said, "Let it be to me according to your word" (Luke 1:38, RSV), she followed through on that "yes" all the way to the end. Power like this borders on the divine.

The Wannabes on the Road to Emmaus

If we look to the end of the Luke's gospel, we see that Jesus encounters two would-be disciples walking away from Jerusalem toward Emmaus (24:13-35). They are disoriented and going in the wrong direction. They know a lot but they don't know how to make sense of things. They're awfully chatty and don't listen very much. Their hope is in the past tense. And what does Jesus do to them and for them? He transforms them into disciples according to the pattern already established in his Blessed Mother. He silences them: "O foolish men" (24:25). He reconfigures their memories by teaching them the Scriptures aright: "beginning with Moses and all the prophets" (24:27). He teaches them how true power—divine power—comes as mercy by schooling them in his own suffering: "Was it not necessary that the Christ should suffer these things . . . ?" (24:26). And finally, he feeds them with himself—the Word made flesh—and frees them to take on a new mission of great joy, in haste: "And they rose that same hour" (24:33, RSV). They become what Mary is: ones who hear the Word of God and act on it.

Like those disoriented, confused, chatty, and sad wanderers whom Jesus transformed into missionary disciples, Mary is for all Christians and would-be Christians both the image of discipleship into which we shall be transformed and the embodiment of the dispositions in which we must be tutored in order to become fully human and fully open to the Word of God, ready to act on it.

Mary can't be ranked between passivity and activity because she breaks the mold. She *is* the scale on which all maturing disciples are measured, while also being the one who never ceases to pray for those whom her son claims as his own. Upon her, the Holy Spirit works in full, while she works fully in cooperation with the Spirit. Grace and virtue grow in direct proportion in the life of a disciple, unto everlasting glory. Mary is the source of goodness for all Christians and would-be Christians—her "yes" never ends, as she always receives the ones to whom her son directs her, and she acts in mercy for them, with great haste.

chapter twenty-two

The Mystery and Motherhood of the Church

"I will not leave you orphans" (John 14:18, NABRE). Indeed, Jesus gives us his mother, who teaches us how to say "Our Father" with her son. Herein lies the mystery and motherhood of the Church.

When bishops and others from around the world gathered in Rome for the Second Vatican Council in the early 1960s, their charge was to proclaim the identity of the Church and recommit the Church to its sacred mission in the modern world. A primary task, therefore, was to give an account of what the Church is. The document that serves as the Dogmatic Constitution on the Church—*Lumen Gentium*—gets right to this task in its opening paragraph:

> Christ is the light of the nations and consequently this holy synod, gathered together in the holy Spirit, ardently desires to bring to all humanity that light of Christ which is resplendent on the face of the church, by proclaiming his Gospel to every creature (see Mk 16:15). Since the church, in Christ, is a sacrament—a sign and instrument, that is, of communion with God and of the unity of the entire human race—it here proposes, for the benefit of the faithful and of the entire world, to describe more clearly, and in the tradition laid down by earlier council, its own nature and universal mission. (LG 1)[1]

1. Quotations of Vatican II documents are taken from Austin Flannery, ed., *Vatican Council II: Constitutions, Decrees, Declarations; The Basic Sixteen Documents* (Collegeville, MN: Liturgical Press, 2014).

What is the very first thing the council fathers say the Church is? A sacrament. The Church herself is a sacrament. The Church finds her identity "in Christ," and that identity is as a "sign and instrument." As a sign, the Church receives her meaning and refers herself to who and what Christ is. And who is Christ? The one who, in his person, is communion with God and brings into unity the entire human race. As an instrument, then, the Church hastens and works to bring about that to which it points: the communion with God and the unity of the human race in Christ.

The title of this first chapter of *Lumen Gentium* is "The Mystery of the Church," because the Greek word that corresponds to the Latin word *sacramentum* is *mysterion*. To say the Church is a "mystery," in this sense, is to say the Church is a sacrament. That does not mean the Church is a puzzle that we cannot figure out, but rather that the Church signifies Christ and makes him present. In saying that, you have said everything that the Church is, and yet the journey into understanding what that means is unending.

As *Lumen Gentium* itself draws to a close, its final chapter focuses on "Our Lady." This means that the articulation of what the Church is begins with a statement about mystery and ends with a statement about Mary. In particular, Mary's motherhood is highlighted, for "she is clearly the mother of the members of Christ" (LG 53, quoting St. Augustine). This means that the gift that Christ gave to the beloved disciple from the cross—the gift of his own mother—is indeed the gift given to all who are joined to Christ. To be joined to Christ is to receive his mother.

Mary's motherhood is an enduring gift to all those whom Christ claims as his own:

> This motherhood of Mary in the order of grace continues without interruption from the consent which she loyally gave at the Annunciation and which she sustained without wavering beneath the cross, until the eternal consummation of all the elect. (LG 62)

Her motherhood began when she gave her "yes" to the angel and will not stop until the end of time, when all the saints are gathered together in heaven. Her motherhood is constant. And who is this mother, Mary, if not the one who signifies Christ and makes him present? She is the one who always hears the Word of God and acts on it. Her motherhood in the order of grace builds upon her discipline and freedom as the first and perfect disciple.

Christ promises his disciples he will not leave them orphans and then gives them his mother. Where is her maternal care given for disciples in century after century, including today? In the Church: "The Church contemplating [Mary's] hidden sanctity, imitating her charity and faithfully fulfilling the Father's will, by receiving the word of God in faith becomes herself a mother" (LG 64).

The mystery and motherhood of the Church is typified and fulfilled in the person of Mary; the Church is Marian. Like a mother, the Church births, feeds, and empowers her children, whom Christ entrusted to Mary from the cross. She heals and binds up the wounds of her children. She prepares her children and sends them into their missions in life. In summary, the Church—as sacrament, in Christ—gives her children the sacraments.

"All of the faithful must willingly hear the word of God and carry out his will by what they do" (LG 42). This is the universal call to holiness, initiated in Mary who never fails to hear the Word of God and act on it. By her identity and mission, the Church proclaims this call and nourishes this call in her children. The Church exists to form a people who become what Mary already is: one who is in communion with God and united to each of us through her son Jesus Christ.

In the three chapters to follow, I will guide us through an exploration of the seven sacraments of the Church. The next chapter is on the sacraments of initiation, by which we become Christ's Body. The subsequent chapter is on the sacraments of healing, by which we are healed as members of Christ's Body. The final chapter is on the sacraments in service of communion, by which we build up Christ's Body. Each of these sacraments and all of these sacraments are the Church at work: being what the Church is called to be and doing what the Church is called to do. When Jesus gave his beloved disciple to his mother, he meant for Mary, in her maternal care, to form that disciple into complete union with the son she herself carried and birthed, nourished and raised, sacrificed for and loved unto the end. The sacraments are the gift of that maternal care, forming all those whom Christ has claimed into one body, in him.

chapter twenty-three

Becoming Christ's Body: Baptism, Confirmation, Eucharist

"Through him, and with him, and in him, . . . in the unity of the Holy Spirit," all those whom Christ gathers become one body to share his communion with the Father. The Church is the "sign and instrument" of this union, which is made present now and will be made complete in the heavenly kingdom (LG 2, 3). Salvation means healing and wholeness, being restored to the unity we have lost in sin and perfected for the unity God desires for us as we come to share in his own life. The Church's mission is to herald and harken toward salvation, so that, as Jesus prayed on the night before he died, "they may all be one; even as you, Father, are in me and I in you, that they also may be in us" (John 17:21, RSV). "Since the sacraments are the means of salvation," as the twentieth-century theologian Henri de Lubac explains, "they should be understood as instruments of unity. As they make real, renew or strengthen man's union with Christ, by that very fact they make real, renew or strengthen his union with the Christian community."[1]

In the sacraments of initiation, the union of the Church is made real, renewed, and strengthened, both in terms of union with God and union with others. The *Catechism of the Catholic Church* teaches that "[t]he faithful are born anew by Baptism, strengthened by the

1. Henri de Lubac, *Catholicism: Christ and the Common Destiny of Man*, trans. Lancelot Sheppard and Elizabeth Englund (San Francisco: Ignatius Press, 1988), 82.

sacrament of Confirmation, and receive in the Eucharist the food of eternal life" (1212). When, through the ministry of the Church, the newly initiated become members of the Body of Christ, the entire mystery of the Church is celebrated as the Church reveals what she is and does what she is called to do.

Baptism

All six of my children have been baptized in the same font, at the entrance of our home parish, right in the middle of the Sunday liturgy. Of all the things our parish does well liturgically, the baptisms in the middle of Mass might be the best. In a single photo of the baptism of our fifth child, Gianna, I can see and recall the whole drama that takes place every time a child, whether one of my own or someone else's, is taken to those waters.

In this photo, the priest is standing in the (walk-in) font holding baby Gianna in his arms. He just immersed her three times in the water, "in the name of the Father, and of the Son, and of the Holy Spirit." Around the font arranged in spontaneously organized concentric circles, children of various ages and heights look on, with the youngest and the smallest pressed right up to the edge of the font. Behind the children, parents and other adults look on too, some of them holding their own children in their arms. Some of these people have lived their whole lives in this parish community, including the now-deceased ninety-three-year-old man to the right. Some are in the parish for just a few years, and some are just there today for this baptism. Regardless of who they are or where they come from, the image they create together expresses a great mystery. They are a visible sign of the whole Church.

If you were to look at this photo and I were to ask you what has just occurred, you would likely say that this child—my daughter—has just become a member of the Body of Christ; she has just entered the Church. This is, of course, correct. Baptism is the "in-corporation" of a new member—that is, Gianna was brought into the body (*corpus*). But the rest of the photo represents the other side of the same mystery, which is that baptism is also "con-corporation"—that is, it is a work of the whole Church, *with* the whole body. Something happened *to* Gianna, while something also happened to every member of the Church and to the entire Body of Christ. In an act of unity, the whole

Church works to bring in a new member, and those who were gathered that day, many of whom are seen in that photo, represent the whole.[2]

Indeed, those who gathered that day heard something that this photo cannot convey; they heard the names of the saints sung in a litany as the entire parish community processed toward the font. Those saints were invoked to gather with this community for this one work of the Church, where this new member was joined with the other members in the one Body of Christ. Those saints we named were themselves representatives of the whole communion of saints, because the whole communion of saints is involved in every baptism, every work of the Church in the sacraments. Each sacrament is the work of Christ through his Church, and Christ is never divided. Those whom he gathers as his Body work through him, with him, and in him, in the unity of the Holy Spirit, in every sacrament. The particular sights and sounds, movements and rituals of this particular baptism express that sacred mystery: the faithful are born anew through the motherhood of the Church.

Confirmation

The Body of Christ is a living Body; to become a member of this Body is to share in the life of the whole Body. Members of Christ's Body share in the identity of Christ, who makes us adopted children of his Father, and share in his mission.[3] The sacrament of confirmation imprints that mission upon the baptized, making them "true witnesses of Christ, . . . more strictly obliged both to spread and to defend the faith by word and deed" (LG 11, quoted in CCC 1285).

In following the narrative of St. Paul's conversion and transformation, we caught a glimpse of this twofold mystery, where a Christian receives a new identity in Christ and shares in Christ's mission. Paul was separated from his old way, entered into a period of blind waiting, and then became a new man when Ananias baptized him. Then, as Acts recounts, Paul, "took food and was strengthened" (9:19, RSV). That strengthening continued in Paul to the point that he became

2. For more on this, see de Lubac, *Catholicism*, 83–85.

3. On adoption in Christ, see Eph 1:5; Gal 3:26 and 4:5-7; 1 John 3:1-2; Rom 8:14-19 and 9:8; and John 1:12.

a source of goodness for others. Not only did he cease persecuting Christians when he joined them as a member of the "the Way," but he also became an instrument of Christ's saving grace both to members of the Church and to those outside the Church. Paul's mission was conformed to the mission of the Church. In confirmation, the baptized receive this same mission.

The sacrament of confirmation takes the name "Christian" and turns it into a verb. For one who has become a Christian in baptism, confirmation represents and makes present the reality that there is no such thing as a lifeless Christian. To be a Christian means to live in Christ, to participate in his healing and charity, and to take on as one's own mission the mission of the Church in the manner appropriate to one's own character and gifts. To be confirmed is to be anointed, which is signified in the perfumed oil that is put upon the *confirmandi* along with the laying on of hands. "This anointing highlights the name 'Christian,' which means 'anointed' and derives from that of Christ himself whom God 'anointed with the Holy Spirit'" (CCC 1289, quoting Acts 10:38).

In the original order of the sacraments of initiation, confirmation came second, right after the sacrament of baptism and before the sacrament of the Eucharist, which completed Christian initiation. This is still seen, of course, with adults who are brought into the Church at the Easter Vigil, receiving all three sacraments at once. Even for those who are baptized as infants, receive Eucharist, and then, later, are confirmed, the full character of Christ is imprinted on the Christian in these three sacraments. The identity of Christ conferred in baptism is sealed with the mission of Christ conferred in confirmation.

Eucharist

"The holy Eucharist completes Christian initiation" and "The Eucharist is 'the source and summit of the Christian life'" (CCC 1322, 1324, quoting LG 11). The keynote of Christianity is communion: the gift and task of communion with God and with one another in Christ. The Eucharist is the sacrament of that twofold communion in Christ; it is therefore the sacrament at the heart of the Church. To receive the gift of this sacrament is to already taste the heavenly bliss God intends for us, where communion will be complete and unending.

The Eucharist is at once total gift and essential task. In the Eucharist, Christ gives himself freely—body and blood, soul and divinity—but the task is, as St. Augustine preaches, "to become what you receive." If the Eucharist is Christ's gift of communion, those who receive are called to foster communion. This communion is the same communion of which the Church herself is a sacrament in Christ: communion with God and the unity of the human race.

In order to grow in appreciation of the sacred mystery, it is helpful to understand the three elements or stages of depth presented in the Eucharist. These are the *sacramentum tantum*, the *sacramentum et res*, and the *res tantum*. The *sacramentum tantum* is "the sign itself," which, in the Eucharist is the bread and wine. Bread and wine are the only acceptable "signs" of the eucharistic mystery. The *sacramentum et res*, then, is the "sign and the reality," which is the body and blood of Christ. His body and his blood are the true signs of the Father's saving love for the world, *and* his body and his blood really make that love present. The sign and the reality are inseparably joined in him: there is no way to remove the Father's love given for us from Christ's body and blood, or vice versa. Lastly, the *res tantum* is "the reality itself," which is charity. This is the fruit of the sacrament: God's peace, God's charity that becomes our own peace, our own charity.

In holding on to these three elements, we better recognize what it is that a communicant receives in the Eucharist. Yes, the communicant receives the bread and wine consecrated on the altar, and yes, this bread and wine has become the Body and Blood of Christ. But Christ gives everything that he is, which means he gives the Father's love, everlasting peace, in and through himself. To receive him means to receive this entire gift, and to receive that gift means to receive the mission of becoming that charity, that peace for the world. The Church's entire mission is contained in this one sacred gift.

Above, I mentioned St. Augustine, who taught his flock to "become what you receive" when they receive the Eucharist. In those few words, Augustine touches on the layers of mystery of this sacrament that completes Christian initiation and nourishes the Church. To receive Christ's Body means to become Christ's Body, and to become Christ's Body means to be conformed to what Christ himself signifies and makes present: charity. Excerpts from two of Augustine's eucharistic sermons prompt us to contemplate more fully this sacred mystery:

> "The Body of Christ," you are told, and you answer "Amen." Be members then of the Body of Christ that your Amen may be true. Why is this mystery accomplished with bread? We shall say nothing of our own about it, rather let us hear the Apostle [Paul], who speaking of this sacrament says: "We being many are one body, one bread." Understand and rejoice. Unity, devotion, charity! One bread: and what is this one bread? One body made up of many. Consider that the bread is not made of one grain alone, but of many. During the time of exorcism, you were, so to say, in the mill. At Baptism you were wetted with water. Then the Holy Spirit came into you like the fire which bakes the dough. Be then what you see and receive what you are.[4]

> Now for the Chalice, my brethren, remember how wine is made. Many grapes hang on the bunch, but the liquid which runs out of them mingles together in unity. So has the Lord willed that we should belong to him and he has consecrated on his altar the mystery of our peace and our unity.[5]

Augustine teaches his own flock and us how the bread we receive teaches us what we are to become when we receive the Body of Christ. Just as bread is made up of many grains that have been ground down in the mill and then baked into one loaf, so we, who receive this one Eucharist, are to be united to one another in love. This is hard, as the work of bringing many grains into one loaf is hard. It is, however, what has already been initiated in the Christian at his baptism, when he is separated from the isolating way of Satan and freed to live by God's own life. So now this bread, by which Christ gives his own body, is the sign of the charity to which those who receive are to be conformed.

Likewise with the wine. Augustine appeals to what everyone knows, which is that wine comes not from one grape but from many grapes. Those grapes are squeezed and pressed so that their juice flows together, and only together are they made into this new thing. The wine of the chalice signifies what Christ himself does to and for those he claims in this sacrament: he takes the many and makes them one. His blood is the sacrifice of that new communion.

4. St. Augustine's Sermon 272, quoted in de Lubac, *Catholicism*, 92.
5. St. Augustine's Sermon 234, quoted in de Lubac, *Catholicism*, 92.

In the sacraments of initiation, communion in the one Body of Christ is the gift and the call represented and made present in these works of the Church. The unity of the Holy Spirit is the fruit of these works of Christ through, with, and in his Church. As a sacrificial and nourishing mother, the Church forms the faithful in the image of Mary's son, for the life of the world.

chapter twenty-four

Healed as Members: Penance and Anointing of the Sick

All sins are social and all wounds are shared. This is a fact of the Catholic Church. To become a member of Christ's Body means that, as the earliest Christians knew even before they were called Christians, "all who believed were together and had all things in common" (Acts 2:44). To be in Christ, as St. Paul teaches, means that "[i]f one member suffers, all suffer together; if one member is honored, all rejoice together" (1 Cor 12:26; RSV). The Church holds to this truth because it takes Christ seriously. He who gathers others to himself suffers with those who suffer, rejoices with those who rejoice, and gives others the power to suffer and rejoice together as one.

The sacraments of penance and of anointing the sick are sacraments of healing in which members of the Church are healed precisely as *members*. Like all sacraments, these sacraments are both the work of Christ and the work of the whole Church. To be healed as a member means to be healed with and for others, and never merely as a private event. Healing in the Church is an exercise of communion—one that restores lost communion and strengthens us for renewed communion.

Penance

Jesus spoke to his disciples in terms of a vine and its branches. Here is what he said:

> I am the true vine, and my Father is the vinedresser. Every branch of mine that bears no fruit, he takes away, and every branch that does

> bear fruit he prunes, that it may bear more fruit. You are already made clean by the word which I have spoken to you. Abide in me, and I in you. As the branch cannot bear fruit by itself, unless it abides in the vine, neither can you, unless you abide in me. I am the vine, you are the branches. (John 15:1-5, RSV)

The basic imagery here shows that branches only grow when connected to the vine. If they are unconnected, they wither and begin to die. Jesus then makes certain that his disciples know what he means, as he tells them, in no uncertain terms, *you* are the branches. "If you are cut off from me," Jesus says, "you will die. If your connection to me is tenuous, you will weaken." Perhaps we could think about mortal and venial sins in those two ways.

There is more going on here, though, than simple imagery communicating the dependence of the branches on the vine. Have you ever seen a disconnected branch reinserted into a vine? By the horticultural technique of grafting, the tissues of plants are joined together so that they may grow together. A branch that has no connection to a life source may, in this way, share in the life of the vine to which it is inserted. But if you were to go to a vineyard or even just search online for pictures of grafting, you would see that the vine does not remain unchanged in this process. In fact, the vine is split open in order to make space for the branch to be inserted. This, too, is contained in the imagery Jesus uses to describe his relationship to his disciples and their relationship to him: the vine allows itself to be wounded so that the branches might have life again. Even those who have been cut off may, through the sacrament of penance, enter back into Christ's pierced side.

What this all means is that every branch attached to a vine grows on the same root system as the vine itself. All the branches and the vine become one living organism. The point is that the vine receives the branches so that all may grow as one: "As the Father has loved me, so I have loved you; abide in my love" (John 15:9, RSV).

If by sin—whether mortal or venial—disciples cut themselves off from the vine, who has the power to forgive sins, to renew the connection to this vital life of the vine? The answer seems obvious: God alone! Indeed, this is what those who saw Jesus heal and heard him forgive sins proclaimed in protest. As we read in the Gospel of Mark:

> And when Jesus saw their faith, he said to the paralytic, "My son, your sins are forgiven." Now some of the scribes were sitting there, questioning in their hearts, "Why does this man speak thus? It is blasphemy! Who can forgive sins but God alone?" (Mark 2:5-7, RSV)

The scribes are, in fact, correct. Only God can forgive sins, giving new life to those who have cut themselves off. That is what makes Jesus's commission to his disciples when he appears to them in the glory of the resurrection so perplexing:

> Jesus said to them again, "Peace be with you. As the Father has sent me, even so I send you." And when he had said this, he breathed on them, and said to them, "Receive the Holy Spirit. If you forgive the sins of any, they are forgiven; if you retain the sins of any, they are retained." (John 20:21-23, RSV)

The scribes object that Jesus forgives sins because they do not believe him to be God, though a Christian would certainly know and believe what those scribes did not. But nobody—especially not Christians—believes that the disciples are God; they are indeed human and only human. So what gives?

What gives is that Christ deigns that his disciples do not only receive mercy but become agents of mercy. God desires that we become agents of his love, so that our own actions have real meaning. When Christ breathes on his disciples, they receive the Holy Spirit to animate them. They are given the power to forgive by the same Spirit that is the love, the communion of the Father and the Son.

In the sacrament of penance, the priest acts *in persona Christi* and *in persona Ecclesiae*—that is, in the person of Christ and in the person of the whole Church. In doing so, the priest is entrusted with the power to absolve sinners of their sins. The priest is also, therefore, entrusted with the power to reintegrate the sinful member into the believing community: the Church. In and through the priest, the Church, in the name and by the command of Christ, forgives sins.

The words of absolution in the Rite of Penance express this mystery:

> God, the Father of mercies, through the death and resurrection of his Son has reconciled the world to himself and sent the Holy Spirit among us for the forgiveness of sins; through the ministry of the Church may

> God give you pardon and peace, and I absolve you from your sins in the name of the Father, and of the Son, and of the Holy Spirit.

Notice what the priest does not say. He does not say, "I pray that God absolve you" or "I believe God has absolved you." No, the priest says, "*I* absolve you from your sins . . ." The power, the ministry that Christ entrusts to his Church is real: "If you forgive the sins of any, they are forgiven."

Looking back at all of this, including the imagery of the vine and the branches, we can see the awesome mystery of the sacrament of penance. Yes, the mystery is with a God who forgives and gives new life. Yes, the mystery is Christ's mercy bestowed upon his fearful, guilt-ridden, sinful disciples. But the mystery is also that Christ gives the Church the power to suffer for sinful members, so that we may be healed as one. In the sacrament of penance, not only Christ but also the Church is wounded in the side so as to make space for the injured, withered member to rejoin the communion of life.[1]

Anointing of the Sick

From where does God know you? Where does God's knowledge of you begin, and where does it end? Psalm 139 paints the picture for us:

> O Lord, you have searched me and known me!
> You know when I sit down and when I rise up;
> you discern my thoughts from afar.
> You search out my path and my lying down,
> and are acquainted with all my ways. . . .
> Where shall I go from your Spirit?
> Or where shall I flee from your presence?
> If I ascend to heaven, you are there!
> If I make my bed in Sheol, you are there!
> If I take the wings of the morning
> and dwell in the uttermost parts of the sea,
> even there your hand shall lead me,
> and your right hand shall hold me. (Psalm 139:1-3, 7-10, RSV)

1. I am grateful to my friend and colleague Dr. Anthony Pagliarini, whose lecture on the sacrament of penance was influential to me in what I have articulated above.

God knows you from everywhere, in every place from the deepest depths to the highest heights. God's knowledge—God's personal knowledge—has no beginning and no end. In the heavens, God knows in full, and because Jesus has descended to the dead, even in "Sheol"—the land of non-existence, cut off from life—God is there, opening a path to return to him. Every place is a suitable place to cry out to the Lord.

It is not difficult to imagine various forms of suffering as God-forsaken. Even for those who might, with their minds and even with their desire, grasp and assent to what the psalmist proclaims about the inescapability of God's knowledge, when someone is in the midst of suffering—especially prolonged suffering, chronic suffering—it is far easier to imagine God as absent than as present. The faith of the Church, however, holds fast to the following belief:

> On the cross Christ took upon himself the whole weight of evil and took away the "sin of the world," of which illness is only a consequence. By his passion and death on the cross Christ has given a new meaning to suffering: it can henceforth configure us to him and unite us with his redemptive Passion. (CCC 1505)

This is a remarkable, marvelous claim. In faith, the Church professes that suffering is itself transformed in Christ. It is not just on the heights that union with God in Christ is possible, but also in the depths. Suffering, illness, dying, and even death are places of communion in Christ because Christ has suffered for us. He has claimed our suffering in his so that we can offer our suffering with him to the Father.

Throughout history and even today—in different ways in different parts of the world—the sick and dying are cut off from participation in the fullness of life. They do not share fully in the life of the community. In Jesus's day and later, we might think of lepers, who were cast off from society in fear and for the sake of security. In the 1980s and 1990s, those with HIV were treated similarly. In 2014, it was Ebola victims in West Africa. Regardless of the reasonableness of such societal separation, the point remains that the sick and dying in these cases and others are kept apart. Even in "developed countries" without widespread epidemics, we see signs of this in nursing homes and hospitals, in those who suffer silently from alcoholism and anxiety alike, or in those who lose their vivacity due to some chronic illness and thus can no longer be active in the way they once were. We live in a world that values activity above almost anything else.

The sacrament of anointing of the sick proclaims that even from here—from this illness, this infirmity, this form of dying—the power of Christ meets you. In this sacrament, the sick and dying are claimed as members of Christ, united together in the Church. Through this sacrament what St. Paul announces is enacted: when "one member suffers, all suffer." In the name of Christ, the Church joins with those who suffer and claims that suffering as her own.

What Christ bestows upon the Church, the Church bestows upon the sick and suffering members through the sacrament. In particular, the Church offers the gifts of the Holy Spirit: peace, strength, and courage. The Church offers union with the passion of Christ. The Church offers ecclesial grace, by which the suffering member is again claimed as a member of the Body of Christ through the communion of the Church. And the Church offers preparation for the final journey, into the heavenly kingdom.[2]

The Grace of Healing

Along with the sacrament of penance, the sacrament of the anointing of the sick heals the sick and suffering members of the Church. Whether it is through the sins of the members themselves or the illnesses and associated forms of alienation that afflict people in a world marred by sin, these "instruments of unity" restore, nourish, and strengthen not only the individual members but also the communion of the whole Church. These are indeed "means of salvation," as the *Catechism* eloquently and succinctly concludes:

> The Lord Jesus Christ, physician of our souls and bodies, who forgave the sins of the paralytic and restored him to bodily health, has willed that his Church continue, in the power of the Holy Spirit, his work of healing and salvation, even among her own members. This is the purpose of the two sacraments of healing: the sacrament of Penance and the sacrament of Anointing of the Sick. (CCC 1421)

2. See sections 1520–1523 of CCC regarding these effects of the sacrament.

chapter twenty-five

At the Service of Communion: Marriage and Holy Orders

We have seen that none of the sacraments of initiation or the sacraments of healing are merely about the individual. Baptism is about the incorporation of the new member and the concorporation of the whole Church, at the same time. The Eucharist is the gift of Christ's Body and Blood, given to produce the fruit of charity in the communicants and the Church, and through them in the world. Penance heals the sinner through the Christ and the Church's gift of making space for all the members to grow together again. Nothing is private, everything is social, and it is all a matter of communion.

Does the same hold true for the final two sacraments—matrimony and holy orders? It can sure look like these sacraments are at least principally about individuals: what they become and what they do. Could it be that one or even two sacraments actually are, in the end, more or less private matters, different in character from the other sacraments? (Hint: the answer is "no.")

In this final chapter on the sacraments, our task is to see if this same social character, this same mystery of communion, is made manifest in matrimony and holy orders, as it is in the others.

Matrimony

Let's begin with a couple questions. First: Whom does marriage serve? And second: What is a married couple—the husband and wife—a sign of? It is worthwhile to try to answer these questions on your own, before consulting sources (or looking down below).

In response to the first question, one might reasonably expect that marriage serves the couple, or that each of the spouses serves each other, or maybe that it serves children. It is for *their* good, we might reasonably think. If so, we might be surprised to read how the Church understands this sacrament, alongside that of holy orders, which together are recognized as sacraments at the service of communion:

> Holy Orders and Matrimony are directed towards the salvation of others; if they contribute as well to personal salvation, it is through service to others that they do so. They confer a particular mission in the Church and serve to build up the People of God. (CCC 1534)

This sounds a little bit crazy. Like holy orders (which we will get to shortly), matrimony is not chiefly concerned with the salvation—the well-being and wholeness—of the spouses themselves. Or, to put it in better terms, the sacrament is *only* concerned with the spouses to the extent that they are sanctified in their service to others.

The sacrament of matrimony does not make spouses into greater or fuller members of the Church than others, since full membership is effected in the sacraments of initiation. What the sacrament of matrimony confers is a particular mission, and this mission is at the service of communion. This mission is expressed in the procreative and unitive dimensions of marriage, or the mission to give life and provide stability in charity.

As we discussed already in chapter 15 on God's creation of human beings as male and female, the power and responsibility of procreation brings human beings to share in God's own character. God is the one who gives life and nourishes the life he creates. Every generation has this power and responsibility relative to the next generation, but husband and wife receive this mission as particular to them. The creation and care for new life is indeed a gift to the couple, but it is a gift to be shared for the good of the world. Their children are not theirs alone. The creativity of a married couple's mission to give life is expressed in myriad ways, including but not limited to adoption, fostering, and godparenting.

The other side of the particular mission conferred in the sacrament of matrimony concerns the stability and the charity of marriage's unitive dimension. Especially in a world where private interests shift and it is all too common for people to seek their own imagined good rather than a common good, the fidelity of the married couple—the discipline of abiding together—creates a new possibility within society. This is the possibility of remaining constant in serving the good of others, come what may. In fact, this is so essential to the character of matrimony that marriage is based on the consent of the husband and wife to each other (see CCC 1662). Their consent is, so to speak, that which is taken, blessed, broken open, and shared through this sacrament.

As for that second question regarding what the husband and wife are a sign of, we saw how in the Eucharist the bread and wine are indeed signs of the reality the sacrament makes present. The husband and wife are signs of God's fidelity, who weds himself to his creatures in Christ. Christ is the one who is the union of two natures that are neither confused (one doesn't become the other) nor separated (their union is real and permanent). God and Israel are the first image of this marital union, but the fulfillment of that image is Christ and his Church. We have been created male and female to point to the mystery of Christ and the Church, specifically the relationship between them. This is not to say that the man is Christ and the woman is the Church, or that the man is God and the woman is Israel. Instead, it is the other way: as Christ loves the Church, so the husband loves his wife and vice versa (see Eph 5:25-33). The primary reality is Christ and the Church; the sign and instrument of that reality is husband and wife, particularly in the sacrament of matrimony.

What is therefore true of the mission of those who receive the sacrament of matrimony is first of all true of the mystery of the Church. The Church gives life to the world in union with Christ, principally through evangelization and the celebration of the sacraments. And the Church provides stability in union with Christ through its memory and hope. The Church remembers the passion, death, and resurrection of Christ and hopes for his coming again at the end of time. Both its memory and its hope are held within the Church's fidelity to her spouse, Christ the Bridegroom. In a world that forgets and often despairs, the Church remembers and hopes because Christ is faithful to his bride.

As it says in the passage from the *Catechism* quoted above, marriage serves the people of God and manifests the mission of the Church: to bring about the communion with God and the unity of the human race (LG 1). The unitive and procreative gift of the married couple is both the sign and the instrument of Christ's fidelity to and fruitfulness in the Church.

Holy Orders

We ought to ask the same questions about holy orders that we asked about matrimony, except I would like to reverse their order. First: What is an ordained man a sign of? Second: Whom does ordination serve—that is, the sacrament is for whose good?

He upon whom the sacrament of holy orders is conferred becomes a sign of Christ the Bridegroom; he is a sign of Christ, the Head whose members we are. The priest does not *become* Christ, but rather he represents him and makes him present. This is most apparent at certain times, such as during the words of institution during the eucharistic prayer, where a priest speaks the words of Christ as his own: "Take this, all of you, and eat of it, for this is my Body . . . Take this, all of you, and drink from it, for this is . . . my Blood." When the priest speaks, he speaks *in persona Christi Capitis* (see CCC 1548–51). Likewise, as we saw in the previous chapter, during the absolution in the sacrament of penance, the priest says, "*I* absolve you . . ." Indeed, in all the ecclesial service of the ordained minister, "it is the same priest, Christ Jesus, whose sacred person his minister truly represents" (CCC 1548).

While he who receives the sacrament of holy orders is not preserved from sin or cured of his human weaknesses, it is indeed true that God calls and blesses this *person* through the sacrament. Who he is changes. It is not as if only his functions are blessed, but rather he himself becomes a sign of Christ. If he errs and sins, he errs and sins while representing Christ to the Church. Scandals regarding ordained ministers are, therefore, especially grievous, as we all know.

If the ordained minister is himself a sign and instrument of Christ the Head, then the answer to the second question becomes apparent. Whom does ordination serve? It serves the Church, Christ's bride, his members. All Christians share in Christ's priesthood, but in different ways. By virtue of baptism, all the faithful share in the common priesthood, but by holy orders, the ordained man shares Christ's ministerial priesthood. They are related to each other simply in this:

> The ministerial priesthood is at the service of the common priesthood. It is directed at the unfolding baptismal grace of all Christians. The ministerial priesthood is a *means* by which Christ unceasingly builds up and leads his Church. (CCC 1547)

Holy orders is at the service of communion—the communion of the Church. The sacrament is conferred on particular men—bishops, priests, deacons—so that they may, in Christ's name, serve and strengthen the union of the members of the Church to Christ.

Each of these sacraments—matrimony and holy orders—confers particular missions within the common mission of the Church. Each is ordered to the love of God and the love of neighbor in a distinctive way. Each is ordered to being and building up communion.

Epilogue

The Keynote of Communion

Saul of Tarsus was a man set apart, not as someone sacred and blessed but rather as a man in opposition to Christ. He was set apart from the source of life. By the grace of Christ and through the ministry of the Church—at the hands of Ananias, in the waters of baptism, by the teaching of the apostles—he was freed from his old way and brought into "the Way." This changed and affected everything: how he viewed the world, how he listened, and how he spoke. His dispositions and actions were transformed. He himself became a source of goodness for others in "the Way." From his starting point in opposition to Christ, he was drawn deeper and deeper in Christ's life, and became a man of communion.

There is no other way to be a Christian than to become a person of communion. The reason for this is simple: Christ himself is communion and all those whom Christ claims share in his life. Christ is the one who, as Son of God and Word Incarnate, eternally prays to the Father: "that they may all be one; even as you, Father, are in me, and I in you, that they also may be in us, so that the world may believe that you have sent me. . . . Father, I desire that they also, whom you have given me, may be with me where I am" (John 17:21, 24, RSV). Christ offers those he claims as his own to the Father (in the Spirit). He offers us so that what God has set out to do may become complete: to "share in his own blessed life" (CCC 1). In uniting us to himself, Christ unites us to his Father, so that we may call *his* Father "Our Father." In doing so, Christ unites us to one another as children of God who, together are "heirs of his blessed life" (CCC 1). St. Paul shows us what that transformation looks like, whereby we become what we were not. In the Blessed Mother, we see the gift and destiny of sharing God's life revealed in full, through her whom Christ gives us as our Mother.

In contemplating the mystery of our creation principally in Genesis 2, we have seen how this gift and destiny corresponds to how we are created. We are created in harmony, for harmony. That harmony includes our harmony with the earth out of which God forms us, with each other for whom God intends us, and with God himself who breathes his breath into us so that we may have life. The dignity of our creation as human beings is itself the pledge of our future glory as sharers in God's life: the life of communion. It is our sin that tears us apart—from each other, from ourselves, from God—and God who heals us and pulls us back together as members of one Body. The life of that Body is the Holy Spirit, who is charity.

The practice of and growth in virtue is part of our work toward cooperating with the grace of God, who makes us one in Christ Jesus. It is, after all, *our* minds and *our* hearts and *our* tongues that must be transformed, and that work cannot be done without us. At the same time, though, we cannot transform ourselves. And so our work in growing in virtue is aided by and completed in the gift of the sacraments, by which God draws us into his very life through the ministry of the Church. Each sacrament and all of them together are instruments of unity, by which and through which our communion with God and union with one another is both represented and made present.

Catholicism is about the whole because God gives everything. "God, infinitely perfect and blessed in himself, in a plan of sheer goodness" (CCC 1) seeks to make us whole—each of us and all of us together, as one. There is no such thing as an individual Christian because Christians are all one in Christ, who makes us members of one another. Catholicism professes and serves that mystery and nothing less. To grow in the Catholic faith, therefore, is never a matter of many different things in isolation from one another; it is, instead, always a matter of being made whole, in every sense. To form others in this faith requires us, therefore, to give everything, to witness to the beauty of God's plan, and to make the manner of formation as holistic as the gift and mission Christ imparts to his Church.

Part Two

Reflection and Practice

Introduction

The Conditions of Formation

Catholic Formation Group

In today's world, most things feel like just "one *more* thing to do." Many of us often encounter preparation for confirmation or, perhaps to a lesser extent, RCIA formation in just that way. It can easily feel like just one more class to take, one more set of requirements to fulfill, one more thing to complete. Rather than a sacrament of initiation, confirmation comes off like the sacrament of inconvenience.

I know this from experience. A few years ago, my wife and I were preparing to send four kids back to school, leaving two little ones at home. Our eldest son was starting a new school for seventh grade after he chose to move on from our parish school at the close of the previous year. It was a good change for him and a mostly seamless transition; even our drop-off-and-pick-up routine for all the kids was easily adjusted. But when I read the letter from our parish about enrolling him in the religious education program for the first time now that he was no longer in Catholic school, I did not see it as an important sacramental formation opportunity. My immediate reaction was that this was indeed "one *more* thing to do."

Our son's outlook was no more favorable. He had long disliked his religion class in school not because he is unreligious but because the textbook-based curriculum oscillated between triviality and banality. In his words, it was "boring" and "easy," and everything was "obvious." Needless to say, he was less than eager to go back for more of the same, except now it would be worse because class was on Sunday morning . . . *early* Sunday morning.

It was not hard to figure out that my son's peers and their parents shared similar feelings. Our pastor and director of religious education (DRE) were more than willing to find a better way to form young people for confirmation, but no better way was on offer. I think we could all agree that reluctance and disinterest are not the ideal conditions for welcoming the Holy Spirit.

Fortunately, a friend and fellow parishioner, Bill Mattison, had come upon the same problem the previous year, and rather than complain he decided to initiate something new. He approached our pastor and offered to lead a formation group himself—one that would meet at his home. He wanted to create a better setting, build stronger community, foster more conversation, and include families in the process. Our pastor thought it was a great idea; besides, pastors are not accustomed to turning down volunteer catechists.

Here is the unsurprising but crucial thing I heard in the subtext of my conversations with Bill: if you want something different, *you* have to do something different. As parents, Bill and his wife Courtney opened their home as a place to form their son and other young people in faith, preparing them for the sacrament of confirmation. My wife and I followed their lead and then built on what they started. Not only did we open our home as the environment for the formation of our son and his peers but also I cast aside the textbook approach and designed a new way for reflecting on and practicing the faith with them. At minimum, this new approach aims to avoid being "boring," "easy," and "obvious," and seeks to prepare each candidate to respond to their full initiation in the Church by becoming a source of goodness for others.

In the pages that follow I present a new proposal for forming people for full initiation in the Catholic Church, through what I call a "Catholic Formation Group." This proposal is not a theoretical undertaking but rather an approach to formation developed in a concrete faith community with real families and a wonderful group of young people, one of whom is our son. I received my pastor's permission to develop this approach with our parish's young people. I collaborated with Sean Driscoll, our DRE, and promised to pass on to the parish everything I developed. I conferred with the diocesan office for catechesis and likewise pledged to share this approach with the diocese. This book, in part, comes from my debt of gratitude to all of them for supporting the Catholic Formation Group that I established with the other parents and their young people in our home.

The Room Where It Happens

The first time I taught a confirmation class we met in a school classroom. I was not a school teacher; I was a volunteer catechist—in fact, I was a sophomore in college working alongside another sophomore. It was very clear to us that the classroom where we met was not our own; we were just borrowing it. Come Monday morning, no one should have been able to tell that we had been there. Needless to say, neither we nor our students ever felt at home.

My current parish is fortunate enough to have a parish center with good meeting spaces. When our religious education program meets on Sunday mornings, every room is filled. The catechists do not feel like squatters as I did during my first year teaching confirmation. All the same, no one would say they feel "at home" in the space. It is a meeting space; at best, a parish classroom. It is hard to allow young people to feel like this is something other than just another morning at school.

The Catholic media scholar Marshall McLuhan famously wrote that "the medium is the message." What he meant is that we all spend so much time trying to determine the meaning of *what* is communicated that we fail to recognize the most powerful message of all is actually the *way* something is communicated. As he shows, a radio *program* is one thing, but radio itself is the predominant message in what it does to soundwaves and to you as the listener. We might consider how every web page presents message after message, and yet the internet itself is the stronger message. The *medium* is the message.

Considering the physical spaces used for faith formation endeavors, as well as how people are instructed to conduct themselves in those spaces, is not just an ancillary concern. These spaces and the habits formed therein are indeed part of the message. In fact, they are often the most powerful part.

In laying out this approach to Catholic formation, therefore, I first draw attention to the space itself where formation activities take place. Along with the physical space, the importance of the environment that is fostered in that space cannot be overestimated. Following my friend Bill's lead, my proposal to bring formation into a family home is a significant dimension of this overall approach. While I would not go so far as to say that this approach *only* works if it is done in a home, I am confident in claiming that hosting a Catholic Formation Group in a home is ideal.

Since March 2020, when most of our civil institutions were shut down due to the COVID-19 pandemic, every one of us has become aware of how precious and surprisingly tenuous our ability to gather together really is. Not only were parishes and schools almost universally affected by this shutdown but so were family homes. For weeks and even months on end, we really could not gather anywhere except maybe outdoor venues with generous spacing.

The approach I am advancing here in which gathering together in a family home is highly recommended was developed before COVID-19 changed our consciousness about the potential limitations to gathering. While there may again be times when gathering together anywhere for even religious formation is unwise or suspended, privileging the family home as the primary site of this formation remains in place. In fact, this approach allows for greater flexibility over the standard model of meeting in a parish or school under the guidance of one designated minister or teacher, because a Catholic Formation Group that meets in a home can be subdivided into smaller "pod" groups that can then meet in separate family homes as necessary. For example, a group of twelve that meets together in a home could become two groups of six that meet in two different homes, or even three groups of four spread across three homes. If the circumstances are really restrictive or situations dire (whether for reasons like a pandemic or even personal reasons unrelated to global events), this book and the approach it presents empower parents as competent and confident primary educators of their children in faith, and the same could be said of spouses for one another or even a sponsor for an RCIA member.

Since the content of part 1 of this book is available as a one-part companion book that allows everyone involved in and surrounding the formation process to engage the study of the faith themselves and part 2 offers guidance for anyone (teacher, parents, sponsors, etc.) to lead sessions for a Catholic Formation Group, there is a natural and even ready-made flexibility to this approach. Therefore, even though this approach in full calls for regular, face-to-face gatherings ideally conducted for an entire group in a family home, the very nature of this approach itself grants more power of adaptability and improvisation to parishes, schools, and families alike. This investment in broad-based, shared leadership redounds to the benefit of the entire community in ordinary as well as extraordinary times.

With that caveat in mind, I will move in the next section to lay out this approach to Catholic formation, along with some rationale for each aspect of the approach. The setting itself—the family home—is the first aspect in the whole approach, followed by the regular pattern or rhythm that is developed therein for the meetings of the Catholic Formation Group. The truly Catholic way is to put equal emphasis on the medium *and* the message, and since interest and attention ineluctably tend toward the "message" end of things, I am overemphasizing the "medium" end to make up for it.

Laying Out the Approach

For the most part, we have become dependent on textbooks and third-party programs to run religious education in Catholic schools and parishes alike. I think this is because no matter how passionate any of us might be about the faith, most of us feel unqualified to teach it or form others in it. By and large the options for those in a position of catechizing others is to either attempt to teach what we do not know or merely "press play" on what someone else prepackaged.

What I want to do is equip the person in the room to actually teach, witness to, and mentor those preparing for full initiation in the Catholic Church. This requires something different than just providing resources for you to pass on. It requires a resource to inform and empower you yourself so that *you* become *the resource* for your students.

This is not to say that every catechist, every teacher, every parent is expected to develop their own approach and design all their own lessons. Part of what I am providing in this book is the approach I developed with the specific lessons that comprise it. You will therefore be given the substance of what to teach and guidance in a way of teaching. But the entire approach is built on an investment in *you.* This resource is a support for your leadership. At most, this is sheet music for you, the orchestra conductor.

There is no magic or secret formula in what follows. We are going to invest in basic, simple Catholic things. All of these investments are specifically chosen. In a world that is increasingly fast-paced and adverse to silence and reflection, we are going to invest in the practices of prayer and journaling. In a media environment where fleeting soundbites are how we communicate with each other, we are going to invest in face-to-face conversation. In a religious milieu where Scripture is at most appealed to for proof-texting or as a repository of moral platitudes, we are going to invest in slowly acquiring a scriptural imagination; indeed, the Bible is our primary text for this approach, alongside the *Catechism of the Catholic Church*. And in a cultural moment where everything seems subject to change, we are going to invest in the foundational realities of the Christian faith that provide us a solid ground on which to stand: the person of Christ, the sacraments, and the meaning of life as communion.

Home (duration: approximately 90 minutes weekly)
If we want people to feel at home in the mission of the Church, then why not use a home to form them for it? When you have guests over for dinner, you open your home and use it intentionally. When you celebrate Christmas at home, you use your home intentionally. When you put your house on the market, you prepare it intentionally. The same can be true of opening a home for the purposes of religious formation: use it intentionally.

The intentional uses of a home for this particular purpose include the following: a place to pray, a place to reflect, a place to study and learn, a place to eat together, and a place to welcome families. With the exception of meeting for things like Eucharistic Adoration, our Catholic Formation Group always meets at our home. When the young people arrive, they just hang out for a while, shooting hoops or chatting. We have a basement in our house, where I put some tables together to use as our primary meeting space. When we break for personal journaling time, the young people scatter a little bit to have some privacy. When they eat together in smaller groups (lunch every time), they sit at the dining room table or the kitchen table. Their parents are able to join in the lessons, mingle in the kitchen, and chat over a light meal, while siblings who often come can play together inside or outside. A home is a natural setting for all these activities.

Moving from one kind of space to another, all for different aspects of one complete formation session each week, establishes an atmosphere of integration. A school classroom or a parish center cannot easily provide for this. Since a primary aim of this period of formation is the further integration of faith into each person's everyday life, the setting of a home establishes the conditions for reinforcing that very message. The medium—the environment—serves the message.

Within this setting, we established a regular pattern for our 90-minute meetings, which we held on Sunday:

11:30 a.m.	Arrival
11:45–11:55	Opening prayer and prayer journaling
11:55–12:10	Lunch and small group conversations
12:10–1:00	Lesson and discussion
1:00 p.m.	Closing prayer

Opening Prayer

The opening prayer each week is an opportunity to introduce group members to common but sometimes neglected Catholic prayers. Our regular opening prayer is the Angelus, which is traditionally prayed thrice daily: 6 a.m., noon, and 6 p.m. The regular recitation of this prayer within our group gives each person something to carry with them not just for a year but for life.

While this particular prayer does not necessarily need to be used, there is a certain genius to the Angelus and that genius is twofold. On the one hand, the prayer invites regular contemplation of the central mystery of our salvation: the Incarnation. On the other hand, it is incredibly brief. After a few weeks of praying this prayer once, twice, or even thrice daily, the words of Luke 1 and John 1 that give the prayer its basic structure are impressed upon your memory, while the rhythm of the three Hail Marys draw your heart and mind into God's gentle presence. In our case, we pray it together once a week with the recommendation to pray it at least daily. The Angelus is a simple practice of regular formation into the mystery of the Incarnation.

Prayer Journaling

Rare is the person who says they have enough time to themselves, with plenty of time to think. It is no secret that people today feel busier and more hurried than ever before. As a counter-practice, our formation group commits to 7–10 minutes of prayer journaling at the beginning of each meeting. My hope is that this habit becomes part of their regular, perhaps even daily lives.

Many times, I do not provide the group members with any prompt other than to suggest that they begin with the words, "Dear Jesus." This is part of what makes this exercise "prayer journaling" and not just writing to yourself. It is an address to the Lord. At other times, as you will see in the sessions that follow, I do provide prompts to which the members can respond. Sometimes those prompts tie in to the group conversations or lesson to follow, and sometimes not. The primary objective here is simply to give the time for writing directly to the Lord and, secondarily, to build up this habit of silence and reflection.

Meal and Conversation

Two other regular practices to incorporate into the regular rhythm of this formation are the practice of eating together and the practice of face-to-face conversation. Both of these practices have become even more desired and appreciated after the suspension of group gatherings due to the COVID-19 pandemic. Even before this virus disrupted our lives, I chose the meeting time I did for this group in part so that we would be able to eat a simple meal together. The group of parents agreed to take turns in providing the meal each week. We provide enough food not only for the group members but also for the parents and other family members who might join from week to week. Our group members sit together in smaller groups of four or five to eat together *at a table*. This meal time together is a time for nonfrivolous conversation, meaning that they are prompted to talk to each other about things that actually matter. As you will see in each session to follow, oftentimes I give them a prompt for the conversations or ask them to share with each other a "high and low" from the previous week. This is simple, not necessarily pious stuff. But it is an important part of the formation we hope to provide: reclaiming the skills for direct, interpersonal communication.[1]

1. Among many other possible sources, you may be interested in the following two works about the loss of the skills for direct communication in the modern world: Sherry Turkle, *Alone Together: Why We Expect More from Technology and Less from Each Other* (New York: Basic Books, 2012); and Sherry Turkle, *Reclaiming Conversation: The Power of Talk in a Digital Age*, reprint ed. (New York: Penguin Books, 2016).

During this time for meal and conversation, parents in our group also sit and eat together. As you might imagine, this is a valuable way to build community among parents and foster meaningful though organic conversation among themselves. In the first few movements of each meeting, we have set an important tone by giving our attention to the Lord through prayer and journaling, and to each other through meal and conversation.

Testimonials

Beginning with the mini-unit that explores the question "Who is Jesus?," there is an important opportunity to add personal testimonials to group meetings. As you will read, the complementary question of "Who is Jesus *for me*?" goes right along with the question we explore in sessions 7–10. Therefore, for sessions 8, 9, and 10, I invite parents of my teenagers preparing for confirmation to offer short testimonials in response to that personal question of faith. For groups forming adults for full initiation into the Church, these testimonials could be from sponsors, spouses, or other family members.

In the second semester or unit of the Catholic Formation Group's meetings, the group members themselves (those preparing for initiation in the Church) share their own testimonials. By that point, they have benefitted from listening to the testimonies of more mature disciples (parents, sponsors, etc.) and have been given the time and opportunity to consider their own response. These are not intended to be the *final* testimony to faith in Jesus that each person will provide in their life; instead, these are often the *first* testimony someone gives. This means, of course, that these are not intended to be perfect; they are intended to be sincere. Since each testimonial is only meant to be 2–3 minutes, and since there are typically two and no more than three testimonials shared in a session, these take about 10 minutes of the group meeting time. In terms of the importance of this practice, studies show that Catholics are, by and large, "incredibly inarticulate about their faith."[2] This is a small, direct, intentional practice aimed at building up articulacy.

2. Christian Smith, *Soul Searching: The Religious and Spiritual Lives of American Teenagers* (New York: Oxford University Press, 2005), 131.

Lesson

The chapters to follow will include details on each of the lessons. For now, it suffices to say that my approach to developing these lessons begins with narrative (hence, the story of St. Paul) that then introduces us to the centrality of the person of Jesus followed by a focused preparation for Advent. In beginning this way, we also begin an immersion into Scripture, slowly building up our skills of biblical literacy and developing a scriptural imagination as we go along. In the second semester, this scriptural imagination is then expanded and opens up to an exploration of the meaning of creation, the gifts of the Holy Spirit, the development of virtue, the conditions of discipleship, and the sacraments.

Especially throughout the "Lesson" portion of these Reflection and Practice sessions, I want to *avoid* providing an overly scripted "lesson plan." My job is to give the leaders of various Catholic Formation Groups enough material and direction for *you* to lead well. I want you to claim and trust in your own competence and creativity, and I hope that part 1 of this book helps build up your knowledge, interest, fluency, and imaginative energy. What I provide in these lessons, then, is the fruit of my own leadership of a Catholic Formation Group. If we were each directors of our own theatrical companies, I would be one director offering performance notes to other directors. I know full well that textbooks tend toward taking the agency away from a catechist or teacher by over-scripting. Again, I am fully committed to *avoiding* a textbook approach, so if at times I come close to over-scripting myself, please accept my apology in advance and by all means, use what is useful and leave the rest.

Closing Prayer

I have incorporated many different kinds of closing prayers for each of our meetings, sometimes specifically chosen because of what we are studying and sometimes not. This is an appropriate time to share personal intentions, especially when closing with the Lord's Prayer. As you will see, though, this is also an opportunity to immerse ourselves in the prayers of the saints or invite different people to occasionally lead spontaneous prayer.

Forming Catholics for Mission

When I led my first Catholic Formation Group, ten young people and their families were part of the group. This is a really good number for one of these groups, which could easily grow to fourteen or fifteen and maintain the same effectiveness, or even run smaller if necessary. I would consider twenty members to be the absolute maximum for an effective group. The size of the group is of course left to the leader's and the parish's discretion but keeping these groups to a more modest size means that everyone can sit at the same table (literally) and that everyone can be part of the conversation. It is also difficult to host larger groups in a family home. In parishes with a larger population, I could easily imagine multiple groups of about this size running simultaneously, perhaps on different days of the week.

When initiating a Catholic Formation Group and inviting people to join, it is important to let them know what is entailed and what is expected. This is especially important for the parents of teenagers preparing for confirmation. A Catholic Formation Group is *not* a drop-off-and-pick-up kind of religious education. Instead, this intends to draw families in, empower and partner with parents, and bridge the divide between parish (or school) and home. In my email to parents of my first Catholic Formation Group, I shared with them what I later reinforced at our first meeting:

> I believe it is crucial for parents to be personally involved in this formation with their sons and daughters. While this does not mean that I would expect parents to sit in on all our sessions, I will welcome the regular contributions of parents, including asking people to share some of their own personal faith stories with the young people throughout the year. Mentoring and modeling is crucial, and as parents I think we have the opportunity to offer those things in an especially powerful way. As compared with other ways of faith formation, this one will require more from us parents on a regular basis.

The setting and basic approach that I have described above intends to create conditions conducive to the formation of Catholics toward the end of becoming a "source of goodness." It is about instilling within them the mission of the Church as their own life mission and empowering them to claim ownership of that mission. The leaders of the Catholic Formation Group *lead* this effort, but those leaders are not solely responsible. It takes a parish (or school) and it takes families. The sacraments of initiation should no longer be encountered as sacraments of inconvenience. These are gifts of Christ to his Church, and these gifts immerse us, strengthen us, and nourish us into *his* life.

If we want to form Catholics who are committed, courageous, and charitable, then we need to form them better to receive and respond to the gifts of Christ through the Holy Spirit. We need to do better than we have been doing; we need something different. By "we," I mean the Church. People are leaving the Catholic Church in droves. According to one recent study, the typical age of disaffiliation is now thirteen.[3] We need to form those who are being fully initiated in the Church to become agents of renewal who live lives that inspire *other people* to believe and to offer their lives to the love of Christ. We need Catholics to be sources of goodness and witnesses to the gospel. But as I learned from my friend Bill, if we want something different, then *we* need to do something different. So let's do it.

3. Robert McCarty and John Vitek, *Going, Going, Gone: The Dynamics of Disaffiliation in Young Catholics* (Winona, MN: Saint Mary's Press, 2018).

chapter one

The Way

Overview

A Look from Above

For each session, I will use this "look from above" to address the context of this particular session within the progression of sessions throughout the year. Oftentimes, this will include looking back and looking ahead, as well as identifying various "mini-units" within the two larger units of the whole (those two larger units are sessions 1–12 and sessions 14–25, respectively, with session 13 serving as a "reorientation" at the midway point). Since this is the first session of our time together, what precedes this session is, undoubtedly, inviting and communicating basic information with members of your Catholic Formation Group, recruiting and communicating with other leaders for the group (including parents for confirmation preparation or spouses/family members for RCIA prep), establishing the schedule of meetings for the year, and securing a meeting space, which is preferably in a home.

A Closer Look

The "closer look" is an opportunity to introduce this particular session more specifically. In this first session, the general objectives are twofold: first, to introduce the group to the idea of this approach to formation along with how sessions will be structured, and second, to teach about baptism and confirmation in relation to what we know about the way of life in the earliest Christian communities. The second objective provides the rationale—the "why"—for the first objective. In other words, because of the basic pattern for Christian formation that goes all the way back to the first Christian communities, our Catholic Formation Group will proceed the way it does.

In the following sessions, a basic three-part schema will be employed for organizing these "Reflection and Practice" chapters. Following an introduction like this one, the first movement will be entitled "Holy Conversation" that includes opening prayer, journaling, and conversation/meal; the second movement will lay out the lesson (this is the longest section); and the third movement deals with the closing prayer. For this first session, though, the organization will be a bit different since everything is just getting started and explaining the format of the group meetings is itself one of the tasks of this session.

For teenagers preparing for confirmation, all parents should be present at this introductory session, while families are welcome as always. For adults in RCIA, significant others and family members are welcome, as always, while including godparents/sponsors would be ideal.

1st Movement – Getting Started

1. Welcome and Introductions

2. Opening Prayer: the Angelus (see online resource; this is the regular opening prayer for our sessions)[1]

   Brief Catechesis on the Angelus: It is a traditional Catholic prayer that meditates on the mystery of the Incarnation. In large part, this prayer is drawn from the Angel Gabriel's Annunciation to Mary in the Gospel of Luke. Traditionally, Catholics pray this prayer three times a day—6 a.m., noon, and 6 p.m.—in order to mark the beginning, middle, and end of the day. Since we will be praying this together, there is a part for the leader and then responses for the whole group. Within a few months, we should all have this entire prayer memorized.

3. Basic Introduction to the Catholic Formation Group (by leader)

   Sample intro: We gather together as preparation for receiving the sacrament of confirmation (or sacraments of initiation for RCIA), but we should not view this merely as a "class." This is a "Catholic Formation Group" because together we are accompanying and assisting each other in our formation as Catholics. This formation is in part about preparing to

1. As a reminder, the online resource is available at leonardjdelorenzo.com/turn-resources.

receive the sacrament(s), but Catholic formation itself is lifelong. Together, this group is meant to help us all in our lifelong formation as Catholics.

2nd Movement – Getting Our Bearings

1. Opening Exercise: On Baptism

   Brief Large Group Discussion: What do you think happened to you at your baptism? (For RCIA: What do you think *will* happen to you at your baptism?) Share responses.

   To Teach (by leader; distribute handout for this session from the online resource)
   Three things happen right in a row in the baptismal rite:
   - Renunciation of sin, of the "way of Satan"—i.e., like three "Nos"
   - Profession of faith in the Father, Son, and Holy Spirit —i.e., like three "Yeses"
   - Immersion into this *life* of the Father, Son, and Holy Spirit

   First, a person is separated from the "old way" of sin. Second, a person is committed to the "new way" of God. Third, the immersion makes the words true.

   Takeaway: Baptism is the gift of new life in God, given for *our own good.*

2. This "Way" of Life

   To Teach:
   To become a Christian in baptism is not just to receive some*thing* but to be immersed into a *life.* We could even say this is a "way of life."

   In fact, before Christians were called "Christians," they were recognized for their "Way" of life. Christianity was initially just called "The Way." We want to see what this "Way" of new life in God was.

   Read Together: Acts 2:42-47 (on handout "The Way" in online resource)

   Question for the Group: From this passage, what did Christians do from the very beginning? There are four things:
   - They studied the teachings of the apostles (the gospel, the tradition).
   - They shared in a communal life (they were together, sharing needs and gifts). Notice: they sold their property and gave to the poor (v. 45) and practiced charity.
   - They broke bread together (an early indication of the Eucharist).
   - They prayed regularly.

Connect to our Catholic Formation Group:

The four pillars of "the Way" in the earliest Christian community are the four pillars of our Catholic Formation Group:

- We will study the faith together, from Scripture and the tradition passed down from the apostles.
- We will practice being together and sharing things with each other, supporting each other, challenging each other, and holding each other accountable to practicing charity in our lives.
- We will share meals together.
- We will pray together.

Notice the end of verse 47: "And every day the Lord added to their number those who were being saved."

- Those who are formed in and practice the Christian life—this "Way"—give life to others.
- This is a way to think about confirmation: If baptism is a gift given for *our own good*, then in confirmation we are given the grace to become *a source of goodness for others.* A Catholic Christian receives life from God and shares that life with others. Our formation this year is about each of us becoming *a source of goodness.*

3. Structure of Catholic Formation Group Sessions

We will practice a basic rhythm for our sessions that builds off of those four pillars of "the Way":

- Opening Prayer: Angelus (some variations possible for Lent)
- Prayer Journaling for 7–10 minutes
- Meal and conversation in small groups for about 20 minutes
- Lesson, with discussion, with a lot of attention to reading Scripture (40–60 minutes)
- Closing Prayer

To every session, group members should bring a Bible, journal, pen, and their full attention.

3rd Movement – Encouraging Buy-In

Note: If your group is comprised of teenagers preparing for confirmation, then the teens and the parents will be separated for this next period. If your group is for adults in RCIA, then you may want to do both parts with the whole group.

1. Teenagers Break Off into Small Groups (four people in each)

Prepare questions for each member to write about for several minutes on their own. It is recommended that you have the members turn in what they write here to the group leader, so that the leader can be aware of what each member is interested in, worried about, and hoping to do. Therefore, it may be best to distribute a handout (see online resource) with questions and room for them to write. Allow time in small groups for members to discuss what they wrote about, and what they think of this whole thing.

2. Parents of Teenagers Remain with Leader (to share expectations, answer questions, elicit buy-in)

   Emphasize: As the leader—or as a group of leaders—you want to create an *environment* that is conducive to members both growing in faith and integrating faith into their lives.

   Emphasize: This is an *environment* that all of you must nurture together, although you (as leader) are taking the lead.

   Name: The kind of contributions you hope/expect parents to make:
   - At times, teach on certain topics or help with leadership of certain sessions, as people are able and comfortable.
   - Share personal witness of your own faith, for which there will be several opportunities.
   - Participate in group sessions, learning alongside group members.
   - Follow up on discussions at home.
   - Read along with the first part of this book as part of your own study. (This is doubly important since this form of study also prepares parents to contribute to and guide their children's formation throughout the year, and especially to take on a more active role should unforeseen circumstances arise that preclude the group from meeting.)
   - Regarding meals for the group (since eating together is important), here is the ideal arrangement: Choose one parent who will coordinate a meal schedule. Families take turns providing simple meals for the entire group.

   Ask: What are their own expectations or concerns or interests? Invite questions and feedback.

4th Movement – Closing Prayer

Pray the Lord's Prayer, possibly after inviting people to share their intentions.

chapter two

Saul of Tarsus and the Witness of St. Stephen

Overview

A Look from Above

This is the first "regular" session of the Catholic Formation Group, following the introductory session. This session and the four that follow it focus on the person of St. Paul, beginning before his conversion and continuing all the way through his transformation as a source of goodness who leads others to Christ. The most famous episode relating to Paul is undoubtedly that of his conversion on the road to Damascus. That episode will be the focus of the next session (3). Since that episode is all-too-often imagined as something like a spectacular, one-off event, we will begin preparing the context for that episode in this session (2) and follow up on it later to see what Paul's thorough transformation yields (4). A film study will follow (5), before the final session in this Pauline "mini-unit," which connects us directly to the person of Jesus Christ (6).

A Closer Look

This session introduces us to Saul of Tarsus (later known as "Paul") by setting our attention on the events immediately preceding Saul's introduction. These events concern Stephen, the first martyr of the Church. By heeding what the Acts of the Apostles tells us about Stephen, we will discover in him a kind of power that is not at all like the power that Saul exercises, though Stephen's power is no less impressive. Stephen serves to present Saul to us as he was *before* his conversion, and it is important to take stock of this profile. What we are seeing in this session is what Saul will have to *renounce* when he is baptized into "the Way."

1st Movement – Holy Conversation

1. Prayer
   Angelus recommended: see online resource

2. Journaling (approximately 7–10 minutes)

   Getting Started: Remind group members that they will be given time to journal at the beginning of each session. This is individual time, with the option of playing soft music in the background. Group members are always welcome to write about anything they want, though the intention is to allow this journaling to be "prayerful," which will often mean writing directly to the Lord.

   Prompts for Journaling Session:
   - Consider something you are grateful for and why, then thank the Lord for it.
   - Consider someone you want to pray for, then ask the Lord.
   - Consider how you are doing in general, then tell the Lord.

3. Conversation (and Meal)

Introduce yourselves to each other and spend time getting to know each other. Consider sharing something you wrote about during your journaling.

2nd Movement – Lesson

1. Review from the First Session (briefly, done by leader)

   In baptism
   - We receive the good gift of new life in God.
   - The rite of baptism includes renunciation, profession, and immersion.

   In confirmation
   - We receive the grace to become a source of goodness for others.
   - The gift received in baptism becomes the mission to share that gift.
   - By living "the Way" of Christ, Christians contribute to the well-being of others.

What's Next: In the next five sessions, we are going to see this whole drama play out in one person: St. Paul, who was one of the first people to convert to "the Way" from an "old way" that was very different.

2. The Story of Paul Begins with Stephen

To Teach:
As the early Church grew rapidly in Jerusalem, the apostles appointed seven disciples to serve the needs of the poor in the community—Stephen was one of these seven.

Stephen was so successful in his ministry as a servant and healer that he became known to the religious authorities, who sought to put him down.

Read Together: The arrest of Stephen (Acts 6:8-15)

- Notice the power of his speech (v. 10).
- Notice how those who seek to silence him must resort to false witnesses (v. 13).
- Notice the description of his face: like that of an angel (v. 15).

Questions for the Group:

- What do you think the face of an angel is like?
- What is almost always the first thing angels say when they appear to someone in the Bible?

Answer: "Do not be afraid!" or "Fear not!"
If any of the responses to the first question have to do with anything "cute" or "cuddly," perhaps the response should be reconsidered since angels are always telling people to *not* be afraid when they see them. You might share a passage about an angel from the Book of Daniel (10:5-6).

Takeaway: Stephen is powerful, persuasive, and effective, whether in word, action, or appearance.

Exercise for Group Members:
The following chapter of the Acts of the Apostles—chapter 7—contains Stephen's long speech before his accusers. Just glance over it for a minute or two. What does Stephen talk about? (Invite responses.)

Summary: He re-presents the entire Old Testament (the history of Israel) as leading to this person of Jesus. He also shows how God's people have always rejected God's prophets, just as they have now rejected Jesus.

To Teach:
Show how Stephen makes Jesus present in his own death (see Acts 7:54-60):

- He looks to heaven and sees Jesus at the right hand of the Father (v. 55)—we can imagine that glory now reflected on Stephen's face.

- He hands over his spirit to the Lord (v. 59) just as Jesus handed over his spirit to the Father (Luke 23:46).
- He forgives his executioners and asks the Lord to pardon them (v. 60) just as Jesus forgave and asked his Father to pardon his executioners (Luke 23:34).

Whatever power or influence Stephen has, it is a reflection of Christ's power and influence.

Question for the Group: Who oversaw Stephen's execution?

Answer: Saul (see Acts 7:58 and 8:1).
This is the first we hear of Saul of Tarsus. Consider that Saul heard all that Stephen said; Saul saw what Stephen looked like (his face like an angel, the glory of Christ reflected on him); and the memory of Stephen likely stayed with Saul.

3. The Initial Profile of Saul of Tarsus

Read Together: The initial introduction to Saul in Acts 8:1–3

- Ask what kind of man he was.
- Notice there is violence in Saul, who drags men and women out of their homes to bring them to prison.
- There is passion in Saul, who "laid waste" to the Church.
- This is a man of power and purpose.

Exercise for Smaller Groups (3–4 members each)

- Read two additional passages that come later in Acts, where Paul is recalling the kind of man he once was (Acts 22:3-5 and Acts 26:9-11).
- Take notes on Paul's characteristics from these accounts.
- Try to think about the following, then share responses in large group: How did Saul see the world, and especially Christians? How did he listen for or to others, especially Christians? What is the manner of his speech? How does he use language?

In Conclusion: Keep this profile of Saul in mind, because this shows us the kind of life he must *renounce* before receiving new life in Christ. This is the "old way."

3rd Movement – Closing Prayer

Offer the "Litany of St. Stephen," the first martyr (see online resource under "Prayers").

chapter three

The Conversion of St. Paul

Overview

A Look from Above

We are now in the middle of a five-lesson "mini-unit" focusing on St. Paul. In the previous session, we saw how the martyrdom of St. Stephen is the beginning of Paul's own life in Christ, though at first that life is a life lived in rebellion. In the following three sessions, we will see how Paul is thoroughly transformed in Christ in his mind, heart, and tongue, before following Paul's lead to the person of Jesus Christ himself. Between the man Paul had been and the man Paul becomes is the great turn in his life: his conversion on the road to Damascus, which moves to centerstage in this session.

A Closer Look

This session concerns Paul's conversion, begun on the road to Damascus and facilitated through the ministry of Ananias. Paul's conversion is perhaps the most famous conversion is Christian history, though too few actually pay close attention to what happens in his life-altering encounter with Christ. Our aim is to slow down to both heed and wonder about how this change in Paul takes place and how the man he was is put into crisis. In doing so, we will highlight the way he sees, the way he hears, and the way he speaks, all of which were drenched in rage in his "old way"—the way that he must now renounce so as to be refashioned as a new man.

1st Movement – Holy Conversation

1. Prayer
   Angelus recommended: see online resource

2. Journaling (approximately 7–10 minutes)

   Prompt: Write directly to the Lord about whatever is on your heart. Begin with "Dear Jesus . . ."

3. Conversation (and Meal)

   Prompt: Share with one another a high and low from this past week.

2nd Movement – Lesson

1. Review from Previous Sessions (briefly, done by leader)

   In baptism
   - We receive the good gift of new life in God.
   - The rite of baptism includes renunciation, profession, and immersion.

   In confirmation
   - We receive the grace to become a source of goodness for others.
   - The gift received in baptism becomes the mission to share that gift.
   - By living "the Way" of Christ, Christians contribute to the well-being of others.

   St. Stephen at the Beginning of the Story of Paul
   - Stephen was powerful in his testimony to Christ: he spoke in terms of the entire Old Testament, his face was like that of an angel, by his death he resembled Christ.
   - Paul oversaw Stephen's execution and therefore witnessed everything.
   - Paul's character was filled with anger, violence, passion, and purpose.
   - Paul was in a sense fearful, because he needed to be right and could not tolerate any other way, especially "the Way" of Christians.

2. The Conversion of St. Paul

   Questions for the Group: What do you already know about Paul's conversion? Who else was involved in his conversion? Invite responses.

   Read Together: The first half of Paul's conversion (Acts 9:1-9).

To Teach (by questioning):
Looking to verses 1-2, what is Paul's mission (or the "way" he is going)? Points to establish (it is crucial to see what is going on with Paul's eyes, ears, tongue):

- With his *eyes*, Paul is looking for Christians and looking for them with anger, suspicion, and hatred.
- With his *ears*, he is *not* listening to the prayers, words, and pleas of Christians with understanding, but only hearing those things as an invitation to bring them harm.
- With his *tongue*, he is speaking venomous threats, spewing anger.

Looking to verses 3-9, what does Paul see and hear? How does he speak? Points to establish (again, focusing on eyes, ears, and tongue is key):

- Paul *sees* the blinding light of Christ, then he cannot see anything. When Christ appears, the way Paul had seen is taken away.
- Paul *hears* the voice of Christ: "Why are you persecuting me?" Jesus identifies himself with the ones Paul is persecuting. What Paul does *not* hear are his companions—they are "speechless" (v. 7). When Christ speaks, the voices that have surrounded Paul are mute.
- Paul *speaks* only in a question: "Who are you, Lord?" (v. 5). In response to Christ, the once mighty Paul is reduced to a confused seeker.

By the end of verse 9, what has changed about Paul? Points to emphasize:

- The proud, motivated, powerful Paul is made weak. He is blind and uncertain. He does not eat or drink. He must be led by others and he cannot make *his own way.*

Read Together: The second half of Paul's conversion (Acts 9:10-20).

To Teach (by questioning):
In verses 10-14, Ananias is called by the Lord to minister to Paul—how do you think Ananias felt? Points to emphasize:

- Obviously, Ananias would be fearful to seek out the very man who was seeking to persecute people like him. Consider how much trust in the Lord and how much courage Ananias must exercise to follow this call.

In verses 17-20, what does Paul hear, see, and say? Points to emphasize (this is the third time looking at this triad):

- The *first* thing Paul hears is Ananias calling him "brother." Ananias claims Paul as his own. This is really quite shocking. Paul begins to *hear* anew.
- Paul regains his sight when his blinders are removed and, after initially blinded by the light of Christ, begins to *see* anew.
- When Paul speaks again, he begins proclaiming Jesus (v. 20). Paul begins to *speak* anew.

In verses 18-19, it says that Paul was baptized and took food and was strengthened—what do you make of that? Invite responses. Points to emphasize:

- His baptism separates him from his old way and immerses him in this new way of Christ.
- To take food is a eucharistic action.
- To be strengthened resonates with confirmation.
- These are images of the sacraments of initiation: baptism, confirmation, Eucharist.

3. Reflecting on Paul's Conversion

To Teach:

The conversion of St. Paul has to do with every part of who he is:

- How he *sees* changes. This has to do with the *renewal of his mind*. It is about how he views things, what he is looking for, how he sees other people. He has begun to see in the light of Christ.
- How he *hears* changes. This has to do with the *renewal of his heart*. Yes, we hear with our ears, but the most profound listening happens with our hearts. How he is willing to listen to others, to receive their words, and identify with them changes. He is moving from anger to charity.
- How he *speaks* changes. He begins to speak in order to build up others, and to spread Good News rather than threats.

When the gospel is proclaimed at Mass, we ask the Lord to "be on my mind, on my lips, and in my heart." It is a moment of continual conversion to Christ.

Perhaps the most remarkable thing about Paul's conversion is that he becomes humble:

- This was the proudest of men, and he learns to follow and be healed by others (especially, Ananias).
- Humility is *not* weakness; it is honesty. Paul needed to be healed of his old way.
- Humility is the basis of the Christian life: the willingness to heed *the Lord's Way* and be joined to others.

3rd Movement – Closing Prayer

Pray the "Litany of Humility" (see online resource under "Prayers").

chapter four

St. Paul: The Source of Goodness

Overview

A Look from Above

In the previous session (3), we explored Paul's conversion as concerning his eyes, his ears, and his tongue—or, in short, all of who he was. Paul's conversion is not the end of his story, though, just as it was not the beginning. Paul's story began with St. Stephen's martyrdom and it continues through to the thoroughgoing transformation of who Paul becomes for others.

A Closer Look

This session concerns Paul's transformation, which begins but does not end in his conversion on the road to Damascus. By reading and reflecting on selected passages from Paul's epistles, we will discern just how complete and profound the change that the Lord worked in Paul really was. Paul is not just saved from being the hateful man he was but he also becomes a source of goodness for others. And as with his conversion, this transformation concerns how he sees, hears, and speaks.

1st Movement – Holy Conversation

1. Prayer
   Angelus recommended: see online resource

2. Journaling (approximately 7–10 minutes)

   Prompts:
   - Write directly to the Lord about whatever is on your heart. Begin with "Dear Jesus . . ."
   - Consider offering one prayer of gratitude to the Lord for something in your life.
   - Consider offering one prayer for someone else's wellbeing.

3. Conversation (and Meal)

   Prompt: Share with one another a high and low from this past week.

2nd Movement – Lesson

1. Review from Previous Sessions (briefly, done by leader)
   Paul's conversion concerned how he saw, how he listened, and how he spoke.
   - He had seen the world through anger and vengeance, but the Lord blinded him and when he could see again, he started to see the world in the light of Christ.
   - He had listened for Christians' prayers and words in order to identify and persecute them, but then he heard the voice of the Lord and Ananias claim him as "brother," which opened him to a new way of listening that went all the way to his heart.
   - He had spoken with murderous threats, but then he was shocked by the Lord and could only question, and immediately after his baptism he began to proclaim Christ Jesus.

2. Paul Becomes a Source of Goodness (Setup)

   To Teach:
   Before his conversion, everything about Paul was part of his "old way." The man Paul was had a significant effect on other people: he persecuted lowly ones and he directed other people to participate in his way of violence. Paul's conversion, therefore, has to do with everything about him. The man Paul ultimately becomes also has a significant effect on other people, just as much or even more than before. We want to read some of Paul's letters to see who he becomes according to how he sees, hears, and speaks.

3. Paul's Transformation of Mind: How He Sees

   Question for the Group: From what you might know of the great apostle and saint that Paul eventually becomes, what reasons would he have for being proud and even boastful?

Possible Answers (share ones that are not otherwise mentioned):

- He traveled more than 10,000 miles to proclaim the gospel, by foot and by sea.
- He endured enormous hardships (see 2 Cor 11:24-28 for a list).
- He was a powerful evangelizer who converted many and started churches all over the world.
- He was given a mystical experience, raised to the "third heaven" (see 2 Cor 12:3-6).

Emphasize: Paul says that "I will boast of the things that show my weakness" (2 Cor 11:30). That is an odd thing: to boast of weakness.

Read Together: Selection from Paul's Second Letter to the Corinthians (12:7–10).

Question for the Group: What do you think might have been this thorn in his flesh that keeps him humble? Points to consider:

- No one knows for certain, but possibilities include: a lingering temptation, speech impediment, physical deformity, severe headaches, false teachers or teachers who oppose him.
- What about his own memory? Could that be what afflicts him? (a) Paul remembers the violence he enacted on others. (b) Paul remembers what he has done to ruin others. (c) Paul has blood on his hands.

Key Takeaways:
God's "grace" is what God has done for Paul. The Lord tells Paul to trust in his grace more than Paul trusts in what he himself had done and who he had been. It is like the Lord says, "Believe in my love more than you believe in what you are ashamed of."

The key to Paul not becoming too proud but instead to remain grateful is remembering what the Lord has done for him. Paul practices *seeing* through God's grace. This *renews his mind.*

Suggested Exercise: Group members spend a few minutes writing in their journals about something they are ashamed of or do not like about themselves. When they are done, invite them to write—in big bold letters above and below what they journaled—"Your grace is enough, Lord."

4. Paul's Transformation of Heart: How He Listens

Question for the Group: How did Paul listen to or for Christians, before his conversion?

Answer: He listened for them in order to identify and persecute them; their prayers and needs were invitations to him to seek their ruin.

Read Together: Selection from Paul's Letter to the Philippians (1:3-9).

Question for the Group: What does it mean to hold the Christians at Philippi "in his heart"?

Possible Answers: Paul seeks after their own good, their joy. They are intimate with him. His own heart is filled with faces and names; it is a space for bringing them all together and nurturing them.

Takeaways: Consider how profound Paul's change in heart is. Consider how he now rejoices in what is good *for others* and suffers when they suffer.

Suggested Exercise:

- Have group members sketch an image of their own heart, then draw or write the faces and names of people they hold in their heart in the image.
- When complete, invite group members to now think of who else they can work on putting in there—e.g., someone they do not yet hold in their heart, who might be difficult to love or care for—and then draw or write that person's face or name in their heart.

5. Paul's Transformation of Lips: How He Speaks

Question for the Group: From what you know about St. Paul, what do you think might be the most important experience or event of his life, for him to tell others about?

Read Together: Selection from Paul's First Letter to the Corinthians (15:3-10).

To Teach:
What Paul considers "of first importance" is what was handed on to him. He does not pass on first his own experiences—his conversion, his works, even his own mystical experience. The most important thing is the faith of the Church he has received. The life, death, and resurrection of Christ is most important.

Takeaways:

- Paul uses his words to preach Christ Jesus.
- Paul accepts himself as the person the Lord has made him to be ("by the grace of God I am what I am").
- The man who once spoke "murderous threats" now proclaims "Good News."

3rd Movement – Closing Prayer

Offer the "Prayer for the Intercession of St. Paul" (see online resource under "Prayers").

St. Paul gave his life to preach Christ Jesus, so let us pray in the words Jesus taught us: *Our Father* . . .

chapter five

Paul, Apostle of Christ

Overview

A Look from Above

In our three preceding sessions with St. Paul, we moved from the martyrdom of St. Stephen that Paul witnessed (2), to Paul's conversion through the Lord's encounter and Ananias's ministry (3), and eventually to Paul's transformation into a source of goodness through his mind, heart, and lips (4). In Paul, the entire drama sacramentally effected in baptism and then sealed in confirmation is made evident. He is freed from an "old way" and immersed in a new life, and he gives of himself in order to hand on to others the gift he has received. Soon enough, we will follow Paul's lead to gaze upon the person of Jesus Christ, but before making that transition two additional sessions on St. Paul will allow us to reflect on the witness of this saint and apostle.

A Closer Look

This session is dedicated entirely to viewing the film *Paul, Apostle of Christ.*[1] This film may be viewed together in an extended meeting (the film is 108 minutes), or members may watch on their own, preferably with family members or friends. Since the film focuses on the end of Paul's life with flashbacks to earlier moments, including especially his time as a persecutor of Christians, it works nicely as a capstone for this mini-unit on Paul. The following session (6) is built around discussion about the film.

1. For information on the film, visit http://www.paulmovie.com/.

chapter six

The Life of Paul and the Love of Jesus

Overview

A Look from Above

Having now viewed the film *Paul, Apostle of Christ,* the previous five sessions have come together both chronologically and thematically. In terms of chronology, we have moved from Paul's "old way" in the session about St. Stephen (2), to the conversion of St. Paul (3), to the transformation of St. Paul (4), to his last days and martyrdom (5). Since everything about Paul ultimately leads others to Christ, we ourselves will move to studying the person of Jesus Christ beginning in the next session (7).

A Closer Look

In this session we make a transition from Paul to Christ. The majority of this session is dedicated to discussing the film, while the final and shorter portion introduces the two key questions for the following sessions: "Who is Jesus?" and "Who is Jesus for me?"

1st Movement – Holy Conversation

1. Prayer

   Angelus recommended: see online resource

2. Journaling (approximately 7–10 minutes)

   Prompts:

   - Write about something that inspired, challenged, or troubled you in the film about St. Paul.

- Feel free to also use this time to write directly to the Lord about anything that is on your heart.

3. Conversation (and Meal)

   Prompt: You may choose to incorporate this portion of the meeting into the discussion about the film, which is detailed below. Otherwise, you might choose to allow group members to have a check-in conversation over the meal, then setup the discussion groups for the film.

2nd Movement – Lesson

1. Discussion about the Film *Paul, Apostle of Christ*
   Smaller discussion groups of four to six people are ideal. Family members and others can be included along with the regular group members. For groups of teenagers preparing for confirmation, it is especially wise to incorporate parents into these discussions, both for guidance and for intergenerational discussion. Give groups 20–30 minutes for discussion, and encourage people to take notes either during or after the discussion. See the PDF of suggested discussion questions in the online resource under "Paul Film Questions."

2. Summing Up and Looking Ahead (Full Group)

   To Teach:
   St. Paul's conversion initiated a change in everything about him, his transformation touched every part of him, and his witness to Christ ultimately included his entire life (including his past) all the way to his death.
   - Transformation of seeing: "My grace is sufficient for you" (2 Cor 12:9).
   - Transformation of hearing: "I hold you in my heart" (Phil 1:7).
   - Transformation of speech: "I handed on to you as of first importance" (1 Cor 15:3).

   In the film—and we can see this in Scripture, too—Paul's love for and witness to Christ took dedication, struggle, and sacrifice, all the way to the end. Though his witness may be challenging, it is also reassuring to know that even a great saint like Paul struggled to live the Christian faith and entrust himself to Jesus until his last day.

   Takeaways:
   - Everything about Paul points to Jesus. In pointing us to Jesus, he urges us to discover over and over again who Jesus is. The question Paul leaves us with is "Who is Jesus?" We will study who Jesus is together in the following sessions.

- A second question goes along with that first one, which each of us must respond to ourselves. It is the question of "Who is Jesus for me?" No one can answer that for you, though we can support each other in giving a response.
- The next four sessions are about the question "Who is Jesus?" but keep in mind the second question "Who is Jesus for me?" at the same time.

3rd Movement – Closing Prayer

Offer intentions and the Lord's Prayer.

chapter seven

Who Is Jesus? The Son of the Father Drawn Near to Us

Overview

A Look from Above

The five-session mini-unit on St. Paul, which included the viewing of and discussion about the film, was all a preparation for encountering the person of Jesus Christ. Paul's entire life was one ultimately made into a single offering to Jesus, who claimed Paul in love. Paul turned to the Lord, and so in following Paul, we are led to the person to whom Paul directed everything. The next four sessions—including this one—are all about rediscovering who Jesus is. This requires more than affection and piety, though affection and piety certainly have their rightful place in the Christian life. To discover Jesus for who he is, we must study Scripture so as to first of all *receive and ponder* who Jesus reveals himself to be. Our contemplation of Jesus will yield a fourfold response to that question: the Son of the Father (7), I AM (8), the Power and Wisdom of God (9), and the Gift of Beatitude (10). All the time while studying who Jesus is in and through Scripture, we will also keep in the forefront of our minds that deeply personal question to which each disciple must respond: "Who is Jesus for me?"

A Closer Look

As the first of four sessions in this mini-unit on "Who is Jesus?" this session presents Jesus as the "Son of the Father drawn near to us." Two things are said in that one response. First, Jesus is the Son of the Father. This speaks to his divine identity, which is hidden in God and only made accessible to us through faith. Second, the movement of Jesus's life—that is, the entire drama of the Incarnation—is noted when we say that he has "drawn near to us." There is a danger in having this all sound abstract, which is why the testimony of Scripture is so important. In this session, then, we will focus on two scenes from the gospel (specifically, Luke's gospel) to train our vision on and open our imaginations to who Jesus is: his baptism and his transfiguration.

Special Note

Starting in either the next session or the one after (7 or 8), group leaders should have parents/sponsors (for teenage confirmation groups) or sponsors/spouses (for RCIA and adult confirmation groups) share short testimonials in response to the question "Who is Jesus for me?" These testimonials are typically 2–3 minutes long and, of course, personal in nature. The idea is that these more mature disciples offer to those in sacramental preparation both a model for how to take responsibility for responding to that critical question of discipleship and an example of the courage and trust necessary to share that response with others. These testimonials should be included at the beginning of the next several sessions, and then later in the year (beginning in session 15), those in sacramental preparation (*confirmandi* and RCIA candidates) share their own testimonials. See online resource for samples of parent testimonials.

1st Movement – Holy Conversation

1. Prayer

   Angelus recommended: see online resource

2. Journaling (approximately 7–10 minutes)

   Prompts:

   - At the end of the last session, we brought up the very personal question of "Who is Jesus for me?" Spend some time writing directly to the Lord, offering a first response to this question. Write in the following manner: "Lord, you are . . . " (that is, write directly to the Lord).
   - Alternatively, if you have trouble coming up with a response, write directly to the Lord asking him to help you respond to this question. Again, write directly to Jesus: "Lord, help me to . . . "

3. Conversation (and Meal)

   Prompt: Share about at least one of the following things: someone who has been a blessing in your life within the past few weeks, and why; someone whom you have been concerned about or want to pray for, and why; someone whom you have had a hard time getting along with or loving, and why; someone who brings you joy, and why.

2nd Movement – Lesson

1. Review and Introduction (briefly, by leader)
   By St. Paul's own words, what he considered most important of all was what he received in faith: the person and the work of Jesus Christ (see 1 Cor 15:3-10).

   Everything about St. Paul points to Christ. We are following Paul's lead in looking to Christ, and for four sessions we will stay with the question "Who is Jesus?" Our study together will help us to learn more. While we do this, keep in mind the second, very personal question that goes with it: "Who is Jesus for me?"

2. The Baptism of Jesus
   This is the first place we will look to seek an answer to the question "Who is Jesus?" (Option: share icon of Jesus's baptism—see online resource.)

   A. Reimagining Jesus's Baptism

   Read Together: Luke's account of the baptism of Jesus (3:21-22).

   Question for the Group: Why are people being baptized by John the Baptist?

   Answer: To repent, to be turned away from their sins.

   Question for the Group: So what does it mean if Jesus is being baptized?

   Consider: It would *seem* like he is just another sinner, except for this voice from heaven and the descent of the Holy Spirit.

   Key Point: He is *not* a sinner but he mixes in with sinners and goes under the same waters as sinners.

   Propose:
   - Notice that it sounds like Jesus is baptized at the end (v. 21).

- Now imagine him standing in line with all the other people, waiting for John to baptize him. Everyone would assume he was just like everyone else: a sinner.
- But in the end, the voice of the Father from heaven proclaims him as the "beloved Son," with whom the Father is "well pleased" and therefore without sin.
- This *should* be troubling to us: he who is united to the Father in love (that is what and who the Holy Spirit is, by the way) has put himself in the position of being confused with sinners.

Takeaway: Jesus is the Son of the Father who draws near to sinners (and is even confused for one).

B. From Baptism to Genealogy

Look Together: See what comes immediately after Jesus's baptism in Luke's gospel (glance at 3:23–38).

Question for the Group: Could this long genealogy possibly have anything to do with what just happened in Jesus's baptism?

Consider: The one who is proclaimed as the "Son of the Father" and who is joined to sinners in those waters of baptism is now linked in this genealogy to the entire history of Israel (back to Abraham in v. 34) and even further to all of humanity (back to Adam in v. 38).

Takeaway: The Son of the Father is connected to all of Israel and all humanity.

C. From the Genealogy to the Desert

Question for the Group: Where was John the Baptist performing his baptisms?

Answer: The River Jordan. (Option: show images of the River Jordan—see online resource.)

Question for the Group: And where is the River Jordan in relation to Israel's homeland?

Answer: It is the easternmost border of Israel's homeland. Show map of Israel—see online resource.

To Teach:
Geography is important here. After Israel was freed from slavery in Egypt by passing through the Red Sea, they wandered for forty years in the desert where they had to be healed of their sin and they struggled with

temptation. After those forty years, they entered their Promised Land by passing through the *River Jordan.*

Read Together: Luke 4:1-2.

Question for the Group: What is curious about Jesus's movement after his baptism?

Answer: He goes in the *other direction*. He moves from the Promised Land (full of the Holy Spirit), across the River Jordan, and into the desert of sin, where temptation abounds.

Takeaway: See here again the same mystery, which is that the one who is united to the Father moves toward the sinfulness of the people. In this case, he goes back to the place where all of Israel suffered in sin and was tempted.

Final Takeaway: Who is Jesus? The Son of the Father who goes to the place of temptation where sinners dwell.

3. The Transfiguration of Jesus

This is a second event, connected to the first, where we will seek an answer to the same question: "Who is Jesus?"

Read Together: Luke 9:28-36.

To Teach (either by discussion or direct guidance):

- As with the baptism, Jesus is again claimed as "my Son" by the Father.
- Here, the glory of Jesus is not just audible but in fact visible: he appears in dazzling white, the cloud of God's presence surrounds the mountain, Moses and Elijah appear, Jesus is literally "high up."
- Peter knows this is the glory of God, but he does not understand.

Question for the Group: So what happens immediately after the transfiguration? (They will need to look at Luke 9:37-43.)

Answer: Jesus goes down the mountain toward the crowd, where he drives an unclean spirit out of a child.

Takeaway: Jesus, who is the Son of the Father "on high," willingly "goes down" toward the sin and mess of the crowd to drive out the unclean spirit. The setting is different but the movement is the same as in his baptism and temptation in the desert.

Final Takeaway: These episodes show us who Jesus is and what Jesus does. Jesus is the Son of the Father who draws near to us, even in our sin, our mess, and under the control of unclean spirits.

3rd Movement – Closing Prayer

For this and the next three sessions, we will pray with the words of different saints, as they each in their own way testify to "who Jesus is for *them.*" Offer the prayer of St. Gianna Beretta Molla in part 1, page 35 (also in online resource under "Prayers").

chapter eight

Who Is Jesus? I AM

Overview

A Look from Above

We are now in the midst of four consecutive sessions devoted to contemplating the question "Who is Jesus?" In the previous session (7), we moved from the baptism of Jesus to the transfiguration of Jesus in order to see that Jesus is the Son of the Father who draws near to us, even in our sin and our messiness. In the following two sessions (9–10), our appeals to Scripture will help us respond to this question by marveling at the power, wisdom, and joy of Jesus. While each of these four sessions puts the question of "Who is Jesus?" at the forefront, we are also keeping in mind the more personal question that goes alongside that one: "Who is Jesus for me?" Beginning in this session and continuing for at least the next two sessions, short testimonials from parents, sponsors, or other mature disciples will be shared with the group, partly as edification for the members of the group and partly as models for how group members will later share their own testimonies (beginning in session 15).

A Closer Look

As the second of four sessions in this mini-unit on "Who is Jesus?" this session presents Jesus according to the name of God: "I AM." We will seek to make a clear and direct connection between the revelation of God's name in the Book of Exodus and Jesus's claiming of that name for himself in the Gospel of John. Whereas the previous session sought to show how Jesus is the Son who is in union with the Father but freely moves toward us in mercy, this session focuses on how who Jesus is and what Jesus does is in continuity with what God has done for Israel, as revealed in the Old Testament.

1st Movement – Holy Conversation

1. Prayer

   Angelus recommended: see online resource

2. Testimonies: "Who is Jesus for me?"

   It is best to have two or three parents, sponsors, or other more mature disciples share their short testimonies in response to this question. Limiting the number helps listeners to remain attentive. Again, these testimonies should be about 2–3 minutes, brief and direct, perhaps with a short narrative. They should be shared in this session and the following two (i.e., 8–10). This *should* take no more than 10 minutes.

3. Journaling (approximately 7–10 minutes)

   Prompts:

   - Write to the Lord and reflect on at least one thing shared in the testimonials.
   - Write directly to the Lord about what is going on in your life.

4. Conversation (and Meal)

   Prompt: Reflect together on the testimonials you heard. Check-in with each other about how you are doing, including perhaps something you are excited about and something you are worried about these days.

2nd Movement – Lesson

1. Review of the Previous Session

   Brief Exercise: Give group members 1 minute to write about something they remember or that made an impact on them regarding both Jesus's baptism and his transfiguration, which we studied last week. Share responses.

   Reaffirm the Main Takeaway: Jesus is the Son of the Father who draws near to us, even in our sin, our mess, and under the control of unclean spirits.

2. The Name of God in the Book of Exodus

   Setting the Scene (done by leader): Today we want to consider the importance of the "name" of God. God gives his name to Moses in the Book of Exodus. Provide group members with a summary of the first two chapters of the Book of Exodus—see the third paragraph of chapter 8 in part 1 for guidance.

A. Introducing God

Read Together: The passage that is "God's introduction" in Exodus 2:23-25.

Question for the Group: What are the Israelites doing?

Answer: Crying to God for help, because they are suffering in slavery.

Question for the Group: If this is the introduction about God in the Book of Exodus, what is the first thing we learn about God? What does God do?

Answer: God hears the cries of the people, God remembers the covenant (so God connects this people now with their ancestors), and God perceives and notices this people in their suffering.

Question for the Group: What direction are the Israelites cries moving, and therefore what direction would God have to move to respond?

Answer: Their cries *go up*, so God would have to *go down* to respond.

Question for the Group: What do you think it will mean for God to take notice of and respond to this people?

Answer: That is what we are about to find out.

B. The Revelation of God

Read Together: Exodus 3:1-15.

Question for the Group: From what we read here, what is God's response to the sufferings of the people?

Answer: To personally come down to liberate them (see vv. 7-8).

Question for the Group: In order to know exactly who it is that is promising to save them, Moses asks God for his name so that he can tell it to the Israelites. What is the name God reveals and what does this name mean?

Answer: "I AM" (or "I AM WHO AM") is how we typically translate this name. It could also be translated as "I WILL BE WHAT I WILL BE," which means something like "what I do will tell you who I am." So this name is itself a mystery because it means both something like "you must see what I do to know who I am" and "you must know who I am to understand what I do."

C. Naming God

Read Together: Exodus 15:1-3.

To Teach:
This is the song the Israelites sing to God once they have been freed from slavery to the Egyptians. What they are doing is proclaiming the *name of the Lord.* "The Lord is my strength and my song, and he has become my salvation" (v. 2). The Israelites have learned God's name because they have seen what God has done *for them.* The Lord has saved them, and that shows them who God is.

Takeaway: With the Book of Exodus, we see that God reveals who he is through what he does.

3. The Name of Jesus in the Gospel of John

Setting the Scene (done by leader):
The primary question of the gospels is "Who is Jesus?" We are going to look at a few scenes from just one of the four gospels to see how Jesus presents himself.

A. "I AM" in the Storm

Read Together: John 6:16-21 (the disciples in the storm and Jesus walking on the sea)

Question for the Group: How would you describe the condition of the disciples here?

Answer: They are in the dark, they are being tossed about, and they are afraid.

Question for the Group: What does Jesus do in response to them?

Answer: He comes to them and he says, "It is I; do not be afraid."
- Note: This is all he does; moves toward them and says who he is.
- Note: "It is I" is otherwise translated as "I am."

Takeaway: In response to the disciple's suffering, Jesus says "I AM."

B. "I AM" from Above

Read Together: John 8:23-30 and verse 58.

To Teach:
- The question about Jesus here is about two things: who he is and where he is from.

- Regarding *where* he is from, Jesus says he is “from above” whereas they are “from below.” Notice: for them to meet Jesus, they must “go up” and for Jesus to meet them, Jesus must “go down” (the same directions as between the Israelites and God in Exodus).
- Regarding *who* he is, Jesus says: “I AM (he)” in verses 24 and 28. And then at the very end of this episode (v. 58), he announces who he is even more forcefully in direct connection with the name of God: “I AM.”

Takeaway: Jesus announces that he is “from above” and that he is “I AM.”

C. “I AM” in the Garden

Read Together: John 18:1-8 (the arrest of Jesus).

To Teach:

- The question Jesus asks is “Whom do you seek?” When they say “Jesus of Nazareth,” he says “I AM.” Notice that when he says “I AM,” the force of that name knocks them to the ground.
- Consider: They came looking for a mere man and what did they find? The name—and the presence—of God! “I AM.” Jesus repeats this name—“I AM”—in verse 8.

Takeaway: Jesus reveals who he really is: the one whose name is “I AM.”

4. Jesus and the Name of God

Final Takeaways:

- In the Book of Exodus, God reveals that his name is “I AM” and “I WILL BE WHAT I WILL BE,” which means that what he does reveals who he is.
- What God does in the Book of Exodus is come down to the people who are suffering to liberate them, so who he is is their salvation.
- Jesus claims the name “I AM” for himself; he is God’s saving action.

Main Point: Jesus is one with the God of Israel; Jesus is “God with us.”

3rd Movement – Closing Prayer

For each session on “Who is Jesus?” we conclude with a prayer from one of the saints who testifies to who Jesus is *for them*. Offer the prayer of St. John Vianney in part 1, page 42 (also in online resource under “Prayers”).

chapter nine

Who Is Jesus? The Power and Wisdom of God

Overview

A Look from Above

In the previous two sessions we studied how Jesus is the Son of the Father drawn near to us (7) and how Jesus claims the name of God as his own: "I AM" (8). To put these together, we might say that who Jesus is *is* God's saving action. Now this third session on the question "Who is Jesus?" builds on what we have already discovered, specifically by seeing the manner in which Jesus acts. In the next session (10), we will tie the manner of Jesus's own acting to the beatitudes, which identify those who will inherit everlasting joy. Moreover, with the previous session we began to incorporate testimonials from parents, sponsors, or other mature disciples in response to the question "Who is Jesus for me?," and those testimonials will continue in both this session and the next.

A Closer Look

As the third of four sessions in this mini-unit on "Who is Jesus?" this session reckons with St. Paul's heralding of Jesus as the "power of God and the wisdom of God" (1 Cor 1:24). This designation seems straightforward and wholly acceptable, until we allow ourselves to really notice how Jesus acts and what he allows to happen to him. Power is made to look quite weird in Jesus, while wisdom looks more like foolishness. The heart of this session concerns four episodes from the gospels that should trouble our commonplace notions about power and wisdom.

1st Movement – Holy Conversation

1. Prayer

   Angelus recommended: see online resource

2. Testimonies: "Who is Jesus for me?" (see instructions in lesson 8)

3. Journaling (approximately 7–10 minutes)

   Prompts:
   - Write to the Lord and reflect on at least one thing shared in the testimonials.
   - Write directly to the Lord about what is going on in your life.

4. Conversation (and Meal)

   Prompt: Reflect together on the testimonials you heard. Share something about whom you are learning or discovering Jesus to be.

2nd Movement – Lesson

1. Review of the Previous Session
   - The name that God gives to Moses in the Book of Exodus is "I AM." The other translation or meaning of that name is "I WILL BE WHAT I WILL BE."
   - In the Gospel of John, we saw how Jesus claims this name as his own.

   Question for the Group: If you had to choose, would you say that this name that Jesus claims is a name of *power* or of *weakness*? (Most if not all people will say it is a name of "power.")

2. Regarding Power and Wisdom

   Exercise: Give group members a minute or two to write down their thoughts in response to the following two questions, and then share these thoughts in a brief large group discussion (possibly making a list together as a group).
   - What are people with power in our world usually like?
   - What do people with power in our world usually do?

   Note: It is likely that people will identify some of the following, though the group leader might also share these points:
   - People with power are usually in control, confident, and bold in their action.

- People with power usually get their way, influence others, and "win."
- People with power can usually avoid discomfort, certain kinds of suffering, and being subject to other people's wishes.

To Teach: St. Paul calls Jesus "the power of God and the wisdom of God" (1 Cor 1:24).

Question for the Group: Does this mean that Jesus is like those who have power in this world, and that he acts like people with power usually act?

3. Small Group Exercise

Setting the Scene: If Jesus is the power and wisdom of God, we want to see what power and wisdom looks like in Jesus. We are going to look at four episodes from the gospels. If Jesus really is the power of God, then power will look strange here.

Instructions for Exercise:

- Form small groups of three to four members each.
- Each group will read together one of the following four episodes (if there are not enough group members to make at least four groups, then each group can do more than one of the four episodes).
- The task is to describe what Jesus does in this particular episode.
- Small groups meet for 3–5 minutes, then the large group comes back together.
- These are the four episodes, all of which come near the end of Jesus's ministry:

  John 11:28-35 (the Death of Lazarus)
  John 13:1-14 (the Last Supper)
  Luke 22:39-46 (the Agony in the Garden)
  Luke 23:33-38 (the Crucifixion)

Small Group Work (3–5 minutes)

Large Group Work:

Since different groups dealt with different episodes, take one episode at a time and have the corresponding groups describe what Jesus does in this episode. By the end of conversation about these episodes, it is important to be very succinct about what Jesus does. The descriptions should be similar to these.

- For the Death of Lazarus (John 11): Jesus weeps.
- For the Last Supper (John 13): Jesus serves.
- For the Agony in the Garden (Luke 22): Jesus suffers.
- For the Crucifixion (Luke 23): Jesus is mocked.

Question for the Group: If Jesus is the power of God, what is strange about power in these episodes?

Answer: The power of God looks like weakness (weeping, serving, suffering, and being mocked).

4. The Strange Wisdom of Jesus's Power

Read Together: Mark 10:35-45.

Question for the Group: What does this have to do with "power"?

To Teach:
James and John want to ascend in power next to Jesus (they want a promotion). The other disciples get angry with them because of James and John's ambition, but that's because the other disciples do not want to let those two get ahead of them and have more "power."

Jesus teaches them all that the way they are thinking about "power" is all wrong. They are thinking about "power" as we typically think about "power" in the world (control, influence, getting your way, etc.), but Jesus reveals that *his* power is *not* like the power of the world.

Jesus's power is the power to serve and even to suffer.

To Teach: Returning to St. Paul
St. Paul finally learned what Jesus's power is when he heard the Lord say to him: "[my] power is made perfect in weakness" (2 Cor 12:9). The truly odd thing is that both of Paul's statements about Jesus are true.

- Jesus is the "power of God and the wisdom of God" (1 Cor 1:24).
- Jesus shows "[my] power is made perfect in weakness" (2 Cor 12:9).

Jesus is the power of God made perfect in weakness. That is God's strange wisdom, which looks like foolishness to the proud of this world.

Takeaway: The will of God is powerful enough to weep, serve, suffer, and be mocked in order to save us.

5. The Power and Wisdom of God

Final Takeaways:

- In the previous chapter we saw that Jesus claims the name of God—"I AM"—as his own name. Jesus is God-with-us; he is God's "coming down" to sinners, to the suffering, to those in need of mercy.
- Jesus is the power of God, but this power is not what we would otherwise expect power in this world to look like.

- Instead, the power of God in Jesus is the power to *refuse* to give in to the world's ways of power, which would just make God into one more tyrant, one more boss like all the others.
- Instead, Jesus is willing to weep, serve, suffer, and be mocked in order to save.

Main Point: In Jesus, God has given everything to the point of weakness, and that is the power of God. That is God's wisdom.

3rd Movement – Closing Prayer

For each session on "Who is Jesus?" we conclude with a prayer from one of the saints who testifies to who Jesus is *for them*. Offer St. Catherine of Siena's "Prayer before the Eucharist" in part 1, page 48 (also in online resource under "Prayers").

chapter ten

Who Is Jesus? The Gift of Beatitude

Overview

A Look from Above

In the previous three sessions we have explored complementary responses to the decisive question, "Who is Jesus?" In sum, he is the revelation and presence of God-with-us, in whom all power and wisdom reside, but not as we would otherwise expect power and wisdom to be. In drawing this central four-part mini-unit to a close, we will see that Jesus is also the point of decision for everyone. By who he is, he forces a choice between the power of God and the power of the world. In addition to concluding these sessions on the question of "Who is Jesus?," this session therefore also provides a segue to the final two sessions of the first half of this journey where we will give our attention over to how to prepare the way of the Lord (sessions 11–12).

A Closer Look

As the fourth and final session in this mini-unit on "Who is Jesus?" this session presents Jesus as the gift of beatitude, meaning that he himself brings everlasting joy to those in need. We will pick up directly on what we established last time, where we saw how strange power is in the person of Jesus as he weeps, serves, suffers, and is mocked. Those four aspects of the power of God will reappear in the blessings of the Beatitudes as recorded in the Gospel of Luke, while the opposites of those four will align with the corresponding curses.

1st Movement – Holy Conversation

1. Prayer

   Angelus recommended: see online resource

2. Testimonies: "Who is Jesus for me?" (see instructions in lesson 8)

3. Journaling (approximately 7–10 minutes)

   Prompts:
   - Write to the Lord and reflect on at least one thing shared in the testimonials.
   - Write directly to the Lord about what is going on in your life.

4. Conversation (and Meal)

   Prompt: Reflect together on the testimonials you heard. Share how you are doing with others, perhaps offering a "high" and "low" from the past week.

2nd Movement – Lesson

1. Review of Previous Three Sessions (done by leader)
   - In Jesus's baptism and transfiguration, we saw that Jesus is the beloved Son of the Father who draws near to us, as we are.
   - In Exodus, we learned that God's name of "I AM" also means that what God does will reveal who he is, and that Jesus claims this name as his own in the gospel.
   - In reflecting on St. Paul's proclamation of Jesus as the "power of God and the wisdom of God," we saw in the gospels how strange God's power and wisdom look to us, since Jesus weeps, serves, suffers, and is mocked.

2. Power and Its Undoing

   For this part and those that follow, refer to the "Who is Jesus?" worksheet in the online resource.

   Exercise for Large Group: Rather than breaking up into smaller groups, this exercise is done together as a large group. Each person needs a copy of the "Who is Jesus?" worksheet. The top row of the worksheet presents the four episodes we examined last time though in a slightly different order, with Jesus's actions highlighted (suffers, serves, weeps, mocked). The other three rows will be filled in during this session.

A. Part 1 of Exercise: Imagining the opposite of what Jesus does

Instructions: See in the top row the "power" actions of Jesus from the four episodes we looked at last time. For each of those actions, brainstorm as a large group what the opposite action would be. When there is general consensus in the group about each one of these "opposites," everyone should write what the opposite is in the corresponding box. For example:

- The opposite of Jesus who suffers is to live it up, do what you want.
- The opposite of Jesus who serves is to command, consume, use others.
- The opposite of Jesus who weeps is to laugh, to be unbothered, to care only about one's own happiness.
- The opposite of Jesus who is mocked is someone who is praised or who ridicules or laughs at others.

B. Part 2 of Exercise: The blessings and curses of the Beatitudes

Read Together: Luke 6:20-26.

Instructions: Complete the remaining boxes in the worksheet together by rereading the four blessings and the four curses:

- The order of the four blessings (third row, from left to right on the worksheet): poor, hungry, weep, hated/excluded/reviled
- The order of the four curses (bottom row, from left to right on the worksheet): rich, filled, laughing, praised

To Teach (either by discussion or direct guidance):

- To be poor is to have to depend on others and trust, while to be rich is to take what you want and rely on yourself.
- To be hungry is to be unsatisfied and wait for fulfillment, while to be filled is to be settled and without longing.
- To weep is to share in sorrow and be troubled, while to laugh (when others are sorrowful) is to cling to your own pleasure in place of others' needs.
- To be mocked humbles you, while to be praised flatters you and puffs you up.

C. Part 3 of Exercise: Reflection on the Beatitudes, and choosing one side or the other

To Teach:

Notice how Jesus's actions unite him to the lowly who are poor, hungry, sorrowful, and reviled. He sides with them and he says that they are on the side of God's power.

Jesus only presents two sides because there is no third option. One side relates to the power of God; the other side relates to the power of the world.

Small Group Discussion (groups of about three):
If the way of everlasting joy (beatitude) is to be on the side of the power of God, and if the power of God is with those who are poor, hungry, sorrowful, and reviled, then how do you practice being poor, hungry, sorrowful, and humble?

Large Group Discussion: Share insights from small groups.

Takeaway: If you yourself are not poor or hungry or sorrowful or mocked, then the important thing is to join yourself to those who are those things. The important thing is to side with the lowly.

3. Reflecting on "Who is Jesus"

Final Takeaways:

- Jesus is the power and wisdom of God.
- Jesus draws near to us, especially to those who are suffering (the lowly).
- Jesus presents to each of us a choice: we can side with either the power of God or the power of the world.
- Siding with the power of God (with Jesus) leads to everlasting joy, or beatitude. Siding with the world's power (against Jesus) leads to everlasting sadness, or woe.

Read Together (optional): Matthew 25:31-46 to hear Jesus present this decisive choice in different words.

Main Point: Each of us professes "who Jesus is" both by what we say and by how we live.

3rd Movement – Closing Prayer

For each session on "Who is Jesus?" we conclude with a prayer from one of the saints who testifies to who Jesus is *for them*. Offer St. Francis of Assisi's "Peace Prayer" in part 1, page 52 (also in online resource under "Prayers").

chapter eleven

Advent: Prepare the Way of the Lord

Overview

A Look from Above

The final two sessions in this first of our two full units draw our attention to the season and the practice of Advent.[1] If your Catholic Formation Group meetings begin with a new academic year at or near the beginning of September, these two sessions should fall at or near the beginning of Advent in late November and early December. These are intended to be the final two sessions before the Christmas break, when meetings are suspended until mid-January. If the schedule of your particular group does not align with this schedule exactly, you may certainly adjust things as needed. It is not even necessary that these two sessions fall squarely in Advent, though then it would likely be better if they came *before* Advent rather than *after* Advent. Following the previous mini-unit in which we heeded the question "Who is Jesus?," these sessions will continue to deal with power and the separation between the power (and wisdom) of God and the power (and wisdom) of the world. In sum, these sessions are about learning how to wait for the Lord and to make room for him in our lives.

1. Corresponding to the two halves of a full year of Catholic Formation Group meetings, what I consider "Unit 1" includes sessions 1–12 that will likely run September–December, while "Unit 2" is comprised of sessions 14–25 that will likely run January–April/May. Session 13 is the midway point and constructed as a time of transition, with a look back to what we have accomplished and a look ahead to what remains.

A Closer Look

The first of these two Advent sessions appeals to a particular section of Luke's gospel in order to juxtapose those who do not prepare the way of the Lord with John the Baptist, who does. Coming at the beginning of the third chapter of Luke's gospel, this particular section continues—or rather, anticipates—the separation between the power of God and the power of the world on which Jesus preaches in the Beatitudes, as we examined in the previous session (10). A good deal of this session depends on reading this portion of Scripture with the aid of an Advent sermon from the German Jesuit martyr, Alfred Delp. The book of his sermons—*Advent of the Heart: Seasonal Sermons and Prison Writings* (San Francisco: Ignatius, 2006)—makes for challenging and illuminating supplemental Advent reading for anyone, whether group members, their families, or others associated with your Catholic Formation Group.

1st Movement – Holy Conversation

1. Prayer

   Angelus recommended: see online resource

2. Journaling (approximately 7–10 minutes)

   Prompt: Advent is a time of waiting for the Lord. What do you think it means to wait for the Lord?

3. Conversation (and Meal)

   Prompt: Do you and your family observe Advent? How?

2nd Movement – Lesson

1. Opening Discussion

   Question for the Group: What do you think it means to wait for the Lord? Share responses and facilitate brief discussion. (This is the question from "Journaling.")

   Try to think about and discuss practices that prepare you to wait for the Lord, as well as dispositions and behaviors to cultivate.

2. A Time of Preparation, or Not

   Read Together: The beginning of Luke 3, which immediately follows the Infancy Narratives in Luke's gospel (when Jesus was a child) and inaugurates Jesus's three years of active ministry beginning at the age of thirty (3:1-2).

Respond to Reading (done by leader):
This seems like a relatively insignificant portion of Scripture (though in fact, no portion of Scripture is insignificant). This is just a list of names tied to a number of places that we have likely never heard of. But what if we learned how to read this passage with all these names through the eyes of someone for whom this passage really mattered?

Introduce to Fr. Alfred Delp, SJ (see part 1 of this book, pages 55–56)

Small Group Exercise: Meditation on Delp's sermon from the Fourth Sunday of Advent, 1941

Break up into small groups of three to four members each. Supply each person with the excerpt from Delp's 1941 sermon (see pages 55–56 in part 1 of this book). A longer excerpt is available in Delp's *Advent of the Heart* (pp. 128–30).[2] The task for each group is to answer—in their own words—the following two questions about each of the people named in Luke 3 (Tiberius Caesar, Pontius Pilate, Herod, Philip, Lysanias, Annas, and Caiaphas . . . but do *not* include John):

- What kind of person is this?
- What does this person want, most of all?

Large Group Discussion:
Go figure by figure and discuss together what kind of person each one is and what each of them really wants. Possibly create a list or a chart together.

Takeaway: Each of these is a figure of the powers of the day, who want to increase their power and prestige if possible, absolutely refusing to lose what they have.

3. The Prophecy of Isaiah and the Witness of John the Baptist

Read Together: John's proclamation, which comes immediately after the introduction to Luke 3 that we just read, and in which John quotes from the prophet Isaiah (Luke 3:4-6; cf. Isa 40:3-5).

Question for the Group: Based on what we were reading earlier, what do you think about this proclamation from John?

2. Alfred Delp, *Advent of the Heart: Seasonal Sermons and Prison Writings, 1941–1944* (San Francisco: Ignatius, 2006).

Main Points to Highlight:

- The high places ("every mountain and hill") are the towering figures of power we just read about. Their names are Caesar Tiberius, Pontius Pilate . . .
- These figures represent "the crooked" and they establish "rough ways."
- The low things ("every valley") are those who are oppressed in this time and place under these crushing powers.
- The prophecy is about the *power of God* overcoming *worldly power* to lift up the lowly, who are oppressed, suffering, and in need.

Question for the Group: What does John the Baptist have in common with those named in the introduction to this chapter, and how is he different from all the rest?

Main Points to Highlight:

- He is like all the others in that he is becoming a person of influence, people are flocking to him and following him, and he has grown in power and prominence.
- He is different from all the others in at least two ways: First, he uses his power and influence to point to someone else: namely, the one who is coming after him (Jesus). Second, when Jesus comes, John the Baptist walks away and gives his place to Jesus. See illustration from Saint John's Bible in the online resource.

Takeaways: None of the other figures dare make room for the coming of the Lord, whereas John the Baptist does. "He must increase, I must decrease" as John says in the Gospel of John (3:30). John puts Jesus at the center of his own life.

4. Waiting for the Lord

Final Takeaways:

- Waiting means preparing to give Jesus the center of your life, today and forever.
- Advent is a time of reckoning for the powers of the world.
- Advent is a time of hope because the Lord comes to this world, to lift up those in need.

3rd Movement – Closing Prayer

Pray "Maranatha!" prayer for Advent (available in online resource under "Prayers").

chapter twelve

Advent: Waiting for the Lord

Overview

A Look from Above

Along with the preceding session, this session focuses on Advent. Following the preaching of Fr. Alfred Delp, we are considering Advent not just as a season but as a way of life for the Christian. Advent challenges us to continually make room for Christ and to side with those with whom the Lord himself sides: the lowly, the forgotten, the weak, and the exploited. Whereas the previous session juxtaposed the towering power figures of Jesus's day with John the Baptist, who made room for Christ, this session will focus even more squarely on those whom Advent urges us to fix our attention and align ourselves. Choosing the power of God over the power of the world is not merely a verbal or mental exercise, but rather an affair of the heart and a commitment of our entire selves.

A Closer Look

The final session of the first unit is intended to precede a longer break for the Christmas holiday. It will therefore conclude with the recommendation for a few specific practices that group members are encouraged to adopt. The primary question for this session concerns what kind of people wait for the Lord—or in other words, who really needs Jesus. To address this question, we will stay with John the Baptist's prophecy but move back to its source in the Book of Isaiah, before returning to Luke's gospel to consider Mary (who is *the* figure of Advent) and the kind of people in our day who are in most need of the Lord's coming.

1st Movement – Holy Conversation

1. Prayer
   Angelus recommended: see online resource

2. Journaling (approximately 7–10 minutes)

   Prompt: Who do you know that really needs the Lord's presence in their lives? Write a prayer to the Lord for that person (or persons).

3. Conversation (and Meal)

   Prompt: What kinds of people most need help from the Lord? Who do you know that needs the Lord to come into their lives?

2nd Movement – Lesson

1. Review from the Last Session

   To Teach:
   - We began last time with the question of "What do you think it means to wait for the Lord?" Quickly review the responses to that question.
   - We read the beginning of Luke 3 and, with Alfred Delp's guidance, we saw how the figures named there are really a list of the worldly powers of Jesus's day, who oppressed the lowly.
   - These towering figures (Tiberius Caesar, Pontius Pilate, etc.) were *not* waiting for the Lord.

   Question for the Group: Why not? Why would they not want to recognize or accept the power and wisdom of God? Brief, open discussion.

2. The Prophecy of Isaiah (see "Isaiah Advent Passages" in online resource)

   A. Background on the Prophecy of Isaiah

   To Teach
   John the Baptist announces the prophecy of Isaiah to prepare the way for Jesus. To understand John's proclamation better in relation to Jesus, we should learn more about Isaiah's prophecy in its original setting. (Note to leaders: this is an example of how knowing Scripture teaches us who Christ is, or, as St. Jerome put it, it is an example of how "Ignorance of Scripture is ignorance of Christ.")
   - When Isaiah announced this prophecy, Israel was in exile, under the power of the Babylonian empire. Israelites were stripped of their land and sent to live in a foreign land under a foreign power.

- The reason for Israel's exile was, in part, due to their own sinfulness and infidelity to God. The Israelites trusted the powers of the world (like Babylon) instead of trusting God most of all.

Question for the Group: What do you think the life of the Israelites was like in exile, under this dominant foreign power?

Main Points to Highlight:

- They had no freedom to practice their religion or express their own culture (Babylon's religion was tied to its culture, which was imposed on the Israelites).
- They were poor and in servitude to the Babylonians (like prisoners of war).
- They felt hopeless (like God had abandoned them, and it was their own fault).

B. Studying the Prophecy of Isaiah

To Teach:
Right in the middle of this desperate situation, God tells his prophet Isaiah to proclaim three things to the Israelites:

- First, that the power of their conquerors cannot last forever.

  Read Together: First selection from Isaiah 40 ("Passage 1" in handout online).

  Main Points to Highlight: (a) Babylon is now in full bloom. (b) But just like flowers and grass that thrive in one season and wither in another, so will the supremacy of the Babylonians come to an end. (c) This is a word of comfort to those under the rule of the Babylonians.

- Second, that the Israelites are known to God himself—God remembers them.

  Read Together: Second selection from Isaiah 40 ("Passage 2" in handout online).

  Main Points to Highlight: (a) Unlike worldly powers, the power of God is without end. (b) The Lord cares for his people Israel like a shepherd who cares for his flock. (c) The wisdom of God is everlasting; he knows what he is about.

- Third, God has not abandoned his people and God is now coming to rescue you.

  Read Together: Third selection from Isaiah 40 ("Passage 3" in handout online).

Main Points to Highlight: (a) As in the time of slavery in Egypt, so too now: God hears the cry of his people and comes to save them. (b) This is the greatest source of joy for those who live in need, on the edge of hopelessness. God comes for them.

3. John the Baptist Proclaims the Coming of God

To Teach (by conversation or direct guidance):

When John the Baptist proclaims the words of Isaiah, he is saying that the God who acted for his people back then is acting for his people again today, except now this is God's final move: the coming of Jesus.

The three parts of Isaiah's prophecy are alive again in Jesus's time:

- First, the power of the conquerors cannot last forever.
- Second, God himself remembers and knows his people.
- Third, God is coming to save them.

How John the Baptist's proclamation goes beyond Isaiah's:

- The powers of the day are not just a foreign power (Babylon), but a foreign power and the corrupt local powers: the Roman Empire (Tiberius Caesar and Pontius Pilate) and the political and religious rulers of Israel (everyone else in Luke 3:1-2, except John the Baptist).
- The good news of God's coming is not just for the people of Israel, but for the people of Israel and for everyone else, meaning the Gentiles (non-Jews), too. (See again how the genealogy in Luke 3:23-38 goes back not just to Abraham but to Adam.)

God's final action begins with Mary (already introduced in Luke 1–2), who is herself the figure of Advent because she is completely on the side of the power of God, not the power of the world.

- She is not in the center of things (Rome or Jerusalem), but Galilee.
- She is not a man but a woman, and not an adult but a young person.
- She is not rich but poor, and not prominent but lowly.

4. Reflecting Together: Who Waits for the Lord?

Question for the Group: With all this in mind, what kind of people wait for the Lord?

Possible Answers: The poor and lowly, the insignificant and needy, the down-and-out (rather than the high-and-mighty), the oppressed and depressed, the humble.

To Summarize: We might think of four kinds of people who are in a position to wait for the Lord: the poor, sick, lonely, and victimized.

Small Group Exercise: For each of the four kinds of people listed above (poor, sick, lonely, victimized), try to identify and name people you know who could be described in one of these ways, or otherwise people you might know about even if you do not know them personally.

5. Wrapping Up

To Teach:

Connecting to the Beatitudes and committing ourselves to God's way:

- When we discussed the Beatitudes and those whom Jesus calls "blessed," we said that if you yourself were not poor, hungry, sorrowful, or ridiculed, the important thing was to side with those who are.
- In the people you have just named who need the Lord, you just identified those with whom you are called to side, in the name of Christ.
- As an Advent practice leading into Christmas, commit to praying for these people daily—by name—and however possible doing good deeds for them.

Praying with the Advent wreath

- As a reminder to side with the lowly in Advent, let each candle of the Advent wreath stand for one of the four kinds of people who need the Lord: the poor, sick, lonely, and victimized.
- Allow your prayers for them and with them to be a way of "renouncing" being for ourselves and "professing" being for others (which is what our baptismal promises demand of us).

Final Takeaway: Waiting for the Lord (as in Advent) is never an individualistic kind of waiting. In waiting for the Lord, Christians are called to wait with and for others.

Note: Encourage group members to think about and even work on their own "Who is Jesus for me?" testimonials, which they will begin sharing with the group several sessions from now.

3rd Movement – Closing Prayer

Offer again "Maranatha!" Advent prayer (available in online resource under "Prayers").

chapter thirteen

Where We've Been, Where We're Going

Overview

A Look from Above

With twelve sessions behind us and twelve sessions in front of us, this session stands precisely at the midpoint of our time together. This is an opportunity to remember and review "where we've been" while also peeking ahead to "where we're going." In the preface of this book, I began by discussing the "coherence factor," by which I stressed the importance of passing on the Catholic faith in a holistic manner. What we are attempting to do through this approach is to form others through a coherent presentation of the Catholic faith, where narrative and theology, Scripture and sacraments, prayer and practice, learning and reflection all go together. This session is the hinge between one continuous presentation (from St. Paul to Jesus) and another (from creation through the sacraments). As we move forward in the next twelve sessions, it is important to hold on to what we reflected upon and practiced in the first twelve sessions, especially since these two larger twelve-session units are really two halves of one whole presentation.

A Closer Look

Since I conceived of this twenty-five-session approach as spanning one full academic year, I anticipate this session as the first session in January, after the Christmas break. The time-off heightens the importance of this kind of review, so as to bring back into mind all that we reflected on and practiced together in the first twelve sessions. It is of course entirely possible to arrange these sessions according to a different calendar depending on the needs of your particular parish, school, or group, so perhaps this session does not follow a longer break for your group. All the same, this seems the most appropriate time for a sort of reorientation in order to get our bearings right in the middle of things.

1st Movement – Holy Conversation

1. Prayer

   Angelus recommended: see online resource

2. Journaling (approximately 7–10 minutes)

   Prompt: Imagine the Lord says to you, "Tell me child, what is on your heart." Respond to him, in writing. Write directly to the Lord.

3. Conversation (and Meal)

   Prompt: Share a high and low from your life since the last time we met.

2nd Movement – Lesson

1. Opening Exercise

   For Individual Reflection/Writing: Looking back at all that we have done together so far, call to mind and write about (a) one thing you learned that you consider important; (b) one thing you have been inspired by; (c) one thing you have been challenged by.

   Large Group Discussion: Share responses as a sort of informal review.

2. Review Conducted by the Leader (to fill in what may have been lacking in the discussion above; this may be done as a presentation or as leading further discussion)

   Baptism (Session 1)

   - Exorcism: saying "no" to the ways of Satan.
   - Profession of Faith: saying "yes" to the way of the Father, Son, and Holy Spirit.
   - Immersion: whereby God does the work of separating us from the "old way" and initiating us into this "new way."

Confirmation (Session 1)

- We become a source of goodness for others.

The Way—i.e., pillars of the Christian community in Acts 2 (Session 1)

- Regular prayer
- Studying and contemplating the teaching of the apostles
- Breaking bread together (Eucharist)
- Sharing all things in common (caring for the poor, almsgiving)

The Conversion of St. Paul (Sessions 2–3)

- The witness of St. Stephen, the first martyr, in Acts 7
- Paul saw others (especially Christians) through anger and vengeance, he listened for Christians' prayers in order to persecute them, and he "breathed" or spoke with "murderous threats."
- On the road to Damascus, he was blinded by the light of Christ, his companions were silenced so he could only hear Christ, and his arrogant speech yielded to questioning before the Lord.
- Paul was healed through the ministry of Ananias, who laid hands on him and called him "brother."
- Paul was baptized, received his sight, took food after his fast, and began preaching Christ Jesus.

The Transformation of St. Paul (Session 4, continuing through 5 and 6)

- Paul's eyes and mind were transformed in Christ, so that he saw the world, others, and especially himself through the grace of Christ (see 2 Cor 12:7-10).
- Paul's ears and heart were transformed in Christ, so that he listened to the needs and joys of others with affection, care, and gratitude, and his heart became a space of communion (see Phil 1:3-9).
- Paul's tongue and words were transformed in Christ, so that he spoke first of Christ Jesus and allowed all he proclaimed to point to Jesus (see 1 Cor 15:3-10).

From Paul to Jesus (Session 6)

- Paul leads us to Jesus, since everything about Paul's life is ultimately focused on the Lord.
- Two related questions become important: Who is Jesus? Who is Jesus *for me*?

Who is Jesus? (Sessions 7–10)

- The Son of the Father who draws near to us in our mess, in our sin, as we are.
- The one who claims the "I AM" of God as his own name. Jesus reveals himself to be one with God as revealed in the Old Testament.

- The power and wisdom of God, but power in Jesus does not look like what the world thinks of as powerful, and his wisdom looks more like foolishness to the proud and arrogant. Jesus weeps, serves, suffers, and is mocked.
- The one who joins the lowly and shows the way to everlasting joy, which we call the "gift of beatitude."

The practice of Advent, or how to wait for the Lord (Sessions 11–12)

- Those who cling to power in the world (like the figures at the beginning of Luke 3) do not make room for Jesus.
- John the Baptist gives up his own power to make room for Jesus.
- To wait for the Lord means waiting with and joining those who are poor, sick, lowly, and victimized.

3. Preview Conducted by the Leader (brief, as overview)

To Teach:
In what we have done, we have placed Jesus at the center of everything. In what we will do, we will reflect on and practice how we ourselves are to be continually transformed in Christ.

In the next twelve sessions, we will explore:

- Who we are created to be
- What it means to be created male and female
- What sin is and what the effects of sin are
- How the gifts of the Holy Spirit heal and strengthen us
- How our own growth in virtue allows us to work with the Holy Spirit
- How to become better listeners
- How to take more responsibility for the power of our words
- How to become more aware of how we see the world and other people
- What discipleship is and how we grow as disciples
- How the Church is called to nurture us as disciples of Jesus
- What the sacraments are and how they form us as members of Christ

In addition to what we learn, we will also:

- Continue to practice prayerful journaling, often writing directly to the Lord
- Continue praying together
- Continue sharing meaningful and attentive conversations
- Reflect on our own areas for growth and our own needs
- Share with each other our own personal testimonies on "Who is Jesus *for me*?"

4. Concluding Exercise

For Individual Reflection/Writing: Thinking ahead to our time together, write about:

- Something you are interested in learning more about
- One way you would like to grow in faith or discipline in the next several months

Large Group Discussion: Possibly share these in the large group or keep these private.

3rd Movement – Closing Prayer

Offer the simple, profound prayer of the father of the sick boy in Mark's gospel (9:24), then a short period of silence, followed by the Lord's Prayer:

Leader:	Let us pray with the words that a man who was learning to trust in the Lord prayed when he met Jesus face-to-face. He prayed: *Lord, I believe; help my unbelief.* Together . . .
All:	*Lord, I believe; help my unbelief.*
Leader:	Let us take a minute in silence to offer this prayer in our hearts. [Silence]
Leader:	In confidence, let us pray the prayer that Jesus taught us . . .
All:	*Our Father* . . .

chapter fourteen

Who We Are Created to Be

Overview

A Look from Above

Over the next three sessions—including this one—we will be exploring a biblical theology of creation, with a particular focus on the creation of the human being. While this will include an examination of what sin is and therefore a sobering look at what is wrong with us, it is important to recognize first the beauty and dignity of our creation, especially since the "Fall" that occurs by sin is a fall *from* something good. Moreover, the best understanding of sin from a Christian perspective includes seeing sin as that which we are being healed from, and therefore we can only ever really recognize sin for what it is in and through Christ's healing mercy. The layout for the next three sessions is as follows:

- Session 14: "Who We Are Created to Be" invites us to slowly and carefully attend to the creation account of Genesis 2.
- Session 15: "Male and Female God Created Them" invites us to rediscover the dignity and mission of the complementarity of the sexes.
- Session 16: "Sin and Its Effects" invites us to recognize the harmony we lost in sin and continue to lose by sinning, while imagining what redeemed humanity would be.

A Closer Look

This session is about fundamental stuff—*really* fundamental stuff. Just because something is "fundamental" does not mean it is easy or obvious. Instead, what is "fundamental" influences everything else so strongly that the possibilities and limits of our imaginations—indeed of our core convictions and driving hopes—are largely established by what we assume as fundamental. To put this another way, what we believe to be fundamentally true about who and what the human being is, who God is, and what the world is influences everything else: how we live, what we consider "good," and how we judge our lives. Think about St. Paul: he changed, fundamentally, because Christ claimed him as his own. Everything else changed because of that: how he saw, how he listened, how he spoke. In Scripture's creation accounts, the Lord speaks to us about what is fundamentally true, if only we would have the eyes to see and the ears to hear. In this session, we attempt to open ourselves to the basic, fundamental stuff that is all too easy to miss but all too important to neglect.

1st Movement – Holy Conversation

1. Prayer
   Angelus recommended: see online resource

2. Journaling (approximately 7–10 minutes)

   Prompts:
   - Spend time preparing for your "Who is Jesus for me" testimony.
   - Ask the Lord to show you who he is and to give you the words to speak about him truthfully.
   - Try completing these lines:
     "Jesus, you are . . . "
     "Jesus, thank you for . . ."
     "Jesus, you bless me . . . "
     "Jesus, I love you for . . . "
     "Jesus, I believe that you . . ."
     "Jesus, when you look at me . . ."

3. Conversation (and Meal)

   Prompt: Share what you are excited or nervous or unsure about with the "Who is Jesus for me" testimony.

2nd Movement – Lesson

1. Creation Begins

   Read Together: Genesis 2:4-7.

Small Group Discussion: In groups of three or four, discuss what this passage tells us about what a human being is (2–3 minutes).

Large Group Discussion: (with guidance—touch on the following)
Human beings as intentionally formed "earth stuff"

- The word for "man" in verse 7 is *'adam* in Hebrew (not a proper name but a description) while the word for "ground" is *'adamah* in Hebrew.
- So, *'adam* comes from *'adamah* (like "earth creature" from "earth" or even "human" from "humus").
- This "earth creature" is therefore created in *harmony* with the earth.

Human beings receive "donated" or "given" breath.

- This breath is given directly from the life of the Creator.
- It is difficult if not impossible to imagine a more intimate action or gift.
- This creature is created in *harmony* with the Lord God.

Human beings live only as "union" of intentionally formed "earth stuff" and "donated breath."

- This signifies the integration of "body" and "soul."
- "Body" without a "soul" is not a living human being, nor is a "soul" without a "body."
- Human beings only exist as this union, this *harmony* of body and soul, which St. Irenaeus calls "the whole man."

Takeaway: *Harmony* is the overwhelming claim of Genesis 2:7:

- Harmony of the human being with the earth/creation
- Harmony of the human being with the Lord God
- Harmony of the human being as a whole creature

2. Creation toward Completion

Read Together: Genesis 2:21-24.

Small Group Discussion: In groups of three or four discuss what you think this passage means and why it's important.

Large Group Discussion: (with guidance—touch on the following)
The body created here (woman) comes of the body (man/*'adam*) created from the good earth (*'adamah*).

- This is again a direct act of creation by the Lord God.
- All human beings are directly willed and created by God, even as we each come from other human beings.

In verse 23, when the "man" speaks, he gives a name to the "woman" that refers to himself, and he renames himself in reference to her.

- In Hebrew, the names in verse 23 are "man" = *'ish* and "woman" = *'ishshah.* These are still not proper names, but rather relational names.

Just as *ʾadam* was a relational name with *ʾadamah*, so *ʾish* and *ʾishshah* are relational names to one another. Upshot (to be continued in future weeks): the two sexes refer to and imply each other.

This provides an image of what comes *before* original sin. We may call it "original solidarity" and its defining feature is *harmony*.

- The harmony of creation includes a given harmony between man and woman.
- This union of man and woman is singular and lasting.
- Man and woman cling to each other and can take refuge in one another. This would be crucial in the ancient world, where security was especially important for women when pregnant or with a young child. Just as Israel makes a preferential choice for widows and orphans (who are vulnerable) so too with all people when in a vulnerable state (as we all are from time to time). The permanence of marriage is a safe haven.
- The "union" or *harmony* of "man" and "woman" recalls and refers back to the *harmony* of the human being with the earth, with God, and as a whole creature.

Takeaway: *Harmony* is (again) the overwhelming message of this creation narrative.

3. Closing Discussion

Large Group Discussion:

- What is beautiful or surprising about the creation of human beings in Genesis 2?
- How does this account compare to or differ from prevalent contemporary ideas about human beings and our "nature"?
- How is this understanding of the relationship between man and woman radical?

3rd Movement – Closing Prayer

Offer intentions followed by *Our Father . . .*

chapter fifteen

Male and Female God Created Them

Overview

A Look from Above

We are in the middle of a three-session mini-unit. In the last session (14), we focused primarily on the creation account of Genesis 2, wherein we studied how *harmony* is the original, created condition of human beings: harmony with the earth, with God, as the union of body and soul, and between one another, especially as man and woman. In the next session (16), we will fully explore what sin is and what the effects of sin are. Linking those two sessions, this session (15) introduces the mission of human beings as created male and female, partly by beginning to notice how the serpent's way of speaking at the beginning of Genesis 3 introduces a dramatic change from the end of Genesis 2 where we hear how human beings are toward one another, as man and woman.

A Closer Look

This session requires us to do two things at once. First, we will pay close attention to the biblical text, even to the point of seeing connections between words that are not apparent in English. Second, we will think creatively together about how the narrative of Scripture is unfolding, and how we see elements of what is presented in our own lives and world. By the end, we will have laid the groundwork for much of what we will study and discuss together in many of the sessions to come.

1st Movement – Holy Conversation

1. Prayer

   Angelus recommended: see online resource

2. Testimonies: "Who is Jesus for me?"

   It is best to have two or three group members share their short testimonies in response to this question. Limiting the number helps listeners to remain attentive. Again, these testimonies should be about 2–3 minutes, brief and direct, perhaps with a short narrative. They should be shared in each of the following sessions, until everyone in the group has shared theirs. This *should* take no more than 10 minutes.

3. Journaling (approximately 7–10 minutes)

   Prompts:

   - Feel free to write any thoughts or reflections based on the testimonies just shared.
   - Write a brief prayer of thanksgiving to Jesus for the faith and courage of those who just shared their testimonies

4. Conversation (and Meal)

   Prompt: Share any thoughts or insights from the testimonies you heard. Talk about one person whose honesty or care for you has been meaningful this week, or recently.

2nd Movement – Lesson

1. Review and Setup

   A. Review:

   Question for the Group: What were some of the important points from last session? (Let the group generate these, then make sure the two points below are covered and emphasized.)

   - Point 1: God intentionally formed human beings from the earth and gave them the breath of life.
   - Point 2: Harmony is the main message of the creation account in Genesis 2. This includes the harmony between human beings and the earth, between human beings and their Creator, of human beings as union of body and soul, and between human beings, especially as man and woman.

B. Setup:

To Teach:
Today's session focuses on the intentionality and beauty of human beings as man and woman. We are going to explore the meaning and mission of the two sexes as being *procreative* and *unitive*.

Working definitions of these two terms (best to establish these at the beginning, even writing them on a board or having these definitions posted in some way):

- *Procreative*: the power and mission to give life
- *Unitive*: the gift and mission of intimacy

By exploring the *procreative* and *unitive* character of human beings as man and woman, we will learn more about what "Christian maturity" looks like. In other words, this is a glimpse of what all of us are being formed for as disciples.

2. What It Means to Be "Procreative"

Read Together: Genesis 1:27-28 (first creation account, which we have not looked at).

To Teach (by lecture or direct guidance):
First, pay attention to what this passage is claiming:

- The two sexes are good, natural, and intended: these sexes are part of God's good creation, which is even called "very good" (Gen 1:31).
- There is *one* image of God yet *two* ways of being that one image of God as human beings: male and female.
- The mission God gives to human beings begins with the words, "Be fruitful and multiply." (And by the way, to "subdue" the world and "have dominion" over it means to keep things in the order God has given to things . . . not to exploit the world for whatever purposes we want.)

Second, think about what it means to "give life," which fulfills the mission to "Be fruitful and multiply":

- On the one hand, to "give life" means to *cause someone to come into existence.* This is the power of procreation.
- On the other hand, to "give life" means to pass on to the next generation what is most beautiful, good, and true. This is the responsibility of procreation.

Third, be clear about whose mission this is—this mission of "procreation":

- Every generation has this mission, with its power and responsibility. It is the mission of every generation to give life to the next generation.

- But in particular, every marriage of man and woman carries within it the mission of an entire generation. This means that man and woman *together* share this power and responsibility to give life.

Questions for the Group: How is "procreation"—"to give life"—related to the "image of God" we hear about in Genesis 1:27?

Answer: Because the power to bring about new life and the responsibility to pass on what is most beautiful, good, and true allow human beings to share in *God's* power and responsibility.

Read Together: Two passages from *Catechism of the Catholic Church* (see online resource, "Lesson 15 CCC Passages").

3. What It Means to Be "Unitive"

A. Remembering the Narrative

Read Together: Genesis 2:21-24 (this is from last session).

Main Points to Highlight:

- See again this intimate union of man and woman in creation.
- See again how they mutually refer to each other, by name and identity (*'ish* and *'ishshah*).

B. Continuing the Narrative:

Read Together: The *next* two verses in this creation account (Gen 2:25 and 3:1).

Question for the Group: What do you think it means to be "naked without shame"? (They may say things like, "to see each other," "not be embarrassed by how you look," "being comfortable with each other," "being vulnerable.")

To Teach:

In Genesis 3:1, the serpent is described as "shrewdest" or else "most cunning" or "most subtle." Here's what we don't see:

- In Hebrew, the word here translated as "shrewdest" is *arum.*
- In Hebrew, the word in 2:24 translated as "naked" is *arummim.*
- This means that to be "naked" is to be "without shrewdness."
- *Arummim* is to *arum* as *guileless* is to *guile.* (The suffix "–mim" basically means without: therefore, "naked" means "without *arum.*")

To Teach:

If we want to know what it means to be "shrewd" or "cunning," the text will show us, especially if we compare the serpent's question in Genesis 3:1 to God's command in Genesis 2:16-17 (since the serpent is supposing to ask about God's command).

- God's command: "Of every tree of the garden you are free to eat; but as for the tree of knowledge of good and bad, you must not eat of it; for as soon as you eat of it, you shall die" (Gen 2:16-17, JPS).
- The serpent's question: "Did God really say: You shall not eat of any tree of the garden?" (Gen 3:1, JPS).

Question for the Group: What is the tone of God's command in Genesis 2:16-17?

Answer: It is overwhelmingly positive! They may eat of *every tree* . . . except for one.

Question for the Group: But what is the hidden message in the serpent's question?

Answer: The entire garden is one gigantic prohibition; God is keeping *everything* from you.

Main Points to Highlight:

- The serpent's question is the very definition of a "loaded question."
- The serpent has hidden motives and a hidden agenda.
- The serpent is really suggesting something about *God's* motives and about what this entire garden really is like.
- Perhaps share examples of hidden agendas, like when you do very nice things for people so they think you care about them and that you are kind, but really you want something from them and this is how you are trying to make them think favorably about you so they will give you what you want.

Question for the Group: If this is an image of what it means to be "shrewd," then what does it mean to be "naked without shame"?

Main Points to Highlight:

- To be honest about your intentions
- To say what you mean and mean what you say
- To be transparent to each other
- To be "intimate"—that is, close to each other, really present to each other, honest and trustworthy in how you act toward each other and what you say to each other
- To be free of self-consciousness about the other person seeing you as you really are, and to be free of fear for seeing the other person as they really are

Question for the Group: Which of these two ways is more common in our world—to be "shrewd" or to be "naked"?

Answer: Obviously, being "shrewd" is more common.

Question for the Group: What is challenging about being "transparent" (or "naked"/"intimate")?

Main Points to Consider:

- Possibility of being taken advantage of
- Possibility of being thought of as gullible
- The challenge of even knowing what you yourself really think and really mean in your actions and words to other people
- The challenge of using words well (saying what you want to say, and having other people hear you correctly)

To Teach (in summary):

What does all this have to do with the "unitive" mission of man and woman?

- In marriage—as the union of man and woman—the husband and wife are intended to practice a way of relationship that is characterized by openness, transparency, honesty, mutuality.
- Man and woman are intended to practice a way of relationship that avoids hidden motives and hidden agendas.
- What happens in this particular relationship—between man and woman in marriage—is intended to introduce a new way of relationship into a world that is so very used to the shrewdness of the serpent.
- The unitive character of man and woman helps restore human beings to how God created us, together in harmony.

To Teach (looking ahead):

In sessions 17–20 we will explore the virtue of chastity, but probably in a way that is different from what most people would expect. We will explore chastity as the power and responsibility of giving your whole attention to another person, in intimacy, and to receive them as they are.

By exploring chastity, we will explore how to become more capable of the "unitive" mission of our creation, especially as man and woman.

Large Group Discussion: Invite the group to share the important points from today's lesson.

3rd Movement – Closing Prayer

That our loving God may teach us, day by day, to trust his Word and follow his will, we pray: Our Father . . .

chapter sixteen

Sin and Its Effects

Overview

A Look from Above

This is the third session in a three-session mini-unit focusing mostly on the accounts of creation and the Fall in Genesis 2–3. In the previous two sessions we moved from contemplating how the creation account of Genesis 2 foregrounds the major theme of harmony, before exploring the procreative and unitive mission of human beings who are created in the image of God as male and female. We have already begun to identify a major shift in the created order when the serpent introduces "shrewdness" in the beginning of Genesis 3.

A Closer Look

In this session we will pick up on what we established last time concerning the serpent's way of speaking, which introduces a new way of being into the created world. Our task in this lesson is to give an account of what sin is and what comes from sin. In doing so, we will hardly leave Genesis 3 at all, but by really focusing on what happens there, we will also see how this narrative is not primarily about what happened "once upon a time" but rather about what is wrong with us *now* and from what we are being healed. For the most part, this lesson is built upon the close and thoughtful reading of continuous segments of the Genesis 3 account, inviting reflection and conversation about what we read and then drawing out key points along the way.

1st Movement – Holy Conversation

1. Prayer

   Angelus recommended: everyone should have this memorized by now

2. Testimonies: "Who is Jesus for me?" (continued; see instructions in lesson 15)

3. Journaling (approximately 7–10 minutes)

   Prompts:
   - Feel free to write any thoughts or reflections based on the testimonies just shared.
   - Write a brief prayer of thanksgiving to Jesus for the faith and courage of those who just shared their testimonies.
   - Write one prayer intention (offer a prayer for someone or something).
   - Write one prayer of gratitude (give thanks for at least one person or one thing, preferably from the past week).

4. Conversation (and Meal)

   Prompts:
   - Share any thoughts or insights from the testimonies you heard.
   - Share the two prayers you offered (one intention and one prayer of gratitude) with others.

2nd Movement – Lesson

1. Review

   Small Group Exercise: In groups of three or four, identify and write down three important things we learned over the past two sessions (the ones dealing with Genesis 2 and the beginning of Genesis 3). Explain why these things are important.

   Note: If quotes or outlines have been written on boards or posted in some other way over the past two sessions, it is best to have those quotes and outlines up for this session so group members can be reminded of what has been discussed.)

   Main Points to Highlight (pick and choose as appropriate):
   - Procreative mission (to give life to and nurture life of others)
   - Unitive mission (to be transparent and honest with each other)
   - Nakedness vs. shrewdness (Gen 2:25 and Gen 3:1)

- Intentional creation of the human being from the good earth (*'adam* from *'adamah*)
- The gift of the breath of life (see Gen 2:7)
- Intentional creation of man and woman, in harmony, with names that refer to each other (*'ish* and *'ishshah*)

2. The Commandment, the Deception, and Misremembering

Read Together: The passage about God's commandment in the garden alongside the passage where the serpent flips this commandment around in its question (see Gen 2:16-17 and 3:1).

Question for the Group: What is peculiar about the woman's response, which is admittedly very close to the original commandment? (See Gen 3:2-3.)

Main Points to Consider (for discussion or to teach):

- The tree alone is now in the middle of the garden. Initially, there were *two* trees in the middle of the garden (see Gen 2:9), but now it seems that only the prohibited tree is in the middle. Isn't this a bit like how the moment something is prohibited, it becomes the most interesting thing to you and occupies the center of your attention?
- The woman adds the words "or touch it" to God's commandment. These words were not there originally.

To Teach:
Since the woman gets the commandment slightly wrong (she at least adds to it), let's consider where the woman was when the original commandment was given:

- Possibility 1: The woman had not been created yet, so the man was responsible for passing on the commandment to her for her own good. He was, in other words, responsible for passing on to her what was most important (this is, quite literally, an act of "tradition," which mean "to hand on"). (a) So why this little addition then, if she was not "there"? (b) Maybe he did not trust her fully or didn't think she could be strong enough, so he added an extra protection to the commandment. (c) That is like a parent telling a child "don't even touch X" because the parent knows that if the child consumes X (alcohol, drugs, etc.), it will harm them. If you doubt the strength or the wisdom of the one you are instructing, you might just put a little extra protection around the thing that is prohibited.
- Possibility 2: The woman was there when the commandment was given since she was not yet separated from the man (his rib) and so

the whole, undivided humanity received this one commandment. (a) So why this little addition, if she was "there"? (b) Maybe this is a sign of the failure or the weakness of memory. If you do not practice rehearsing the most important things word-for-word, pretty soon your memory starts to get fuzzy and you cannot recall even the most important things perfectly.

- We need not choose between these two possibilities; we should keep in mind the importance of both *communication* and *memory.*

Read Together: The serpent's proposal to the woman (Gen 3:4-5).

Main Points to Consider (for discussion or to teach):

- Perhaps the serpent took the woman's words about "touching" the tree as his opening. In fact, ancient Jewish rabbis would imagine the serpent grabbing the tree at this point to show that it is harmless (you might, for example, look at Michelangelo's painting of this scene on the Sistine Chapel ceiling if you want to imagine it better).
- Notice what the serpent is implying: (a) God is a rival who is withholding power from you. (b) God doesn't want you to be like him because he wants to be boss. (c) This whole garden is a prison where God is controlling you. (d) You need to choose for yourself: "You do you."
- The serpent's proposal is telling of his "hidden agenda."

Read Together: The woman's next response to the serpent (Gen 3:6-7).

Main Points to Consider (for discussion or to teach):

- She judges the fruit in three ways: good to eat, pleasant to look at, desirable or useful for wisdom. (Note: these are the three temptations to Jesus in the desert, see Luke 4:1-13.) (a) What standard is she using to make these judgments? (b) The text is silent on that standard, because that's the point! (c) She has made up her own standards. The only standard that was given was God's word in the commandment. The point here is that, in sin, we humans make up our own standards and justifications.
- What was the man doing this whole time? (a) It appears that he was just standing there, silently. (b) He just takes and eats what is given to him (like a dope!). (c) He does not even struggle. (d) He just consummates the sin (he joins her). (e) He does *not* sacrifice for her to bring her back from what she is doing (this is a way of looking ahead to what Christ does for us, by contrast).

Question for the Group: What does it mean that their eyes were opened, that they saw they were "naked," and that they covered themselves? (Good for conversation.)

Main Points to Consider (for discussion or to teach):

- This is where it is crucial to remember the connection between "naked" and "shrewd."
- They see in themselves and in each other that their motives are visible, and that the effects of their trespass are clear to see.
- They were created to be "naked"—that is, transparent in their motives, so that their words and deeds were honest and true.
- Now they hide their motives. They hide their most "intimate parts" from each other and from God.

Small Group Exercise (groups of 3 or 4):
Read what the couple in the garden does next: the effects of sin (Gen 3:8-13). Groups should write down their observations, then share them with the larger group once you come back together.

Large Group Discussion (share from small groups, with attention to points below):

- The couple hides from God.
- They blame each other (and God) rather than confess what they did: (a) "The woman you put at my side" (v. 12). (b) "The serpent [you created] duped me" (v. 13).
- This all initiates a new way of living in the world—a *fallen* way: (a) In place of transparency, hiding yourself and your motives. (b) In place of intimacy, shame. (c) In place of honesty, blame. (d) In place of truthful communication, deception. (e) In place of trust of God, suspicion. (f) In place of love for each other, competition and spite.

To Teach:
This entire narrative shows sin as one slow-motion tragedy, and its effects as being the ways in which we often live in the world now. This shows us what we need to be healed and redeemed from.

Already in this narrative, we see that God does not leave us in our sin but comes to our aid. The first question God asks is: "Where are you?" (v. 9). The man and the woman are lost; they are lost to themselves and lost to God. By responding to that question, they allow themselves to be found. God seeks after his lost creatures, precisely in their sin. This is the beginning of salvation history. Jesus will be God's search for sinners, *in person*.

3. Summarizing Sin and Its Effects

Final Takeaways:

- Sin is not just the single deed, but also all the signs of deteriorating trust throughout this account, the prideful way of seeing (how we judge things on our own, without God), and faulty communication.

- The effects of sin are captured in this new, fallen way of living (blame, hiding intentions, distrust, shame) with which we have all become far too familiar.

3rd Movement – Closing Prayer

Each person shares their intentions from the opening journaling exercise.

Offer all these intentions through the intercession of the Blessed Mother: *Hail Mary* . . .

chapter seventeen

The Gifts of the Holy Spirit and the Strength of Virtue

Overview

A Look from Above

In the previous three sessions (14–16), we followed the creation account of Genesis 2 and then the account of the Fall in Genesis 3. By doing so, first we saw who and how we are created to be, then we saw both the seeds and the bad fruits of sin, which not only change us but also the kind of world we live in. In the following three sessions (18–20), we will focus on the virtue of chastity in three ways: as chastity of the ears, of the tongue, and of the eyes. In sum, we will both study and begin to practice chastity as the gift and ability of attentiveness and presence, and as leading to intimacy. Between the previous three sessions and the next three sessions, we need to establish a link between God's Spirit and our virtue.

A Closer Look

In this session we will do something that seems standard and rather typical of confirmation preparation: we will name and study the "gifts of the Holy Spirit." What is perhaps distinctive here, though, is that we will work on seeing these gifts within the narrative of creation and redemption that we have been developing all throughout, both in terms of the accounts in Genesis 2 and 3 that we just studied, in the narrative of Israel, and even in the narrative of Paul that we examined near the beginning of our sessions. By the end of this session we want to see our growth in virtue—namely, the virtue of chastity—as preparing us to better receive and respond to the Holy Spirit, whom Christ breathes on us and into us. His is the Spirit of life; we are talking about what it means to really live.

1st *Movement – Holy Conversation*

1. Prayer
   Angelus recommended: everyone should have this memorized by now

2. Testimonies: "Who is Jesus for me?" (continued; see instructions in lesson 15)

3. Journaling (approximately 7–10 minutes)

   Prompts:
   - Feel free to write any thoughts or reflections based on the testimonies just shared.
   - Write a brief prayer of thanksgiving to Jesus for the faith and courage of those who just shared their testimonies.
   - Write an entry directly to the Lord, beginning with "Dear Jesus . . ."

4. Conversation (and Meal)
   Before breaking for the meal and conversation, briefly recap the "effects" of sin from last time—namely: pattern of blame, hiding your motives, lack of transparency, making up your own standards, sense of shame.

   Then discuss the following: What do you think it is like to live like that? Do you think you would feel strong, weak, or what?

2nd *Movement – Lesson*

1. Large Group Conversation: Follow-up on Meal Conversations

2. Initial Instruction: On Breathing (leader/teacher guides)

   Read Together: Genesis 2:7 (we have read this before).

   Main Points to Highlight:
   - God breathes his own breath into this earth creature, and only by breathing this divine breath does that earth creature become a "living being."
   - To live in the garden God has created and to live as God creates us to live means to breathe his very breath, not something else.
   - We are going to call this "breath of life" the Holy Spirit.

To Teach:

Offer two examples of breathing something other than oxygen.

- Imagine breathing helium from a balloon. It is fun at first and even funny as it changes your voice. But if you suck in too much helium you get light-headed. If breathe far more of it, you will damage your brain cells, which need oxygen to function. If you tried to breathe only helium instead of oxygen, you would die.
- When climbers ascend Mt. Everest, there comes a point (26,247 feet) where there is not enough oxygen in the air to give the human body what it needs to survive. Everything above 26,247 feet is therefore called "the dead zone." If you stay up at that altitude too long, your body will start to shut down and you will die.

Connect back to where Adam and Eve end up at the conclusion of Genesis 3. They end up outside the garden. They are banished. Why are they banished?

- As punishment? It is easy to see it this way, like they don't "deserve" to live there anymore.
- But also as a consequence of their fallen freedom. They have chosen to breathe something other than God's own breath, God's Spirit. They have tried to live some other way, being animated by something else, and that is deadly.
- Therefore, banishment from the garden is also a mercy because they have turned that garden into the opposite of what it was meant to be. They do not live there in harmony, but in rivalry; not in generosity, but in covetousness. They don't know how to enjoy it because they started living some other way, like they are breathing something else—like something else animates them. They are dying because they don't breathe God's breath.
- God will not leave them like this. Their banishment is part of God's mercy because he won't let them go on as if nothing is wrong.

3. Introduction to the Gifts of the Holy Spirit

Note: It would be best to provide a simple handout (see online resource) for this lesson.

Setup: If the man and woman are *weak* after the Fall as they try to live in opposition to God, we are going to consider the "gifts of the Holy Spirit" as God breathing life back into his dying creatures.

Introduce Activity: To be done in pairs or individually (use handout)

- You are being given a list of the seven gifts of the Holy Spirit.
- Write a quick explanation of what you think each one means.

- Describe how you think each one might make us strong in response to the ways we are made weak in sin.

Large Group Discussion: Group members share their responses while the leader really draws out how each of these are forms of the Lord breathing strength into us through the Holy Spirit. This is the same Spirit that gives us life in the first place: God's own breath. (It might be wise to give members a copy of the descriptions of the gifts of the Holy Spirit from chapter 17 of part 1 after this exercise, or at the end of this session.)

4. The Gifts of the Holy Spirit in Scripture (see handout)

A. The Shoot of Jesse

Read Together: Isaiah 11:1-3.

To Teach (regarding the meaning of this prophecy):
Who is Jesse (v. 1)?

- Jesse is the father of David, and David is the first king of the united monarchy of Israel.
- David is therefore the head or the image of the whole of Israel as one kingdom and one nation, before it was pulled apart.
- "The shoot of Jesse" is David's dynasty.
- This is calling to mind an image of wholeness and health for the *life* of Israel.

This prophecy is speaking about what comes after Israel's fall to the superpowers of its day: Assyria and then Babylon.

- The Assyrians crushed the Davidic monarchy.
- The Babylonians later *exiled* the Israelites from their land (like Adam and Eve banished from the garden).
- In a real way, this is all the consequence of Israel's infidelity to God, as if trying to "breathe" something other than his Spirit of life.

The "shoot from the stump" and the "branch" growing from the same roots is new hope for Israel.

- The prophet is saying Israel will be put back together, renewed, and live everlastingly.
- A "new David" will come from the same roots.
- This is hope for Israel *after* destruction, *after* exile.

"The new king" or "the new David"

- The gifts of the Holy Spirit are listed as forms of *strength* that will be given to Israel through its new king.
- This "new king," this "new David," is Jesus. Jesus is the new David.

B. Jesus, Son of David

Read Together: John 20:20-22 to see Jesus fulfilling this prophecy in the resurrection.

Main Points to Highlight:

- The disciples are locked away in fear. They are broken apart from their "leader," from their "king."
- Jesus comes to them, with new life.
- He *breathes* on them.
- They receive the Holy Spirit.
- They are given the gifts of his life, his strength, by his own Spirit.
- Jesus does what the Creator does when he formed the earth creature and gave it *his* breath of life.
- This is the image of Israel made whole again: the twelve apostles are the twelve tribes of Israel, now with their new king, who will live forever.

5. Summing Up and Looking Ahead

Takeaway (from today's session):
The gifts of the Holy Spirit are ways in which God breathes his life into us, to make us new but also to make us strong.

Connect Back to Earlier Lessons:
Before St. Paul was converted, he was "breathing murderous threats against the disciples" (Acts 9:10). After he was converted, he started to breathe God's breath—the Spirit Christ gave him.

- Paul's conversion required him to become stronger so he could be a source of goodness for others.
- This meant he had to become more receptive and responsive to Christ's Spirit working in him, and through him.

For us to prepare to grow in strength to become a source of goodness like Paul, we must grow as he grew so we can cooperate with the Holy Spirit. Paul changed in how he listened, how he spoke, and how he saw.

- Paul grew in the virtue of chastity, which is about the *power* of attentiveness, of presence, and of generosity.
- Adam and Eve fell into unchastity because they gave their attention over to the wrong things in the wrong ways. Paul was healed of this through Christ.

What's Next (next three sessions):

- Chastity of the ears: how we become better at listening with our whole bodies.
- Chastity of the tongue: how we become better at using words well.
- Chastity of the eyes: how we become better at seeing others charitably.

3rd Movement – Closing Prayer

Offer the Prayer to the Holy Spirit (available in online resource under "Prayers").

chapter eighteen

Chastity of the Ears: Inclining Our Hearts

Overview

A Look from Above

If we remember back to the transformation of St. Paul (3–4), we will recall that his mind, his heart, and his lips were all changed and renewed in the Lord. In other words, everything about him was remade in Christ. And if we remember what we discussed in the previous session, we will recall that the gifts of the Holy Spirit are all moments of Christ breathing his life into us, so that we may become stronger and more cooperative with his grace, for our good and the good of all the Church. If we put these together—the transformation of Paul and the gifts of the Holy Spirit—perhaps we can imagine how our own work and practice in attuning our minds, hearts, and lips to cooperate with the mission of Christ is all part of preparing ourselves to receive and respond to the Holy Spirit. The next three sessions (17–19) are, therefore, more practicums than lessons. In each, a particular set of exercises will give group members the benefit of both assessing and beginning to grow in the quality of their attention through how they listen, speak, and see.

A Closer Look

This session presents a workshop for "listening," keyed to growing in the virtue of chastity of the ears. As we saw with St. Paul in his Letter to the Philippians (1:3-5, 7-9), the deepest and most important forms of listening occur in the heart, but as we will see here, all forms of attentive listening are full-body endeavors. All of this is about the ability and the will to give our full attention to someone else. (For this particular session, the corresponding chapter in part 1—chapter 18—also serves as a close guide for conducting this session)

1st Movement – Holy Conversation

1. Prayer

   Angelus recommended: everyone should have this memorized by now

2. Testimonies: "Who is Jesus for me?" (continued if necessary; see instructions in lesson 15)

3. Journaling (approximately 7–10 minutes)

   Prompt: Write an entry directly to the Lord, beginning with "Dear Jesus"

4. Conversation (and Meal)

   Prompt: Share a high and a low from the past week.

2nd Movement – Lesson

1. Review of Previous Sessions

   To Teach (briefly):
   From last session: The gifts of the Holy Spirit
   - Human beings live by breathing (and living by) God's breath: the Holy Spirit.
   - Sin in the garden had to do with trying to live in another way, breathing something other than God's breath.
   - Gifts of the Holy Spirit revive us from the death of sin and make us strong.

   From way back: The conversion and transformation of St. Paul
   - Paul's conversion had to do with his whole self: ears, tongue, eyes.
   - Regarding the renewal of his ears: In his conversion, his companions were silent so he could only hear voice of Christ (Acts 9:4-7). In his transformation, he hears and holds in his heart the needs and the good of others (Phil 1:3-5, 7-9).
   - The gift of hearing Christ and the work of listening well to others go together.

2. Introduction to Today's Workshop

   Note: This is a workshop on the "chastity of the ears," which is about growing in our power of attention and becoming capable of being totally present to others.

   Question for the Group: Which of the gifts of the Holy Spirit have to do with listening?

   Answer: If we think about it, all of them. Each is about either the seed or the fruit of listening.

   Question for the Group: What is the relationship between hearing and really listening?

   Answer: Happening to hear is the not the same as taking in words and comprehending, or seeking to understand, or empathizing.

   Main Point to Highlight: Attentiveness is the key difference.
   Today we will engage in three exercises that are about paying attention to others (each exercise is about 10–15 minutes, with processing).

3. First Exercise

   Instructions:

   - Pair group members (if there is an odd number, the leader joins in).
   - In each pair, select one person as "speaker" and the other as "listener."
   - The leader chooses a topic that will be of some interest to the whole group (it doesn't really matter what the topic is). Let's say the topic is some trip each person has taken.
   - The "speaker" is going to spend about 2 minutes telling the other person all about a favorite trip they have taken.
   - For 1 minute (the leader keeps track of time) the "listeners" will make it look like they are paying attention with their bodies but try to not actually pay attention (with their ears) to what the "speaker" is saying.
   - For the second minute, then, the same "listeners" will now make it look like they are *not* paying attention with their bodies but they actually will pay attention (with their ears).
   - Switch roles and repeat.

   Processing: Lead the group members in discussion about what they experienced.

   - When you were the one speaking, how did it feel when it didn't look like the other person was paying attention? How about when you knew they weren't paying attention but they were making it look like they were?
   - What do people do when they are trying to *not* focus or pay attention with their bodies?

Takeaways:

- Body posture and bodily expression make a difference in our ability to listen.
- A listener's verbal and nonverbal cues matter to the speaker.
- It is hard to listen when your body is not in it, and it is hard to *not* listen when your body *is* in it.

4. Second Exercise

Instructions:

- Keep the pairs together (or switch partners around, if preferable).
- In each pair, select one person as "speaker" and the other as "listener."
- The leader chooses a new topic, like the best gift you ever received.
- The "speaker" is going to spend about 2 minutes telling the other person all about this great gift: describing the gift and talking about why they loved it so much, who gave it to them, what was the occasion, etc.
- The "listener" is just going to listen, absorbing as much as they can from the other person but without *any* verbal or nonverbal affirmations whatsoever. The "listener," in other words, doesn't do *anything* except listen.
- Switch roles and repeat.

Processing: Lead the group members in discussion about what they experienced.

- What was it like to have someone listening to you like that?
- How did you feel as you were the one listening?

Takeaways:

- We need *feedback* from people when we are talking to them. And we need to give *feedback* in order to process and listen well.
- Nonverbal feedback includes nodding the head, smiling, *appropriate* eye contact, leaning forward, facial expressions, overall posture of openness.
- Verbal feedback includes some reflective comments, things like "oh" or "um-hm," and affirmative statements.
- Of course, both nonverbal and verbal feedback can be taken too far so as to be distracting and counterproductive. There is an appropriateness to all of this.

5. Third Exercise

Instructions:

Keep the pairs together (or switch partners around, if preferable).

- In each pair, select one person as "speaker" and the other as "listener."
- The leader chooses a new topic, like a hobby or game you really enjoy.
- The "speaker" is going to spend about 2 minutes telling the other person all about this hobby or game: how to play it, when they do it, who they like to do it with, great experiences with this hobby or game, etc.
- The "listener" is just going to actively listen. In other words, the "listener" just listens as best they can, with their ears and with their body, using verbal and nonverbal feedback. Everything is allowed.
- Switch roles and repeat.

Processing: Lead the group members in discussion about what they experienced.

- How did it feel to listen this way?
- How did it feel to be listened to this way, especially after the other rounds? Was anything "too much"?

Takeaways:

- Truly attentive listening is "in-sync." It involves the whole body in tune.
- Speaking and listening are intimately connected. When someone is speaking you are not listening to *something* but *someone*, and vice versa. Each person must be aware and considerate of the other person.

6. Reflection on Exercises of Listening

Brief Individual Journaling, then Large Group Discussion, Part 1:

- What can you take away from each exercise?
- What did you learn or what is worth remembering?

Brief Individual Journaling, then Large Group Discussion, Part 2:

- Who is the best listener you know, from your own life? (Or if you can't decide on "the best," then pick someone who is very good at listening.)
- What does that person do when they are listening?
- What can you learn from that person?

Final Takeaway: To truly receive any of the gifts of the Holy Spirit, you must be willing to listen.

3rd Movement – Closing Prayer

Offer the Prayer for Jesus to give us the Spirit (available in online resource under "Prayers").

chapter nineteen

Chastity of the Tongue: Harnessing the Power of Words

Overview

A Look from Above

This is the middle session in a three-session set of practicums. In the first (17), we practiced different ways of listening and not listening—with our ears and really our whole bodies—in order to gain some perspective and begin to experience what truly attentive listening requires. In the next session (19), we will meditate on what we set our eyes on and how we learn to look at others and our world. These are two of the three loci of transformation for St. Paul, whose ears and eyes were renewed in Christ. The other locus of transformation is the focus of this session: the tongue (or lips). In each case, our primary subject is the virtue of chastity, which is the ability and willingness to give one's whole attention to another. Like all the virtues, chastity is a virtue that requires restraint and power.

A Closer Look

This session presents a workshop for "speaking," keyed to growing in the virtue of chastity of the tongue. As we saw with St. Paul in his First Letter to the Corinthians (15:3-10), what he offered to others "as of first importance" is the greatest blessing of all: the passion, death, and resurrection of Jesus Christ. Paul's words were in order: he broke from his old way of speaking (in which he spewed forth "murderous threats") so that he could learn how to build up, encourage, discipline, illuminate, and heal others, all in service of preaching the Word of God. Paul was very intentional about the power of his words, and that is the call to all Christians. By attending to our words, we practice attending well to others and taking responsibility for their well-being, alongside our own.

1st Movement – Holy Conversation

1. Prayer

   Angelus recommended: everyone should have this memorized by now

2. Testimonies: "Who is Jesus for me?" (continued if necessary; see instructions in lesson 15)

3. Journaling (approximately 7–10 minutes)

   Prompt: Consider whose words were meaningful to you this week, for good or for ill. Did someone build you up or cut you down? Did someone encourage or discourage you? Did someone speak honestly to you? Try to focus on one interaction, what the person said to you, and why it mattered.

4. Conversation (and Meal)

   Prompt: Share about one person to whom you find it rather easy to speak kindly, and one person to whom you find it rather difficult to speak kindly. Why so in each case?

2nd Movement – Lesson

1. Review of Previous Sessions

   To Teach (briefly):

   From last session: Chastity of the Ears

   - We practiced listening and *not* listening to each other through our different exercises.
   - We learned how there are both verbal and nonverbal aspects to both speaking and listening, and we learned how we listen both with our ears and with our bodies.
   - In short, listening well is *hard work* and it takes practice to get better at it.

   From way back: The conversion and transformation of St. Paul. Regarding the renewal of his tongue:

   - In his conversion, Paul went from "breathing murderous threats against the disciples" (Acts 9:1) to proclaiming Jesus (9:20), because the Lord spoke to him and Ananias healed him by calling him "brother" (9:17).

- In his transformation, Paul grows more and more in his ability and willingness to share the blessing of Christ with others, which he holds as the most important thing of all (1 Cor 15:3-10).
- In order to learn how to speak anew, we have to break from our unhealthy ways of speaking, listen to Christ and to those who have learned how to speak well in Christ, and then practice new ways of speaking blessings to others.

2. Introduction to Today's Workshop

Note: This workshop is on the "chastity of the tongue," which is about growing in our power of speech, to communicate blessings and not curses to others. In this workshop, we are going to reflect on different parts of Scripture to see and talk about just how powerful speech is—beginning with God's speech but linking directly to our speech. For each of the following exercises, the leader may choose to have group members read the passages on their own, in pairs or small groups or as a whole group. The questions that go with each passage may therefore begin as personal journaling, small group discussion, or immediately as large group discussion. It is, of course, possible to use different arrangements for different exercises. At some point, though, it would be wise to bring at least part of each discussion into the large group, especially so the leader can be sure that some of the key points are discussed.

Read Together (optional): The first half of Proverbs 18:21, then ask the group what they think of this line: "Death and life are in the power of the tongue."

3. First Exercise: God Creates with His Word

Read Together: Genesis 1:1-3, 6-7, 9, 11, 14-15, 20, 24, 26, and 29-30 (see online resource).

Questions for the Group: What do these passages tell us about words?

Key Answer: God creates with his word.

Other Answers: God's word is powerful; God's word is effective (what he says happens immediately); God's word is fruitful (see vv. 29-30); God's word gives order and creates the conditions for life.

Read Together: Genesis 1:26-28.

Question for the Group: In light of the previous passages that we read, what do you think it might mean to be "created in God's image and likeness"?

Key Answer: In order to be "like God," we too are meant to create with our words.

Other Answers: Our words are powerful; our words can be effective; our words are meant to be fruitful; our words ought to provide order and create the conditions of life.

4. Second Exercise: What Comes from Our Mouths Is More Powerful than We Think

Read Together: Matthew 12:34-37.

Question for the Group: What is Jesus saying about words here?

Key Answer: Our words show what kind of person we are. They reveal our character.

Other Answers: Words come from our mouths *and* from our heart (from deep within us). We build up goodness or evil within us, then give what we have stored up when you speak to others. We are responsible for our careless words.

Question for the Group: Why do you think Jesus calls these people "vipers"?

Key Answer: They have stored up venom within them—like vipers—and their speech is therefore poisonous to others.

Share Aloud: Proverbs 18:21. "Death and life are in the power of the tongue."

Takeaway: That's a serious line, and Jesus is taking the power of speech no less seriously.

5. Third Exercise: The Importance of Practicing How We Are to Speak

Read Together: James 3:3-5, 9-10.

Questions for the Group: How is the relationship of a bit to a horse like the relationship between our tongues and our whole selves? How is the relationship of a rudder to a boat like the relationship between our tongues and our whole selves?

Key Answer: Careful and focused direction over the small part (bit for the horse, rudder for the ship, tongue for the whole person), is the most direct, most efficient, and usually the most powerful way to steer the whole thing.

Other Answers: The better the horseman, the better the control of the bit and therefore the direction of the horse; the better the captain, the better the control of the rudder and therefore the better the steering of the whole ship; both the horseman and the captain exercise foresight and learn from their mistakes to become better at what they do; all of this is also true of the person who develops a "well-trained tongue" (Isa 50:4).

Question for the Group: In the end according to James, for what do we ultimately use our tongues—that is, our power of speech?

Key Answer: Either to bless or to curse. Created in the image of God, we either do as God does (create, give life, build up) or we act against God by harming others with our speech.

6. Further Reflection

Question for the Group: What has stood out for you in what we have read about the power of words?

Question for the Group: How do we create life with our words? That is, how do we bless others?

Possible Answers (among others): Offering compliments; encouraging others; praying for others; speaking honestly; using the proper tone of voice; considering how someone else will hear what we say, correcting someone else in a kind way.

Questions for the Group: How do we kill with our words? That is, how do we curse others?

Possible Answers (among others): Gossiping; using harsh language; improper tone of voice; lying or manipulating; being less than truthful; ridiculing or mocking; correcting someone else without kindness.

Question for the Group: If you misuse words, how do you correct this sin and grow in your ability to use words well?

Possible Answers (among others): Apologizing and asking for forgiveness, going to confession, explaining what you meant if you were misunderstood.

Question for the Group: What might be some helpful practices for becoming more careful and more caring with our words?

Possible Answers (among others): Reviewing your day to consider how you spoke to others throughout the day; practicing taking a pause before responding to someone (especially in a heated conversation or when texting); paying attention to how kind and thoughtful people speak (both what they say and how they say what they say); praying for the grace to become more responsible with your power of speech; talking less, listening more.

3rd Movement – Closing Prayer

Offer St. Paul's words to the Ephesians as a prayer for us, today. Paul, who learned how to speak well and to bless others, is instructing us how to allow the Lord to renew our power of speech. This renewal is a lifelong process—we continue to grow in our power of speech, becoming more practiced in the virtue of chastity of the tongue. Read Ephesians 4:25-32.

chapter twenty

Chastity of the Eyes: Risking the Joy of Encounter

Overview

A Look from Above

This is the last of the three-session set of practicums focusing on the virtue of chastity. In each instance, chastity is introduced and explored as power, in terms of the ability and willingness to give one's whole attention to another. The truly chaste person is capable of being truly present. This fullness of presence includes our ears and our hearts, in terms how we listen to each other (17). It includes our tongue and our words, in terms of how we speak to each other, ultimately either blessing or cursing God and neighbor (18). And, of course, it includes our eyes and minds, in terms of how we see other people and the world in which we live.

A Closer Look

This session presents a workshop for "seeing," keyed to growing in the virtue of chastity of the eyes. As we saw with St. Paul in his Second Letter to the Corinthians (12:7-10), the transformation of his mind entailed the ongoing work of learning to see all things new. In the end, Paul trusted the Lord's vision of the world—and especially the Lord's vision of him—more than he trusted in even the things of which he was most ashamed. Our eyes are precious; we must entrust them with care. In this session, we will engage in a workshop that actually extends to a week or two because this workshop invites analysis of how each of us spends our time and what each of us is in the habit of looking at. This is also a session that very well could be used to bring up the corrosive effect of pornography, which immerses viewers in a way of seeing that diminishes the capacity for intimacy. The topic of pornography was introduced and even nuanced in this session's companion chapter in part 1 (chap. 20). There is so much pastoral discretion necessary in addressing this massive issue and the havoc it wreaks in people's lives that it will not be possible to offer a direct guide for how to address pornography and the addiction to pornography here.

1st Movement – Holy Conversation

1. Prayer
   Angelus recommended: everyone should have this memorized by now

2. Testimonies: "Who is Jesus for me?" (continued if necessary; see instructions in lesson 15)

3. Journaling (approximately 7–10 minutes)

   Prompt: Write an entry directly to the Lord, beginning with the words "Dear Jesus . . ."

4. Conversation (and Meal)

   Prompt: Thinking back to the past two workshops on listening and speaking, share with each other what has remained with you as especially important.

2nd Movement – Lesson

1. Review of Previous Sessions

   To Teach (briefly):
   From last session: Chastity of the Tongue
   - We saw in various passages of Scripture just how much power there is in speech, beginning with God who creates all things through his "Word" and ending with our own power to create life or cause death through our speech.
   - We reflected on potential practices for learning how to use our speech better (perhaps share some of the "best practices" that were mentioned in the last session).
   - In short, our words matter and we have to practice using them well.

   From way back: The conversion and transformation of St. Paul. Regarding the renewal of his eyes:

- In his conversion, Paul went from seeing the world through anger and vengeance to learning to see the world anew through charity. In between his old vision and his new vision was his three-day period of blindness (Acts 9:9), where the Lord's light broke him from how he had seen things and prepared him to begin seeing things in Christ (see Acts 9:3).
- In his transformation, Paul slowly but surely allows the Lord's vision of him and of the whole world to become Paul's own vision, to the point where he trusts the Lord's grace more than he clings to the memory of what causes him the most shame—persecuting Christians (2 Cor 12:7-10).
- In order to be perpetually renewed in how we see ourselves, one another, and the world, we have to continually break from our old ways of seeing, and actively practice seeing how Christ desires us to see.

2. Introduction to Today's Workshop

Note: This is a workshop on the "chastity of the eyes," which is about taking greater care both in what we look at and how we look at others. In this workshop, we are going to introduce different ways of examining our own habits in terms of what we regularly look at, but this examination will need to continue for at least a week or two beyond today. This workshop is built around mostly guided, individual reflection. See the last three paragraphs of the companion chapter—part 1, chapter 20—for a brief overview of the following three exercises.

3. First Exercise: The Inventory

Setup: We want to try to think about *how* we spend our time, on a regular basis. We may not be fully aware of this, which is why we have to really study . . . ourselves. The point in what we are going to do is simply to try to get an accurate account of how we spend our time. This is not about judging ourselves or each other for how we spend our time.

Instructions:

- Each member spends 5–10 minutes brainstorming all the ways they spend their time, in a typical day and in a typical week. In particular, each member should try to give extra attention to what they "look at": particular people with whom they spend time in face-to-face settings, their phones or other screens, what kind of content on the internet or in print, etc.
- Each member should then try to estimate how much time they spend in a typical day or week giving their attention to each thing they listed.
- The "assignment," then, is to keep a daily journal for the next week to two weeks in which each member carefully reviews their day and

writes down what they gave their attention to and for how long. They should note whether they gave their undivided attention to each thing or person, or if they were splitting their attention. Every night, each member should spend 15–20 minutes reviewing the day. It might be wise to take notes throughout the day about what you are doing and for how long, and in what manner (undivided attention or split attention). The key with all of this is to try to get as accurate a picture as possible about how each person is spending their time and what they are looking at.

4. Second Exercise: The Meeting

Question for the Group: What is hard about looking into someone else's eyes?

Question for the Group: What do many people do nowadays—maybe you, maybe not you—*instead* of spending time face-to-face, where they can look into one another's eyes?

Main Point to Establish: If we are made for intimacy—as we already learned in Genesis 2—then another way of saying that is we are made to look into each other's eyes, where we are truly present to each other.

Instructions:

- Each person is invited to make a list—it doesn't need to be a long list—of people who live near them, with whom they could spend time but don't regularly, and with whom they would enjoy spending a little more time.
- The "assignment," then, is this: setup a time to get together with one of these people for some time in the next week to two weeks. This "get together" should not be to do something else, like watch a movie or go to a show. The point of the "get together" is to spend time talking, face-to-face. Of course, this can be over coffee or a meal, but the key is to dedicate the entire time you are with the person to paying attention to them. No glances at phones, no checking in on other things.
- After this "get together," spend at least 15 minutes journaling about what your time together was like. What did you enjoy? What was difficult about it? Was it hard for you to keep your attention in this meeting?

5. Third Exercise: The Gaze

To Teach:

There are a surprising number of moments in the gospels where the way Jesus looked at someone is highlighted. Here are just a few examples:

- When the rich young man came to Jesus and wanted to know what he needed to do to inherit eternal life, the gospel says that "Jesus looked upon him and loved him" (Mark 10:21, RSV).
- When Peter denied Jesus for the third time before his crucifixion, it says that "the Lord turned and looked at Peter. And Peter remembered the word of the Lord . . . . [And Peter] wept bitterly" (Luke 22:61-62, RSV).
- When some people brought their friend to Jesus so that Jesus could heal their friend of his paralysis, there was such a crowd around Jesus that they could not reach Jesus. So these friends of the paralyzed man went up on the roof and lowered their friend down to where Jesus was. And it says, "When Jesus saw their faith he said, 'Man, your sins are forgiven you,'' and a moment later he cured him of his paralysis (Luke 5:20, RSV). Notice that it is when Jesus *sees the faith of this man's friends* that Jesus heals the man.

Takeaway: Jesus looks at us, and his look is meaningful. His look is a look of love, a look of honesty, a look of healing. It is a hard but necessary thing to let Jesus look at us.

Instructions:

- Each person is invited to write what, if anything, they have experienced of Eucharistic Adoration. Have you ever done it? Are you comfortable with it? What do you think "the point" is? What are your questions about it?
- Proposal: What if you thought about Eucharistic Adoration as an encounter, like a face-to-face, eye-to-eye encounter? What if it is an opportunity simply to sit before the Lord and let him look at you? That changes things a bit, because we tend to think about what *we* are doing. The point here is to think about what *the Lord* is doing.
- Challenge (and this might take some previous research by the leader): Look over the places and times when Eucharistic Adoration is available in your area. Your challenge is to spend at least 30 minutes—or maybe an hour—in Eucharistic Adoration three times over the next three weeks. You do not have to do anything else; just be there.

Note: Leaders might arrange Eucharistic Adoration for their group, or at least provide group members with a list of Eucharistic Adoration opportunities in their community.

6. Follow up (either with whole group, or in conversation with a mentor)
This workshop gives group members *three* different things to do after this session:

- Keep a daily journal of how they have spent their time, what they have looked at (or given their attention to) and for how long.
- Plan to and then actually meet up with someone to spend time in face-to-face conversation, with a short journaling assignment afterwards.
- Attend three Eucharistic Adoration sessions (of at least 30 minutes each) over the course of three weeks.

It is imperative to follow-up on each of these three exercises.

- The preferred method for follow-up may be to have each group member meet with a mentor (someone who is informed about what the group is doing, or who becomes informed for the sake of this workshop). This mentor may obviously be a confirmation sponsor. It is also possible, of course, to follow up within this group.
- Follow-up should include discussion over the daily journal of how members spend their time: What was surprising? Anything discouraging or any obvious areas where change is necessary? In particular, how do you feel about *what* you are looking at and the amount of time you are spending looking at it? How does the actual account of how you spend your time and what you are looking at compare to the estimate you created when this all began?
- Follow-up should include discussion over the face-to-face meeting. The key with these meetings is to make them a regular, scheduled part of one's life. Put something on the calendar for every week, then cancel it as necessary (rather than always trying to schedule meetings with people you value seeing).
- Follow-up should include discussion about Eucharistic Adoration. How did it go for you? Would you be willing to make this a regular part of your life, perhaps every week or once a month? The key, again, is to put this on your calendar as a regular occurrence, rather than always "trying to find time to squeeze it in." The most important things become the most important things because they are the things we regularly spend time doing.

3rd Movement – Closing Prayer

Pray the traditional Christian hymn of Irish origin, "Be Thou My Vision" (available in online resource under "Prayers"). For a beautiful and prayerful version of this hymn by a modern artist, see Audrey Assad's *Inheritance* album. Her version is also on YouTube as "Be Thou My Vision—Audrey Assad."

chapter twenty-one

The First and Perfect Disciple

Overview

A Look from Above

Looking behind us, we see that we have recently completed two mini-units, each consisting of three lessons. The first mini-unit (14–16), took us through the scriptural witness as to the creation of the human being, particularly our creation as male and female, and then on to an examination of the Fall and the lasting consequences of sin from which Christ heals us. The second mini-unit (18–20), consisted of workshops or practicums on the virtue of chastity, focused especially on the ears, the tongue, and the eyes. In between those two mini-units was a bridge lesson that introduced the Gifts of the Holy Spirit and the virtue of chastity. We come now to another bridge, constructed of two lessons (21–22), which connects the mini-unit on chastity to the last mini-unit on the sacramental life of the Church (23–25). This last "bridge" is neither a concept nor a theme, but a person: Mary.

A Closer Look

In this session we contemplate Mary as the first and perfect disciple. She is the living image of Christian maturity. She, who is the Mother of God, reveals and teaches us what it means to become disciples of her Son, as she is. The primary focus of this session is on the Annunciation narrative in the Gospel of Luke, wherein our attentive reading of the text will lead us to see Mary as the one who "hears the Word of God and acts on it" (Luke 8:21, RSV), which is indeed the very definition of a disciple, especially within Luke's gospel. At the same time, though, we may discern in Mary the embodiment of the virtue of chastity, particularly in terms of how she listens, how she sees, and how she speaks. In her and through her, we discover what true Christian freedom requires and enables. (Alongside this Reflection and Practice chapter, there is also a handout in the online resource that accompanies this lesson, which includes Scripture verses and some important translation notes about the text. It would be helpful to give each group member a copy of this handout. I will refer to this resource throughout this chapter as the "handout.")

1st Movement – Holy Conversation

1. Prayer

   Angelus recommended: especially pertinent since this prayer focuses on the Annunciation

2. Journaling (approximately 7–10 minutes)

   Prompts:

   - Write your thoughts about what you think is required of you to be a disciple. In other words, what is the cost of discipleship, especially on a day-to-day basis?
   - Write your thoughts about what you think being a disciple enables or frees you to do or to become. In other words, what is the gift of discipleship?

3. Conversation (and Meal)

   Prompt: Share what you journaled with one another.

2nd Movement – Lesson

1. Review of Previous Sessions

   To Teach (briefly):

   From last three sessions: Chastity of the Ears, Tongue, Eyes

   - We spent three sessions both exploring and practicing what it means to grow in the virtue of chastity. Chastity is the ability and the responsibility of being truly and fully present, especially to one another.
   - With each of the three dimensions of chastity, we saw that growing in this virtue requires a lot of work from us but also strengthens us to become capable of authenticity, honesty, intimacy, and becoming a source of goodness for others.

From way back: Creation, Sin, and the Gifts of the Holy Spirit

- Before we started exploring the virtue of chastity, we learned from Scripture how God creates us as human beings. In short, God creates us in harmony, for harmony.
- But we also examined what sin is and what the effects of sin are. In brief, we become weak in sin as we cease living by God's own Spirit, breathing God's very life.
- That led us, right before our exploration of chastity, to reckon with the gifts of the Holy Spirit. If nothing else, we might think of these gifts as Christ's way of breathing new life into us, to make us strong and capable of life with him and life in harmony with one another.

2. Introduction to Mary

Sample Introduction: "Today we give our attention to Mary, who is the first and perfect disciple, the image of Christian maturity, and the fullness of the virtue of chastity. We learn who we are called to be as Christian disciples by studying Mary and learning to receive and respond to Jesus as she receives and responds to him. She is fully chaste because she is wholly capable of giving her whole attention to the Lord, and to all those whom the Lord gives us to love—that is, all his disciples."

3. Opening Exercise: Fra Angelico's *The Annunciation*

Present Fra Angelico's The Annunciation *painting to the group. It is preferable to give each person their own copy, which may be printed out in color as high-quality reproductions from the internet (see links in online resource). Fra Angelico painted the Annunciation several times throughout his life. The version to use for this exercise is the one belonging to the collection of the Museo Nacional del Prado (the Prado Museum in Madrid). You will know you are using the right painting when you see on the left side of the painting (as you are looking at it) the figures of Adam and Eve walking away from the garden with three pieces of fruit at their feet and an angel immediately above them.*

Individual Study: Give group members 2–5 minutes to study the painting on their own. Ask them to write down what they notice and what they find interesting.

Group Discussion: Share an open discussion as a group about what you see in this painting.

Possible Points to Highlight:

- Adam and Eve leaving the garden, covered up not only by their clothes and fig leaves but also with Adam partially covering his face. They are averting their eyes.

- The eye contact of Mary and the Angel Gabriel.
- The light shining from God upon Mary, with the Holy Spirit represented as a dove in that light.
- The book open on Mary's lap. What has she been doing? Reading. Reading what? Scripture.
- (There is a lot more here and quite a lot to study. Perhaps some leaders in your group would be interested in studying this painting further in advance, so as to help lead the discussion.)

Key Takeaway: Contemplating this art takes time and requires both our attention and interest. Studying the scriptural text requires nothing less. We are going to try to contemplate Mary as presented to us in Scripture with the patience and care that we would exercise in learning to see well a masterpiece of art.

To Teach (transition): In the Gospel of Luke especially, a disciple of Jesus is defined as one who "hears the Word of God and acts on it" (see Luke 8:20-21, on handout). We want to see how Mary does these two things: hearing the Word and acting on it. We are also going to see how she fulfills the virtue of chastity in terms of listening, seeing, and speaking.

4. On Mary's Hearing and Chastity of the Ears

Read Together: The Annunciation narrative (Luke 1:26-38, on handout).

Question for the Group: How many times does Mary respond?

Answer: Though some people may say once, most people will say twice. But the answer is three times, though we only hear two of them. The first response is her silence (v. 29). The narrative is intentionally structured to highlight these three segments: three times the angel speaks and three times Mary responds.

To Teach:

The importance of Mary's first response (in silence, v. 29) is not really clear to us unless we do what Luke wants us to do: compare this narrative to the one that comes before it, which is the annunciation to Zechariah.

The two narratives are remarkably similar, except that Zechariah seems to end up being punished (he is struck mute) where Mary is praised. What gives?

The similarities between the two narratives make the subtle differences all the more important. The first difference is in the "quality of their quiet," or how each first responds to the angel. See the handout that compares their responses in silence:

- Zechariah is troubled, so fear overcomes him.
- Mary is *very troubled*, so we should expect fear to *really* overcome her. But she is not overcome with fear. Instead, she considers.
- Zechariah recoils in fear and is ready to strike; Mary opens up and is ready to listen.

To Teach:
The second subtle but important difference is in what each of them *says* when they first speak. They both ask questions and the questions sound really similar, but we have to notice how they differ (see "The Form of the Question" on handout).

- Zechariah asks, "How can I know this?," which is like saying, "prove it to me." *He* himself is the center of attention and concern. This is what it sounds like when the one who recoils in fear strikes out.
- Mary asks, "How can this be?," which means that she is giving the benefit of the doubt. She grants that "this can be" but she is asking how. This is what it is like to consider and to work on listening deeply.

To Teach:
This deep listening of Mary becomes her defining characteristic in Luke's gospel. Luke calls it "pondering."

Review the three prominent times in the next two chapters when Mary's heart is singled out, and an emphatic point is made about how deeply the word and action of the Lord impacts her (see "Mary's Pondering" on handout).

Takeaway: Mary, the first and perfect disciple, listens deeply, with her whole being.

5. On Mary's Hearing (or Seeing) and the Chastity of the Eyes

Read Together: The last thing that the angel says to Mary (Luke 1:36-37, on handout).

Questions for the Group: Why is the last thing the angel tells Mary not about her but about her cousin Elizabeth? Is this just a newsflash or status update? What do you think?

To Teach:
Let's go back to the beginning of this gospel, to see how Zechariah and Elizabeth are introduced. Imagine this is some kind of social gathering in polite company, and Luke is introducing you to these two nice people. It starts out quite cordially: he introduces them by name, he tells you something about their families, and he tells you about their righteousness.

But then he seems to completely lose his manners when he points out that not only do they *not* have any children but that they cannot have any because *this* woman—right here—is barren. She is infertile. Oh, and they are both super old, in case you didn't notice. So why introduce these two people in this way, especially Elizabeth? Because, introducing her as old and barren presents her in the image of one and only one other person in all of Scripture: Sarah, Abraham's wife.

To Teach:
We have to recall Sarah if we want to understand Elizabeth.

- First, we have to remember that God's covenant with Abraham (Sarah's husband) included two promises: that his descendants would be numerous and that those descendants would inherit a new land. What does Abraham need in order to have a lot of descendants? At least one child.
- Second, all throughout the chapters in the Book of Genesis (chaps. 12–18), the fact that Abraham and Sarah do not bear any children becomes a bigger and bigger issue. On the handout, you see, on the one hand, how the problem of childlessness persists, while on the other hand God just keeps doubling-down on his promise.
- Third and finally, in chapter 18, things come to a head. If we thought Luke lacked manners, listen to what the author of Genesis says about Sarah: "Abraham and Sarah were old, advanced in age; Sarah had stopped having the periods of women" (18:11, JPS). That doesn't leave anything to the imagination. She no longer ovulates, which means she *cannot have children by the natural course of things.*
- Finally, all of this is for one purpose and one purpose only: to pose the question "Is anything too marvelous for the Lord to do?" (Gen 18:14, JPS). This is what the three visitors to Abraham and Sarah ask after they announce that Sarah will bear a son within the year. She laughs, because she knows her own body. But the Lord provides; she and Abraham conceive and bear a son, and name him Isaac.

Question for the Group: What do you think Mary, as a faithful Jew who reads the Scriptures, hears when the angel says that her cousin Elizabeth—who is old and barren—is now with child?

Answer:

- She hears "Sarah." Elizabeth has been presented as the new Sarah. Mary hears that the God *who did great deeds in Israel's history is now doing great deeds in her time.*

- And of course, Mary also knows that what is being asked of her is being asked by the same God but that this is something new, because she herself is *not* old (she is very young) and she is *not* barren (she is just at the beginning of her child-bearing years).
- Elizabeth's pregnancy is a sign to Mary because Mary sees God's continuous narrative, and so she knows how to see herself within that narrative.

Takeaway: Mary, the first and perfect disciple, remembers what God *has done* and so she is free to see what God *is doing*, now.

6. On Mary's Speaking and the Chastity of the Lips

Question for the Group: What did we learn about God's speech—God's Word—in the first creation account (Gen 1)?

Answers: God's word created life. God's word was effective. God's word was fruitful (etc.).

Read Together: Mary's final words to the angel (Luke 1:38, on handout).

To Teach:
Look at how these words are words that give life. In fact, what is translated as "let it be" is, in Latin, the word *fiat.* When God says, "let there be light" in Genesis 1:3, the Latin translation is *fiat lux.* Mary's "let it be" is an echo of God's word of creation.

Read Together: Mary's Magnificat, her song of praise in Elizabeth's house (Luke 1:46-55, on handout).

To Teach:
Look at how her words are a blessing to the lowly and the downcast. See how her words speak of upending the unjust social order, to restore harmony to God's creation. Note how she praises God's mercy and speaks that mercy to others.

Takeaway: Mary, the first and perfect disciple, who listens to God's word and sees God's action, allows her words and actions to bless others.

7. Back to Fra Angelico's Painting

Question for the Group: What is the significance of placing Adam and Eve's banishment from the garden in an adjacent space to the Annunciation to Mary? (really an open question worth pondering and discussing together).

Final Takeaway: Mary is the New Eve in this painting, who through grace and chastity undoes the first Eve's disobedience. So where is the New Adam? He is the "fruit of her womb."

3rd Movement – Closing Prayer

The Hail Mary is a scriptural prayer, drawing upon both the Annunciation and the Visitation narratives. When we pray it, we ask Mary for her intercession *and* we seek to become disciples as she is a disciple of her Son. So let us pray: *Hail Mary . . .*

chapter twenty-two

The Mystery and Motherhood of the Church

Overview

A Look from Above

We are on a bridge, and the bridge is Marian. This bridge consists of two sessions (21–22) that connect our exercises with the virtue of chastity to an exploration of the sacraments of the Church. In the session immediately preceding this one, we contemplated the Annunciation narrative to discern how Mary embodies the fullness of Christian discipleship, while exhibiting the perfection of chastity. Before launching into a three-part study of the Church's sacraments, we must see how Mary's discipleship and motherhood are united, and how in her motherhood of Jesus she becomes the mother of all disciples.

A Closer Look

This session is about the Church and about Mary at the same time, because the Church itself is Marian and Mary herself embodies the Church. A primary text for this session is the Dogmatic Constitution on the Church from the Second Vatican Council, *Lumen Gentium*. While reading and studying this document in full is never a bad idea, for the purposes of this session the opening and closing of that document are presented together, thereby linking the "mystery" or sacramental character of the Church (beginning) with its Marian identity and care (end). This session acts as an introduction to the sacraments themselves by ultimately presenting the sacraments as acts of maternal care, instituted by Christ and mediated by the Church, by which those claimed in Christ are nurtured into Christian maturity. In short, as

Mary cared for and cherished the Son of God, so the Church cares for and cherishes all those called to become children of God in their union in Christ.

1st Movement – Holy Conversation

1. Prayer
   Angelus recommended

2. Journaling (approximately 7–10 minutes)

   Prompts:
   - Whose care for you has been important in your life? How has this person (or these persons) cared for you? Try to name this person (or persons) and express both how they have cared for you and why that care has mattered so much.
   - Write a brief prayer of thanks to the Lord for this person's care.

3. Conversation (and Meal)

   Prompt: Share some thoughts about who has cared for you and how.

2nd Movement – Lesson

1. Review of Previous Session

   Mary is the one who perfectly fulfills the definition of a disciple as one who "hears the word of God and acts on it." In the Annunciation narrative, we witnessed:
   - the virtue of Mary's listening, which began with her silence and trust, and continued through her "pondering" as she welcomes the word and action of the Lord into her heart;
   - the virtue of Mary's seeing as she recognized in the pregnancy of her cousin Elizabeth the sign of God's action, reaching back to Abraham's wife Sarah, because Mary was attentive to the scriptures and to the continuous narrative of God's saving action;
   - the virtue of Mary's speaking as her "Yes" to the angel's announcement—her "let it be"—was itself an act of creation like God's own, and her Magnificat a proclamation of God's mercy.

2. The Mystery of the Church

   Question for Individual Reflection: What is the Church? (Give members 2 minutes to write their thoughts. Share responses in large group.)

To Teach: "What is the Church?" is a question that the Church itself asked and responded to during the Second Vatican Council in the 1960s. Vatican II was a major council that brought together bishops and others from all across the world to address the most important issues of the Church and the world. (A slightly longer introduction to Vatican II is possible but not necessary. The main point is to be able to present the first paragraph of *Lumen Gentium* as expressing the voice of the whole Church in response to the question that the group members themselves were just asked: "What is the Church?")

Read Together: The first paragraph of *Lumen Gentium*, where the Church responds to the question of what "she"—i.e., "the Church"—is (see handout in online resource)

Question for the Group: What is the first thing that this text says the Church is?

Key Answer: "A sacrament" (specifically, "a sacrament in Christ"). FYI: This first chapter of *Lumen Gentium* is entitled "The Mystery of the Church" because *mysterion* is the Greek word for the Latin word *sacramentum*; to call the Church a "mystery" is to say it is a "sacrament," and vice versa.

Question for the Group: How does this text then define a sacrament?

Key Answer: As "a sign and instrument"

Question for the Group: What is the Church a "sign and instrument" of?

Key Answer: "Communion with God and of the unity of the human race"

Question for the Group: What do you think it means for the Church to be a "sign" of the communion with God and the unity of the human race?

Key Answer: What the Church is points to that reality, which is a reality of wholeness (us with God and at one with one another).

Question for the Group: What do you think it means for the Church to be an "instrument" of that communion and unity?

Key Answer: The Church's mission is to bring about that reality, meaning that the Church's whole purpose is to foster communion with God and the unity of the human race.

Question for the Group: And why do you think *Lumen Gentium* states that "the church, *in Christ*, is a sacrament"? Why is the "in Christ" important?

Key Answer: Christ is the one who is always in communion with the Father in the Holy Spirit, and whose mission is to bring us into that communion by making us one in him. The Church's identity and mission come from and go to Christ.

Takeaway: The identity and mission of the Church come from the identity and mission of Christ, whose whole life is summed up in the prayer he prayed on the night before he died: "that they may all be one; even as you, Father, are in me, and I am in you, that they may be one in us" (John 17:21, RSV).

3. The Motherhood of the Church

Transition and Setup: All of *Lumen Gentium* is about the Church's identity and mission. As we just saw, *Lumen Gentium* begins in its first chapter by presenting the Church as "a sacrament" or "a mystery." The final chapter of *Lumen Gentium* focuses on "Our Lady"—that is, Mary.

Read Together: John 19:25-27 to have an image in mind for thinking about why this document about the Church concludes with Mary (see online resource).

To Teach:
Christ unites his own mother to his disciple (and all disciples), and unites his disciples to his own mother.

- This means that Mary is the mother of Jesus *and* all the disciples whom Jesus claims.
- To be joined to Christ means to receive his mother, and his mother joins disciples to her own Son, Jesus.

Read Together: Three passages from the last chapter of *Lumen Gentium* (see handout in online resource).

- The Church takes very seriously what Christ did from the cross in giving his mother to his disciple and his disciple to his mother.
- What began with Mary at the Annunciation—her "yes" to the Word of God, which made her the mother of Jesus—never ends. It is constant and it continues all the way to the end of time, when all the saints (all those joined to Christ) are united together in heaven.
- She is *always* Christ's mother and therefore *always* the mother of those whom Christ claims.
- The identity and mission the Church receives from Christ was first of all realized in the person of Mary. She is the mother who gathers all peoples into union with her Son. The Church's own character is therefore Marian: the Church is given the privilege and responsibility of providing Mary's maternal care for disciples in century after century.

Takeaway: The Church, which is "a sacrament, in Christ," is also Marian. The Church is a mother who calls and nourishes people into union with Christ. Mary is the figure of the Church.

4. The Church's Maternal Care

Question for the Group: What does a good mother do?

Key Answer: She births, feeds, comforts, teaches, supports, corrects, heals, disciplines, loves. In sum, she guides her children all the way to maturity.

Questions for the Group: What did we say defines a disciple? That is, what does a mature Christian continually learn to do?

Key Answer: Hear the word of God and act on it.

Read Together: What *Lumen Gentium* says *every* Christian is meant to do (handout, paragraph 42 of LG is the key).

To Teach:
The Church, as mother to all whom Christ claims, must therefore guide everyone toward being able to do this: hear the word of God and act on it. How does the Church do this? The way a mother does:

- By giving birth, feeding, and empowering her children
- By healing and mending the wounds of her children
- By preparing her children for their mission in life

This is what we are going to see in the Church's seven sacraments.

- They are actions of a mother—the Church—caring for her children.
- They are also actions that come directly from what the Church is in Christ: "a sign and instrument . . . of communion with God and of the unity of the entire human race" (LG 1).

3rd Movement – Closing Prayer

Pray "Hail, Holy Queen" (available in online resource under "Prayers").

chapter twenty-three

Becoming Christ's Body: Baptism, Eucharist, Confirmation

Overview

A Look from Above

Following the introduction to the Church through its mystery and motherhood (22), the final mini-unit of this journey leads us to the Church's sacraments. Three lessons are devoted to the sacraments, with different sacraments grouped together according to what they share in common. The first lesson (23) treats the sacraments of initiation, the second (24) the sacraments of healing, and the third (25) the sacraments at the service of communion. In each case, we must bear in mind what the Church is as the sacrament, in Christ, of the communion with God and the unity of the human race. We will therefore work to apprehend the sacraments as instruments of unity in which and by which the Church is what the Church is called to be: a sign and instrument of communion.

A Closer Look

This first session in this final mini-unit treats the sacraments of initiation: baptism, confirmation, and Eucharist. Baptism and confirmation have of course drawn our attention before, beginning all the way back in the very first lesson and at several other times throughout. As we will see, the main point in the presentation of baptism here is to see both how this sacrament brings a new member into the Church and how every celebration of this sacrament is itself the work of the entire

Church. With confirmation, we will emphasize how the mission of the Church is impressed upon the *confirmandi*—a mission that is all about fostering communion with God and the unity of the human race. Finally, we will contemplate how the Eucharist is both the gift and task of communion, so that in each Eucharist we are divinely called to "become what we receive."

1st Movement – Holy Conversation

1. Prayer
   Angelus recommended

2. Journaling (approximately 7–10 minutes)

   Prompts:
   - Write directly to the Lord. Ask him how he intends for you to change or grow as you become a fully initiated member of the Church. Tell the Lord your thoughts, your hopes, and even your uncertainties.
   - Reflect on a Catholic that you admire, preferably someone you know. Why do you admire them?

3. Conversation (and Meal)

   Prompt: Share about a Catholic you admire and tell why you admire them.

2nd Movement – Lesson

1. Review of Previous Session

   To Teach (briefly, presenting again the final summary from last session): The Church, as mother to all whom Christ claims, must therefore guide everyone toward being able to do this: hear the word of God and act on it. How does the Church do this? The way a mother does:
   - By giving birth, feeding, and empowering her children
   - By healing and mending the wounds of her children
   - By preparing her children for their mission in life

   This is what we are going to see in the Church's seven sacraments.
   - They are actions of a mother—the Church—caring for her children.
   - They are also actions that come directly from what the Church is in Christ: "a sign and instrument . . . of communion with God and of the unity of the entire human race" (LG 1).

2. Introduction to Three Sessions on the Sacraments

Setup of Sessions:
The Church provides seven sacraments. While all seven relate to and mingle with each of the others, it is also true that different ones are related to each other in different ways. We are going to consider the sacraments in three groups, as they are presented in the *Catechism of the Catholic Church.*

- This session: "Sacraments of Initiation," which are baptism, confirmation, and Eucharist. We are going to think about how these form us into Christ's body.
- Next session: "Sacraments of Healing," which are penance and the anointing of the sick. We are going to think about how these heal us as members of the same body.
- Final session: "Sacraments at the Service of Communion," which are matrimony and holy orders. We are going to think about how the mission of the Church is made present in these two.

3. Baptism

Large Group Exercise:
Present a photograph of a baptism. It would be preferable if this photo was from the parish (or one of the parishes) of the group members. The ideal photo will show the person being baptized, the priest (or deacon), and others gathered around the font. See the description of the baptism in the corresponding chapter of part 1 (chap. 23): the more the photo resembles that description, the better.

Large Group Discussion: Ask group members to describe what is happening in the photo. Ask them to describe what has just happened prior to this photo being taken, and what happened afterwards.

Points to Emphasize: Remember what we discussed in the very first session: how there is a minor exorcism (saying "no" to Satan), then a profession of faith (saying "yes" to the Father, Son, and Holy Spirit), and finally the immersion.

Question for the Group: What is happening to the child in this sacrament (or adult being baptized)?

Key Answer: This child/person is becoming a Christian and being brought *into the body* of the Church. They are being "in-corporated" (*corpus* being Latin for "body").

Question for the Group: What is happening to the Church in this sacrament?

Key Answer: This and every baptism is the work of the *whole* Church. Those who are present (parents, godparents, friends, family, minister, parishioners) represent the entire Church. The Church claims this person in the name of Christ, and the Church makes room for this person in its own body. Every baptism is therefore "con-corporation"—that is, done *with the (whole) body* of the Church.

Takeaways:

- Every baptism is the "incorporation" of a new member.
- Every baptism is the "concorporation" of the whole Church (something the *whole Church* does).
- By the sacrament of baptism, the Church—as mother—gives birth to a new child in Christ.

4. Confirmation

Question for the Group: Think back to St. Paul. How did his conversion ultimately benefit other people, besides himself?

Main Points to Highlight:

- In his conversion, Paul was separated from his old way and initiated into "the Way"—the way of Christ.
- In his ongoing transformation, Paul himself became a source of goodness for others, especially by his witness, preaching, healing, and prayer for others.
- We should think of baptism in connection with Paul's conversion, and confirmation in connection with being made into a source of goodness.

To Teach:
In confirmation, baptized Christians receive the mission of the Church as their own mission.

- The mission of the Church includes proclaiming the gospel in word and deed, responding to suffering and healing wounds whether physical or spiritual, and offering others charity, which is the love of Christ in the Spirit.
- The confirmed Catholic is anointed (with oils) and shares in Christ's own anointing. God the Father anointed Christ with the Holy Spirit and his mission of preaching, healing, and charity began.

Takeaways:
The confirmed Catholic shares fully and personally in the mission of the Church.

- The Holy Spirit who comes upon the *confirmandi* in confirmation is the same Spirit that unites the Father and the Son.

- The confirmed Catholic is commissioned to become a source of goodness for others.
- Confirmation is as much about *other people's good* as it is about the good of the one who has been confirmed.

5. Eucharist

To Teach:
The Eucharist is the third sacrament of initiation and "The holy Eucharist completes Christian initiation" (CCC 1322). For adults who enter the Church (RCIA), Eucharist follows baptism and confirmation. For those baptized as infants/children, Eucharist typically precedes confirmation.

Regardless of the order, a Christian is "fully initiated"—meaning they are full members of the Church—when they receive these three sacraments.

The Eucharist, though, is the "source and summit of the Christian life" (CCC 1324, quoting LG 11)—it is the sacrament at the heart of the Church.

In the Eucharist, Christ gives his body and blood to his Church and in receiving this gift the members of the Church become one in *his* body.

Key Point: Christ's body is given to us so we might become Christ's body.

To Teach (Some technical "stuff" to help us understand the mystery of the Eucharist):
There are three "dimensions" or "senses" to the Eucharist:

- *Sacramentum tantum* (or "the sign itself"). The sign itself is the bread and wine. Only bread and wine can be the signs of the Eucharist.
- *Sacramentum et res* (or "sign and reality"). The sign and reality is the body and blood of Christ. His body and blood are the true signs of the Father's love for the world *and* his body and blood make that love present. You cannot separate the Father's love from Christ's body and blood, nor separate Christ's body and blood from the Father's love.
- *Res tantum* (or "reality itself). The reality itself is the fruit of this sacrament—that is, what the sacrament brings about. The reality is God's peace, God's charity, which is to become *our* peace and *our* charity. In other words, we are meant to "become what we receive."

When we call the Eucharist "Communion," this "communion" is both a gift and a task.

- It is the gift of God's "communion" given to us in Christ by the Holy Spirit.
- It is the task (or responsibility) to become this "communion" in the world. That means, Christians living in unity with one another and

exercising charity . . . *and* it means becoming instruments of that unity in the world, *for others.*

Read Together: Two sermons from St. Augustine on the Eucharist (see handout in online resource)

Main Points to Highlight:

- Bread is the appropriate *sign* for the Eucharist because just as many grains are baked into one loaf, so the many members are made into one body in the Eucharist.
- Wine is the appropriate *sign* for the Eucharist because just as the juice from many grapes mingles together to make wine, so the lives of many members are brought together and transformed in the Eucharist.
- "Unity, devotion, charity!" is the *res tantum*—the "reality itself" that this sacrament brings about.
- This gift of the Eucharist is also a task: "be then what you see and receive what you are."

6. Concluding Points

Key Takeaway 1: Each of the three sacraments of initiation has to do with *the individual member* and *with others.* Every sacrament is social in character, just as every sacrament is personal in character.

- Baptism: a new member is *incorporated* and the whole Church is active in each baptism (*concorporation*).
- Confirmation: the confirmed Catholic shares in the mission of the Church; thus, the confirmed Catholic is to become a source of goodness *for others.*
- Eucharist: to receive the gift of communion in Christ means to share life in communion with others.

Key Takeaway 2: A Christian who has received these three sacraments is a *fully initiated* Christian.

3rd Movement – Closing Prayer

Offer a prayer of thanksgiving for the prayer of Jesus, which he prayed to the Father on the night before he died. In reading his prayer—from John 17:20-26—let us seek to dedicate ourselves anew to his prayer for our good and the good of all the Church.

chapter twenty-four

Healed as Members: Penance and Anointing of the Sick

Overview

A Look from Above

We are in the middle of the final three-session mini-unit of our journey. In the previous session (23), we explored the sacraments of initiation: baptism, confirmation, and Eucharist. In the next session (25), we will attend to the sacraments at the service of communion: matrimony and holy orders. In this middle session, we focus on the sacraments of healing: penance and the anointing of the sick. With the sacraments, we are broadening our imaginations in order to see each and all of them as both deeply personal (from the person of Christ through the Church to particular persons) and fundamentally social (concerning the whole Church at once: each member in the whole body of the Church, in union with Christ, the head of the body). The social dimension is, more often than not, the one that is neglected in both the religious imagination and in devotion; therefore, a strong emphasis is being placed on the social dimension of the sacraments.

A Closer Look

This second session in this final mini-unit treats the sacraments of healing: penance and the anointing of the sick. While highlighting that Christ heals sinful members as well as sick and suffering members, respectively, through these sacraments, we will place an additional emphasis on how the Church as a whole bears the sins and the sicknesses of each of its members in order to seek the healing of the whole body. Through the sacraments, the Church makes present the reality about which St. Paul preached when he said that, "If one member suffers, all suffer together; if one member is honored, all rejoice together" (1 Cor 12:26, RSV).

1st Movement – Holy Conversation

1. Prayer

   Angelus recommended

2. Journaling (approximately 7–10 minutes)

   Prompts:

   - Write directly to the Lord: "Dear Jesus . . . " Share with him something about your own burdens, or illness, or fear or doubt. Ask him for strength and healing.
   - You might also share with the Lord your concern for someone else who is suffering in some way.

3. Conversation (and Meal)

   Prompt: Share with each other someone that you want to or ought to keep in prayer, whether for that person's health, healing, peace, faith, or general well-being.

2nd Movement – Lesson

1. Review of Previous Two Sessions

   To Teach (briefly):

   - The Church itself is a sacrament, in Christ—that is, a sign and instrument of communion with God and the unity of the human race.
   - The sacraments are the Church at work: the identity and mission of the Church are made present in the sacraments.
   - The Church births, strengthens, teaches, and heals as a mother for all.
   - The sacraments of initiation include baptism, confirmation, and Eucharist (possibly review the final summary from the last lesson).

2. Introduction to the Sacraments of Healing

   To Teach:

   The Church names two of its seven sacraments specifically as sacraments of healing: penance and anointing of the sick.

- Each of these sacraments heals members of the Church precisely *as members* of a living body: the Body of Christ.
- Like all sacraments, these sacraments are the work of Christ and the work of the whole Church.

3. Penance

A. The Vine and the Branches

Read Together: John 15:1-6, which presents the words of Jesus to his disciples.

Question for the Group: What is the single most important thing for branches if they are to have life?

Answer: To be connected to the vine.

- Life is only possible for a branch if it is connected to a vine; if a branch is not connected to the vine, it withers and dies.
- Furthermore, if a branch has died on its own while still visibly connected to a vine, that branch is cut off.

Question for the Group: What is Jesus teaching his disciples about themselves—that is, about their own life and well-being?

Answer: Their life and well-being depend on their connection to him, because he is the vine and they are the branches.

Question for the Group: How can we use this imagery Jesus provides to think about sin and its effects?

Key Answer: Sins either weaken or sever the connection that disciples have to Jesus—i.e., by sin, the branches loosen or lose their vital connection to the vine.

- "Venial sins" are a weakening of a disciple's connection to Christ by putting other things before Christ and loving those things in the wrong way. Venial sins weaken disciples' capacity to love and live in charity.
- "Mortal sins" break a disciple's connection to Christ by willfully and intentionally acting against God, especially through the breaking of one or more of the Ten Commandments. So long as a mortal sin remains, one cannot live in charity.
- (For more on "venial" and "mortal" sins, see 1854–64 of the *Catechism.*)

Present: Images of branches grafted on to a vine (best to look for images that show the vine split to make room for the branches, as well as images where the branches and the vine have been bandaged together—see examples in online resource).

To Teach:

A branch that has been cut off from the vine can receive life again by being reinserted into a vine. This is a horticultural technique known as "grafting." The branch that did not have a life source receives a life source by being connected to the vine.

Question for the Group: This is clearly good news for the branch, but what does this mean for the *vine*?

Key Answer: The vine has to be opened up—that is, split open—in order to make room for the once-separated branch. The vine is therefore *wounded* so that the branch can have new life.

Takeaways:

- When a vine is split and a branch inserted, the vine and the branch now grow together as one.
- When Jesus speaks of himself as the vine and his disciples as branches, this form of healing or new life is included.
- Notice: Jesus (the vine) is wounded (his side is opened up) to make room for the cut-off branches to receive life in him.
- This also means that the Church—Christ's body—is wounded (opened up) so that sinful members can receive life again and the whole Church grow as one.
- This is a powerful image of the sacrament of penance.

Additional Option: Contemplate icons of Jesus and his disciples as the vine and the branches, or even something as complex as the Apse of the Basilica of San Clemente in Rome (easily searchable online—see examples in online resource).

B. Who Can Forgive Sins? (consider asking this as a rhetorical question)

Read Together: Mark 2:5-7, where the scribes argue that only God can forgive sins, and then read John 20:21-23, where Jesus gives his apostles the power to forgive sins (see online resource).

Questions for the Group: What is potentially troubling about what is being said here? What is the significance of all this?

To Teach:

The scribes are right: only God can forgive sins. As Christians, we believe that Jesus is who he shows himself to be as the Son of God, so he himself has the power to forgive sins. The apostles are clearly *not* God, but Jesus gives them the power to forgive sins—that is the *real* problem here.

- Christ gives his Church the power to forgive sins *in his name.*
- Christ makes his Church—as his body—into an agent of his mercy and not just a recipient of his mercy.
- In the sacrament of penance, the priest acts *in persona Christi* (that is, "in the person of Christ") to forgive sins.
- In the sacrament of penance, the priest also acts *in persona Ecclesiae* (that is, "in the person of the Church") to forgive sins.
- In this act of forgiveness, both Christ and his Church are "split open" or wounded in love to make room for the sinful member to be healed.

Read Together: The words of absolution from the Rite of Penance (see online resource).

Main Point to Highlight: The priest says "I absolve you," showing that the Church accepts and exercises the power to forgive sins that Christ gave to his apostles.

Final Takeaway: Christ gives the Church the power to suffer for sinful members just as he has suffered for sinners, so that we may be healed as one. (Notice how beautiful it is that the Church has the power to suffer for the life and salvation of all.)

4. Anointing of the Sick

Transition Point: Penance has to do with the healing from sin, whereas anointing of the sick has more to do with the healing from sickness and suffering.

Read Together: Psalm 139 (see online resource).

Main Points to Highlight:

- The psalmist confesses that God knows us from our highest of highs to our lowest of lows, even to "Sheol," which is the land of nonexistence (like being totally cut off).
- Nowhere is too far gone, too far away, too sick or suffering for God to lose sight of us.

Read Together: Section 1505 from the *Catechism* on anointing of the sick (see handout in online resource).

Main Points to Highlight:

- By his cross, Christ has united himself to all human suffering.
- All forms of human suffering are places of potential union with Christ, because Christ joins us in our suffering.

- This means that suffering can be meaningful because it can be a way to union with Christ.

To Teach:

- In much of the world both now and throughout time, those who are sick and dying have been cut off from participating in the life of the community. This was true of lepers in Jesus's time, AIDS patients in the 1980s and 1990s, and even of our sick and dying now who are often sequestered in hospitals and nursing homes.
- The sacrament of the anointing of the sick says to those who are sick, suffering, or even dying: "Even from here, the power of Christ meets you. *You* are claimed as members of Christ, united together in the Church. *Your* suffering is made meaningful because Christ suffers with you, and so does his Church."

Read Together: The meaning of the anointing of the sick from section 1503 in the *Catechism* (included in handout in online resource).

To Teach:

The effects of the sacrament of anointing of the sick include:

- Gifts of the Holy Spirit: peace, strength, courage (CCC 1520)
- Union with the passion of Christ (CCC 1521)
- Ecclesial grace—that is, being joined to the Church and claimed as a member (CCC 1522)
- Preparation for the final journey, to Christ in heaven (CCC 1523)

Takeaways:

- By the sacrament of anointing of the sick, the sickness, suffering, and dying of a particular member of the Church is shared by the whole Church and united to the passion of Christ.
- Both sacraments of healing unite the sinful or suffering member to the whole Church and heal all together in Christ.

3rd Movement – Closing Prayer

Pray "Lord Jesus, you have claimed us . . . " (available in online resource under "Prayers").

chapter twenty-five

At the Service of Communion: Marriage and Holy Orders

Overview

A Look from Above

We are at the end of the final three-session mini-unit and therefore the final session of our journey. In the previous two sessions, we explored the sacraments of initiation (23) and the sacraments of healing (24). Throughout this final turn, we have been considering the sacraments as both deeply personal and fundamentally social, as we will continue to do in this session.

A Closer Look

This third session in this final mini-unit treats the sacraments at the service of communion: marriage and holy orders. Two questions will guide our reflection on each of these two sacraments: Whom does the sacrament serve? and What is the person who receives the sacrament a sign of? In addressing these questions with assistance from the *Catechism,* we will discover how both sacraments are primarily aimed at building up communion with God and the unity of the human race.

1st Movement – Holy Conversation

1. Prayer
   Angelus recommended

2. Journaling (approximately 7–10 minutes)

   Prompts:
   - Write about something you have learned this year that is important to you.
   - Write about something you want to learn more about.
   - Write a prayer directly to the Lord to ask for his guidance in your continued preparation and formation.

3. Conversation (and Meal)

   Prompt: Share with each other something you have learned from this year that is important to you, and why it is important.

2nd Movement – Lesson

1. Review of Previous Three Sessions

   To Teach (briefly):
   - The Church itself is a sacrament, in Christ—that is, a sign and instrument of communion with God and the unity of the human race.
   - The sacraments are the Church at work: the identity and mission of the Church are made present in the sacraments.
   - The Church births, strengthens, teaches, and heals as a mother for all.
   - The sacraments of initiation—baptism, confirmation, Eucharist—form us into Christ's body.
   - The sacraments of healing—penance and anointing of the sick—heal us as members of Christ's body.
   - The final two sacraments—marriage and holy orders—are sacraments at the service of communion.

2. Marriage

   Note: This session utilizes an exercise for Small Group Discussion, then Large Group Discussion

   Questions for Small Groups (two to four members, possibly jot down responses):
   - Whom does marriage serve? That is, for whose good is it?
   - What is a married couple—husband and wife—a sign of?

   Share Responses in Large Group (best to collect responses on white board or poster board, etc.)

A. Whom does Marriage Serve? For Whose Good Is It?

Read Together: Section 1534 from the *Catechism* (see handout in online resource).

Main Points to Highlight:

- Marriage, like holy orders, does not make someone a "fuller" member of the Church since full membership is complete in the sacraments of initiation. Instead, this sacrament confers a "particular mission."
- The mission of marriage is a mission to serve others and thereby build up communion, in two essential ways:
  - (i) By giving life—having and raising children: (a) whether through biological reproduction and parenting; (b) or through adoption and fostering; (c) or through godparenting, mentoring, and the like.
  - (ii) By providing stability and charity in the world: (a) Husband and wife are faithful to each other and provide a safe haven for each other and, through their union, to others in a world that is otherwise often unreliable. (b) Marriage is in fact based on the consent of the spouses to give themselves to each other in a bond that is indissoluble (faithfulness) and open to new life (fruitfulness). (See CCC 1662, 1664.)

B. What Is A Married Couple—Husband and Wife—A Sign Of?

To Teach:

- The union of husband and wife is primarily a sign of *God's* fidelity to us. As God is steadfast in his care for us, so husband and wife seek to be steadfast in their care for each other.
- The first image of this marital union is God and Israel, as expressed all throughout the Old Testament.
- The fulfillment of this image is Christ and the Church. Christ is the sign and reality (*sacramentum et res*) of God's fidelity to us.
- What is true of the mission of those who receive the sacrament of matrimony is first of all true of the mystery of the Church.
  - (i) By giving life: the husband and wife give life just as the Church gives life to the world through its evangelizing mission.
  - (ii) By providing stability and charity: the husband and wife create stability and offer charity just as the Church clings to the memory of Christ's passion, death, and resurrection, and remains vigilant in its hope for his coming again at the end of time. The Church's memory and hope *are* stability that make love possible in a world that is fickle and forgetful.

Important Clarification: Human beings are created male and female in order to point to (as signs of) the deeper reality of Christ and his Church.

- This does *not* mean that the man is Christ and the woman is the Church, or that the man is God and the woman is humanity.
- Instead, the *relationship* between man and woman (called to be faithful and fruitful) signifies and makes present the mystery of Christ's relationship to his Church.
- In the union of man and woman, two who are not the same are made one, as an image of the union of God with humanity in the person of Christ.
- As Christ in union with his Church bears fruit and nourishes life, so are man and woman called to bear fruit and nourish life.

3. Holy Orders

Questions for Small Groups (two to four members, possibly jot down responses):

- Whom does ordination serve? That is, for whose good is it?
- What is an ordained man a sign of?

Share Responses in Large Group (best to collect responses on white board or poster board, etc.)

A. What Is An Ordained Man A Sign Of? (second question first)

To Teach:

- The ordained man is a sign of Christ, the bridegroom (and the Church is Christ's bride).
- The ordained man is a sign of Christ, the head of the body (and the Church is to become the body of Christ).
- The ordained man represents Christ and makes Christ present.
- God blesses and calls this *person*, not just his works. An ordained man is changed by this sacrament (i.e., it is not simply about his functions).

Question for the Group: What are some of the clearest times in which a priest, for example, represents Christ and makes him present?

Possible Answers:

- While offering the words of institution at the Eucharist: "This is my body" and "This is my blood" and "Do this is remembrance of me."
- While offering absolution during penance: "I absolve you . . . "

B. Whom Does Ordination Serve? For Whose Good Is It?

To Teach:

- Ordination is primarily for *our* good—that is, the good of the Church.
  - (i) The "sacramental priesthood" which is conferred in holy orders serves the "common priesthood" of all the baptized.
  - (ii) Remember, "all of the faithful must willingly hear the word of God and carry out his will by what they do" (LG 42). The sacramental priesthood serves the faithful by supporting and nourishing them in this mission.
- By holy orders, the ordained man is blessed and called to serve and strengthen the union of the faithful to Christ. The ordained man supports and nourishes the marriage of Christ to his Church.
- The particular mission of the ordained serves the common mission of the Church: the mission to love God and neighbor; to be and build communion.

Read Together (again): Section 1534 from the *Catechism* (on handout from online resource).

4. Reflecting on the Sacraments at the Service of Communion

Final Takeaways:

- Marriage and holy orders are sacraments at the service of the communion of the Church.
- Marriage is ordered to bearing and nourishing new life, and providing stability and charity in the world.
- Holy orders is ordered to nourishing the union of Christ to his Church, and therefore of enabling the faithful to hear the word of God and act on it.

3rd Movement – Closing Prayer

Pray together Psalm 103, which sings of the Lord's faithfulness and kindness: *Bless the Lord, O my soul . . .*

Index

Abraham, 10, 118–19, 184, 208, 259, 263
Acts
2:42-47, 5–6, 7, 161
2:44, 132
6:8, 8
6:8-15, 166
6:10, 9
6:15, 9
7:2, 10
7:54-60, 166–67
7:55-56, 10
7:58, 10, 167
8:1, 10, 167
8:1-3, 167
8:3, 10
9:1, 94, 243
9:1-2, 12
9:1-9, 169–70
9:3, 249
9:4-7, 238
9:9, 249
9:10, 235
9:10-20, 170–71
9:17, 14, 244
9:18-19, 14
9:19, 127
9:20, 14, 243
10:38, 128
20:24, 24
22:3-5, 11, 167
26:9-11, 11, 167
Advent, 54, 55–56, 58, 61–63, 156, 201–4, 205–9, 213
Ananias: relationship with Paul, 14, 15, 18, 24, 112, 127, 143, 168, 170, 171, 172, 177, 212
Angelus as opening prayer in Catholic Formation Group sessions, 153, 160, 162, 169, 172, 178, 182, 188, 192, 198, 202, 206, 211, 216, 220, 238, 243, 249, 255, 263, 268, 274, 279
anger, 11, 12–13, 14, 16, 17, 18
Annunciation, 115–17, 123, 160, 254, 256–57, 262, 263, 265
anointing of the sick, 132, 135–37, 269, 274–75, 277–78, 280
Apostles' Creed, 89, 91
Aquila, 21–22, 23
Assyrian Empire, 92, 93, 234
attentiveness, 69, 82, 96n., 114, 241, 250–51, 256
role in chastity, 94–95, 96–103, 224, 231, 235, 237–38, 239, 242–43, 248
Augustine, St.: on the Eucharist, 129–30, 272

Babylonian Empire, 59–61, 67, 92–93, 206–8, 234
baptism, 64, 141, 159, 172, 209
  as concorporation of whole Church, 126–27, 138, 269–70, 272
  exorcism in, 211, 269
  immersion in, 4, 5, 63, 130, 161, 165, 169, 211, 269
  as incorporation of new member of the Church, 126–27, 138, 269–70, 272
  of Jesus Christ, 29–33, 31n.1, 33n., 57, 182, 183, 184, 185, 187, 188, 198
  of Paul, 143, 171, 173, 177
  profession of faith in, 4–5, 161, 165, 169, 211, 269
  relationship to confirmation, 6–7, 63, 128, 165, 270
  renunciation of sin in, 4, 161, 165, 169
  as sacrament of initiation, 4, 5, 125–26, 128, 138, 267–68, 271, 272, 273, 274, 280
  and sin, 30–31, 31n.1
Beatitudes, 50–51, 50n., 61, 181, 192, 197–200, 202, 209
Benedict of Nursia, St., 102
Benedict XVI
  on baptism of Jesus, 31n.1
  on name of Jesus, 40–41
"Be Thou My Vision," 253

Cain and Abel, 105n.
Campo, Joe, 110–11, 114
Catechism of the Catholic Church
  on anointing the sick, 277, 278
  on baptism, 125
  on confirmation, 126
  on the Eucharist, 126, 128, 271
  on faith, 127, 136
  and four pillars of Christian life, 6n.
  on God's plan, 3, 90, 143, 144
  on holy orders, 139, 141, 279
  on male and female, 75
  on marriage, 75, 279, 281
  on matrimony, 139, 140
  on the sacraments, 269
  on sacraments of healing, 137
  on senses of Scripture, 69n.4
  on sharing God's life, 3, 143
  on suffering of Jesus, 136
Catherine of Siena, St.: "Prayer before the Eucharist," 48, 196
Catholic Church, 4, 5, 25, 28, 52, 89
  as Body of Christ, 7, 64, 124, 125–27, 129–30, 131, 132, 137, 271, 274, 276, 277, 280, 282
  Catholic faith as holistic, 144, 210
  communion in, 132, 135, 137, 138, 139, 140, 142, 143–44, 264–65
  and forgiveness of sins, 134–35
  and healing, 132
  and hope of Christ's return, 54, 140, 281
  identity and mission of, 7, 122, 124, 125, 128, 129, 139, 140, 142, 144, 152, 157–58, 264–65, 268, 269, 270, 272, 274, 280, 281, 283
  as Marian, 124, 262, 265–66
  memory of Christ, 54, 62, 140, 281
  motherhood of the, 122, 123–24, 127, 131, 262–63, 265–66, 267, 268, 270, 274, 280
  mystery of, 122, 123, 124, 126, 262, 263–65, 267, 281
  as sacrament, 122, 123, 124, 129, 264, 266, 267, 274, 280

as sign and instrument of communion with God, 122, 123, 125, 129, 144, 264–65, 266, 267, 268, 274, 280
See also Catechism of the Catholic Church; sacraments; Second Vatican Council
Catholic Formation Group sessions, 98n., 104n., 147–58, 159–63
closing prayers in, 156, 160, 162, 163, 167, 171, 176, 180, 186, 191, 196, 200, 204, 209, 214, 218, 224, 230, 236, 241, 247, 253, 261, 266–67, 272, 278, 283
conversation and meal in, 152, 154–55, 160, 162, 163, 173, 179, 188, 193, 198, 202, 206, 211, 216, 220, 226, 232, 238, 243, 249, 255, 263, 268, 274, 280
journaling in, 153–54, 160, 162, 169, 172, 182, 188, 193, 198, 202, 206, 211, 213, 216, 220, 226, 232, 238, 243, 249, 255, 263, 268, 274, 280
opening prayers in, 153, 160, 162, 169, 172, 178, 182, 188, 193, 198, 202, 206, 211, 216, 220, 226, 232, 238, 243, 249, 255, 263, 268, 274, 279
parents of teenagers in, 157, 160, 162, 163, 179, 182
testimonies in, 155, 182, 187, 188, 193, 198, 209, 213, 220, 226, 232, 238, 243, 249
charity, 15, 18, 23, 48, 89, 129, 130, 138, 139–40, 271–72, 281, 283
in Christian way of life, 6, 7, 16, 63, 161, 162, 171, 212, 250
Holy Spirit as, 144
chastity, 64, 83n.3
and attentiveness, 94–95, 96–103, 224, 231, 235, 237–38, 239, 242–43, 248
of the ears, 95, 96–103, 231, 236, 237–41, 242, 243, 248, 249, 254, 255, 257–58, 263
of the eyes, 95, 110–14, 231, 236, 242, 248–53, 254, 255, 257, 258–60, 263
as power, 94, 95, 248
of the tongue, 95, 104–9, 231, 236, 242–47, 248, 249, 254, 255, 257, 260–61, 263
as virtue, 95, 101, 109, 114, 116, 224, 235, 242, 248, 254–55, 257, 262, 263
Christian discipleship, 156, 213
as embodied by Mary, 115–21, 124, 143, 254–61, 262, 263
Christian way of life
becoming source of goodness for others, 6, 7, 8, 16–20, 63, 126–27, 143, 148, 157, 162, 165, 169, 212, 235, 255, 270, 271, 272
charity in, 6, 7, 16, 63, 161, 162, 171, 212, 250
costliness of, 22–23
in early Christian communities, 5–6, 7, 21–22, 23, 159, 161–62, 212
eucharistic fellowship in, 6, 7, 212
faith in, 6, 7, 13, 23, 28, 29
as gift, 3, 5, 6, 7, 14, 20
humility in, 14, 16–17, 18, 19–20, 29, 171
as lifelong practice, 7
mentoring in, 21–22, 157
prayer in, 6, 7, 13, 63, 161, 162, 212
role of communion in, 124, 128, 135, 138–42, 143–44, 212

as sharing in God's life, 3, 4, 5, 6–7, 20, 63, 64, 90, 143, 144
skin in the game required by, 22–23
transformation in, 6, 7, 8, 15, 23, 24
communication, 81, 82, 85–86, 90, 91, 228
communion
in Catholic Church, 132, 135, 137, 138, 139, 140, 142, 143–44, 264–65
Eucharist as gift of, 128–29, 271–72
with God, 3, 122, 123, 124, 125, 128, 129, 144, 264–65, 266, 267, 268, 274, 280
and Jesus Christ, 3, 64, 125, 128, 129, 130, 134, 137, 143, 264–65
as meaning of life, 152
role in Christian way of life, 124, 128, 135, 138–42, 143–44, 212
sacraments in service of, 124, 138–42, 267, 269, 273, 279–83
communion of saints, 7, 89, 127
confirmation, 127–28, 157, 159, 162, 163, 177, 179, 182, 212, 268, 270–71
relationship to baptism, 6–7, 63, 128, 165, 267, 270, 272
as sacrament of initiation, 125–26, 128, 131, 147–48, 160, 171, 269, 271, 273, 274, 280
1 Corinthians
1:24, 43, 192, 194, 195
1:25, 43
9:21-23, 20
12:26, 132, 274
15:3, 24, 179
15:3-10, 19, 175, 183, 212, 242, 244
2 Corinthians
5:17, 94
11:24-28, 174
11:30, 16, 174
12:2-5, 19
12:3-6, 174
12:7-9, 24
12:7-10, 174, 212, 248, 250
12:7b-10, 16
12:9, 47, 179, 195
counsel as gift of Holy Spirit, 91
COVID-19 pandemic, 150, 154
creating oneself, 66–67, 66n.
Creed, 89, 91

Daniel
8:15, 9
9:18, 102
9:21, 9
10:5-6, 9, 166
10:12, 9
David, king of Israel, 93, 234
death, 4, 91, 92, 105, 136
Decalogue, 104, 275
Delp, Fr. Alfred, 55–56, 202, 203, 205, 206
De Lubac, Henri, 125
Deuteronomy
6:4, 101
15:1-11, 113
Driscoll, Sean, 148

Easter Vigil, 128
Ebola, 136
Elijah, 33, 185
Elizabeth, 118, 119, 258–60, 263
Emmaus, 121
Enuma Elish, 67
Ephesians
4:17-32, 109

4:25-32, 247
5:25-33, 140
Eucharist, 128–31, 140, 161, 212, 268
Augustine on, 129–30, 272
as gift of communion, 128–29, 271, 272
prayer before, 48
res tantum/reality itself dimension, 129, 271, 272
as sacrament of initiation, 126, 128, 129, 138, 171, 267, 269, 271–72, 272, 273, 274, 280
sacramentum et res/sign and reality dimension, 129, 271
sacramentum tantum/the sign itself dimension, 129, 271, 272
words of institution, 141, 282
Eucharistic Adoration, 114, 152, 252–53
evangelical counsels, 83n.
Exodus
1:8, 36
2:23-25, 37, 189
3:1-15, 189
3:4-6, 37
3:7-8, 37
15:1-2, 39
15:1-3, 190
24:15, 33
33:9, 33
40:34, 33

faith, 21, 52, 148, 252
Catechism of the Catholic Church on, 127, 136
in Christian way of life, 6, 7, 13, 23, 28, 29
in Christ's identity, 181
as holistic, 144, 210
of Paul, 24, 175, 179, 183
profession of faith in baptism, 4–5, 165, 169, 211, 269
teaching regarding, 150, 151, 152–53, 163
testimonies of, 155, 157, 220, 226, 232
Favale, Abigail, 73n.
fear of the Lord as gift of Holy Spirit, 91
fortitude as gift of Holy Spirit, 91
foundational beliefs, 66–68
Fra Angelico's *The Annunciation*, 256–57, 260
Francis I
Evangelii Gaudium: The Joy of the Gospel, 19n.
on God's tenderness, 113
on Jesus, 26
on Paul, 19n., 26
Francis of Assisi, St.: "Peace Prayer," 52, 200

Gabriel, 9, 119, 160, 257
Galatians 2:20, 26
Genesis
1:1-3, 244
1:3, 104, 260
1:4, 108
1:6-7, 244
1:9, 244
1:10, 108
1:11, 244
1:12, 108
1:14-15, 244
1:18, 108
1:20, 244
1:21, 108
1:24, 244
1:25, 108
1:26, 104, 244
1:26-28, 244
1:27, 73, 222

1:27-28, 221
1:28, 68
1:29-30, 244
1:31, 108, 221
2:4-7, 216–17
2:4b-7, 68–69
2:7, 87, 90, 217, 227, 232
2:9, 82, 227
2:16-17, 76, 80–81, 222–23, 227
2:21-24, 70, 217, 222
2:22, 71
2:23, 71
2:24, 222
2:25, 75–76, 222, 226
3:1, 32, 75–77, 80, 105, 222, 223, 226, 227
3:2-3, 80–81, 227
3:4-5, 83, 228
3:6, 83
3:6-7, 228
3:7, 84
3:8-13, 84–85, 229
3:9, 85–86
3:12, 85
3:13, 85
3:22-23, 88
11:4, 105n.
18:11, 118–19, 259
18:14, 119, 259
Gianna Beretta Molla, St., 35, 186
God
as Creator, 3, 60, 67–72, 68n., 73–79, 84, 87–88, 90, 92, 93, 104, 108, 139, 144, 156, 215–18, 219–24, 225, 227, 231, 232, 234, 235, 244–45, 249, 254, 256, 260, 263
existence of, 38
as Father, 3, 7, 28–29, 30–31, 33, 39, 43, 45, 46, 52, 53, 89, 127, 129, 133, 134, 136, 143, 166, 184, 187, 188, 198, 212, 264–65, 270, 272
glory of, 10, 29, 34, 185
grace of, 8, 16, 18, 20, 24, 35, 47, 79, 144, 165, 174, 175, 179, 260
knowledge of human beings, 135–36
as listening attentively, 102–3
love for, 42, 142
mercy of, 86, 88, 119, 121, 134, 233, 260, 263
name of, 37–41, 43, 52, 64, 187, 188–91, 192, 193, 195, 198, 212
power of, 43–44, 47–48, 49–51, 63, 64, 121, 181, 187, 192, 194, 195–96, 196, 197, 198–200, 201, 202, 204, 205, 206, 207, 208, 213, 222
as Triune, 61, 63, 64
wisdom of, 43–44, 49, 51, 60, 64, 91, 181, 187, 192, 194, 195, 196, 197, 198, 200, 201, 206, 207, 213
Word of, 104, 119, 120, 124, 244, 249
God's life, sharing in, 4, 5, 6–7, 20, 63, 64
as God's plan, 3, 90, 143, 144

"Hail, Holy Queen" prayer, 266
Hail Mary prayer, 230, 261
Halpin, Colleen, 118n.
Hamilton, 22
healing of the sick, 132, 135–37
HIV/AIDS, 136, 278
holy orders, 138, 141–42, 269, 273, 279, 280, 282–83
Holy Spirit, 127, 128, 130, 184, 264–65
belief in, 5, 89

as breath of life, 89, 94, 232, 238
as charity, 144
descent of, 7, 183
gifts of, 3, 5, 64, 89–93, 95, 116, 137, 156, 158, 213, 233–36, 237, 238, 239, 241, 254, 256, 278
and Jesus Christ, 90–91, 131, 134, 158, 231–32, 235, 237, 256, 270
and Mary, 115, 121
prayer to, 95
as proceeding from Father and Son, 89
human beings
as created in image of God, 48, 68, 70, 73, 75, 78, 104–5, 221, 222, 225, 244, 246
creation of, 48, 68–72, 73–79, 87–88, 90, 92, 93, 104–5, 139, 144, 213, 215–18, 219–24, 227, 231, 232, 234, 235, 244, 246, 254, 256, 282
as creatures of harmony, 69–70, 72, 73, 75, 94, 217, 218, 219, 220, 225, 256
freedom of, 82
God's knowledge of, 135–36
male and female, 64, 70–72, 73–79, 73n., 74n., 139, 213, 215, 217–18, 219–24, 225, 227, 254, 282
procreative character of, 74–75, 74n., 78, 139, 140, 218, 220, 221–22, 225, 226, 281, 283
as union of body and soul, 70, 73, 217, 219
unitive character of, 74, 78, 139, 140, 220, 221, 222, 224, 225, 226
humility, 14, 16–17, 18, 19–20, 29, 171
intimacy, 74, 84, 85, 94–95, 220, 222, 223, 229, 231, 249, 251
and transparency, 77–78, 80, 224
Irenaeus of Lyons, St., 70, 217
Isaiah
11:1-3, 92, 234
37:17, 102
40:1-2, 60
40:3-4, 32
40:3-5, 203
40:6-7, 60
40:9-10, 60
40:11, 60
40:15-17, 60
40:27-28, 60
50:4, 109, 246
53:11-12, 31
Israel
and Babylon, 59–61, 67–68, 92–93, 206–8
and Jesus, 184–85
and Rome, 61, 208
twelve tribes of, 235

James
3:3-5, 108, 109, 245
3:9-10, 108, 109, 245
James and John, sons of Zebedee, 47
Jerome, St., 206
Jerusalem community, 5–6, 7
Jesse, 234
Jesus Christ
adoption in, 3, 127
agony in the garden, 45–46, 49, 194
anointing of, 270
arrest of, 40, 191
baptism of, 29–33, 31n.1, 33n., 57, 182, 183, 184, 185, 187, 188, 198
Beatitudes, 50–51, 50n., 61, 181, 192, 197–200, 202, 209

as Bridegroom, 140, 141
and communion, 3, 64, 125, 128, 129, 130, 134, 137, 143, 264–65
crucifixion, 28, 29, 46–47, 50, 136, 167, 175, 194, 242, 277–78, 281
and death of Lazarus, 44–45, 50, 194
on the eyes, 112–13
as forgiving sins, 133–35, 137, 276–77
genealogy of, 33n., 184, 208
as gift of beatitude, 197, 213
as gift of God's life, 3
glory of, 166–67, 185
and God's glory, 10
grace of, 64, 94, 128, 237
and Holy Spirit, 90–91, 131, 134, 158, 231–32, 235, 237, 256, 270
humanity of, 7, 28, 29, 34
identity of, 25–26, 27, 28–33, 34, 35, 39–40, 51–52, 63–64, 123, 127, 128, 155, 178, 179–80, 181–86, 187–91, 192, 196, 197, 198, 200, 201, 209, 212, 213, 216, 226, 238
as Incarnation, 7, 41, 46–47, 86, 140, 143, 153, 160, 182
as the Lamb, 105
Last Supper, 194
Lord's Prayer, 156, 175, 180, 214, 218, 224
love of, 25–26
as loving, 26–27, 133
and men on road to Emmaus, 121
mercy of, 215
mission of, 127, 128
as mocked, 46–47, 48, 49, 50, 51, 194, 195, 196, 197, 198, 199, 213
as mystery, 25, 28, 29, 31, 34
name of, 39–41, 43, 52, 64, 181, 187, 190, 192, 193, 195, 198, 212
as new David, 93, 234
parable of the Wise and Foolish Maidens, 53
person and work of, 25–26, 27
and the Pharisees, 106–7, 108
as power of God, 43–44, 47–48, 49–51, 64, 187, 192, 194, 195–96, 197, 198–200, 213
on power of speech, 245
prayers to, 27, 35, 42, 48, 52
preparation for, 53–58, 64
resurrection of, 7, 9, 19–20, 31n.1, 90, 105, 134, 175, 235, 242, 281
and sacrament of holy orders, 141–42
and sacrament of marriage, 140, 281–82
and sacrament of matrimony, 140
as savior, 7, 8, 9–10, 17–18, 19–20, 39, 40–41, 61, 84, 94, 136, 196, 229, 254
Sermon on the Mount, 50n., 112–13
Sermon on the Plain, 50
as serving, 45, 47, 48, 49, 50, 51, 194, 195, 196, 197, 198, 199, 213
as siding with the lowly, 51, 199, 200, 205, 208–9, 213
as sign and reality of God's fidelity to us, 281
as Son of the Father, 28–29, 30–31, 33, 34, 35, 39, 43, 46, 52, 64, 89, 105, 133, 134, 143, 181–85, 187, 188, 192, 198, 212, 270, 276
and Stephen, 166–67, 169

as suffering, 45–46, 47, 48, 49, 50, 51, 194, 195, 196, 197, 198, 199, 213
temptation in desert, 32–33, 33n., 34, 83n., 185, 228
transfiguration of, 29, 33–35, 33n., 182, 185, 187, 188, 198
on the vine and its branches, 132–33, 135, 275–76
virginal conception of, 116
waiting for, 58, 59–62, 64
as walking on water, 39, 190
washing of disciples' feet by, 45, 49
as the way, the truth, and the life, 52, 64
as weeping, 45–46, 47, 48, 49, 50, 51, 194, 195, 196, 197, 198, 199, 213
as wisdom of God, 43–44, 49, 51, 64, 187, 192, 194, 196, 200, 213
as Word of God, 7, 41, 86, 105, 118, 121, 143
John
1:14, 41
3:30, 57, 204
6:16-21, 190
6:20-21, 39
8:23-24, 39
8:23-30, 190
8:28, 40
8:58, 40
11:25-26, 45
11:28-35, 50, 194
11:32-35, 44
13:1, 45
13:1-14, 49, 194
13:3-5, 45
14:18, 122
15:1-5, 133
15:1-6, 275
15:9, 133
17:20-26, 272
17:21, 125, 143, 265
17:24, 143
18:1-8, 40, 191
19:25-27, 265
20:19-23, 90
20:20-22, 235
20:21, 134
20:21-23, 276
1 John, 2:16, 83
John the Baptist, 30, 55, 56–57, 58, 59, 61, 64, 183, 184, 202, 203, 204, 205, 206, 208, 213
John Vianney, St., 42, 191
Jonah 1:12, 31n.1
Joshua 24:23, 102

1 Kings 8:58-59, 102
knowledge as gift of Holy Spirit, 91
Kolbe, St. Maximillian, 114

Lent, 162
lepers, 136, 278
life everlasting, 4, 5, 89
listening, 116–18, 172, 213
chastity of the ears, 95, 96–103, 231, 236, 237–41, 242, 243, 248, 249, 254, 255, 257–58, 263
with the heart, 15, 18–19, 101, 102, 103, 173, 174–75, 237–38
"Litany of Humility," 171
"Litany of St. Stephen," 167
Lord's Prayer, 156, 175, 180, 214, 218, 224
love of neighbor, 142, 183
Luke
1:7, 118
1:12, 117
1:18, 117
1:26-38, 257

1:29, 117
1:32-35, 119
1:34, 117
1:35, 115
1:36-37, 258
1:37, 119
1:38, 260
1:39, 120
1:46-55, 119, 260
2:19, 118
2:35, 118
2:51, 118
3:1-2, 54–56, 202–3, 208
3:3, 30
3:4-5, 32
3:4-6, 56–57, 203
3:16, 57
3:21, 30
3:21-22, 29–30, 183
3:22, 33
3:23-38, 33n., 184, 208
4:1, 32
4:1-13, 83n., 228
4:2, 32–33
5:20, 252
6:20-22, 50
6:20-26, 199
6:24-26, 51
8:20-21, 257
8:21, 115, 254
9:28-36, 185
9:29, 33
9:33, 33
9:35, 33
9:37, 34
9:37-43, 185
9:42-43, 34
11:28, 115
22:29, 46
22:39, 45
22:39-46, 194
22:39-66, 49
22:42-44, 46
22:61-62, 252
23:2-3, 46
23:33-38, 50, 194
23:34, 167
23:35-38, 46
23:46, 167
24:13-35, 121
24:25, 121
24:26, 121
24:27, 121
24:33, 121

Magnificat, 119, 260, 263
"Maranatha!" prayer for Advent, 204, 209
Mark
2:5-7, 134, 276
6:50, 39
8:29, 52
9:9, 34
9:24, 214
10:21, 252
10:35-45, 195
10:37, 47
10:38, 47
10:41, 47
10:42-45, 47
16:15, 122
marriage, 74–75, 78, 138–40, 142, 218, 224, 269, 273, 280–82, 283
Catechism of the Catholic Church on, 75, 279, 281
and Jesus Christ, 140, 281–82
Mary, the Blessed Virgin, 61, 64
and Advent, 205, 208
at Annunciation, 115–17, 123, 160, 254, 256–57, 262, 263, 265
chastity of, 256, 257, 263
Christian discipleship embodied by, 115–21, 124, 143, 254–61, 262, 263

Church as Marian, 124, 262, 265–66
Magnificat of, 119, 260, 263
motherhood of, 123–24, 262–63, 266
Matthew
5:3-11, 50n.
6:22-23, 113
12:33, 106
12:34-37, 106, 245
17:2, 9
17:9, 34
24:36, 53
25:10, 54
25:31-46, 200
25:40, 51
25:45, 51
28:3, 9
Mattison, Bill, 148, 150
McLuhan, Marshall: on the medium as the message, 149
memory, 81–82, 91, 228
of the Church, 54, 62, 140, 281
of Mary, 118, 119
of Paul, 10, 17–18, 24, 167, 174, 250
mentoring, 21–22, 157
Moses, 33, 36–39, 43, 101, 185, 188, 189

Noah, 105n.
Noem, Stacey, 98n.

obedience, 83n.3

Pagliarini, Anthony, 135n.
Palmer, Michael, 104n.
Patterson, Kaitlyn, 100, 101
Paul, Apostle of Christ, 21–24, 177, 178–80
Paul, St., 156, 231, 274
baptism of, 143, 171, 173, 177
conversion of, 8, 10, 12–15, 24, 63, 65, 94, 127, 164, 166, 167, 168–71, 172, 177, 178, 179, 212, 235, 238, 243, 249–50, 270
on the Eucharist, 130
faith of, 24, 175, 179, 183
humility of, 14, 16, 19, 20, 171
on identity of Jesus, 28–29
on Jesus as power and wisdom of God, 43, 44, 192, 194, 195, 198
martyrdom of, 178, 179
memory of, 10, 17–18, 24, 167, 174, 250
as mentor to Luke, 21
relationship with Ananias, 14, 15, 18, 20, 112, 127, 143, 168, 170, 171, 172, 177, 212, 244
as source of goodness, 16–20, 127–28, 143, 164, 172–76, 177, 235, 270
and Stephen's martyrdom, 8–11, 13, 19, 20, 24, 166–67, 168, 177, 178, 212
on suffering, 132, 137
thorn in flesh of, 16, 17, 24, 47, 174
transformation of, 15, 16–20, 63, 65, 94, 95, 97, 112, 127, 143, 164, 166, 168, 171, 172–76, 177, 178, 179, 212, 216, 235, 237, 238, 242, 243–44, 248, 249, 250, 270
and virtue of chastity, 235
witness to Christ, 24, 25, 178, 179, 181, 183, 212
on the world, 113–14
penance, 132–35, 137, 138, 141, 269, 274–77, 280, 282
Peter the Apostle, 20, 24, 33–34, 185, 252

Pharisees, 106–7, 108
Philippians
  1:3-5, 18, 237, 238
  1:3-9, 175, 212
  1:7, 97, 103, 179
  1:7-9, 18, 237, 238
  2:6-11, 28–29, 32, 34, 49
piety as gift of Holy Spirit, 91
pornography, 110–11, 248–49
poverty, 83n.
power
  of chastity, 94, 95, 248
  of God, 43–44, 47–48, 49–51, 63, 64, 121, 181, 187, 192, 194, 195–96, 197, 198–200, 201, 202, 204, 205, 206, 207, 208, 213, 222
  Paul on Jesus as power and wisdom of God, 43, 44, 192, 194, 195, 198
  of the world, 43, 47, 49, 50–51, 58, 61, 63, 119, 193–95, 196, 197, 200, 201, 202, 204, 205, 206, 207, 208, 213
Prayer for Jesus to give us the Spirit, 241
"Prayer for the Intercession of St. Paul," 176
Prayer to the Holy Spirit, 236
Priscilla, 21–22, 23
procreation, 74–75, 78, 139, 218, 220, 221–22, 225, 226, 281, 283
Promised Land, 32, 34, 92, 185
Proverbs
  4:20, 102
  18:21, 104, 105, 244, 245
  22:17, 102
Psalms
  17:6, 102
  40:1, 103
  78:1, 102
  103, 283
  116:1-2, 103
  139, 277
  139:1-3, 135
  139:7-10, 135

rage, 11, 12–13, 14, 16, 17, 18
resurrection of the body, 5, 89
Revelation 12, 105
Rite of Christian Initiation of Adults (RCIA), 7, 147, 150, 159, 160, 161, 162, 182, 271
Romans
  4:17, 74
  12:1, 25
  12:2, 113
Rome community, 21–22, 23

Sabbath, 68
sacraments, 156, 213, 254, 262, 266, 268
  of healing, 124, 132–37, 138, 267, 269, 273–78, 279, 280
  of initiation, 4, 5, 124, 125–31, 138, 139, 147, 158, 160, 171, 267, 269–72, 273, 274, 279, 280, 281
  as instruments of unity, 125
  mystery of the, 64, 126, 127, 129–30, 135, 138, 264
  as personal, 273, 279
  relationship to salvation, 125, 139
  in service of communion, 124, 138–42, 267, 269, 273, 279–83
  as social, 138, 273, 279
salvation
  Jesus Christ as savior, 7, 8, 9–10, 17–18, 19–20, 39, 40–41, 61, 84, 94, 136, 192, 195, 196, 229, 254
  relationship to sacraments, 125, 139

Sarah, 118–19, 259, 263
Second Vatican Council
  on Jesus and the Church, 122–23
  Lumen Gentium, 122–24, 125, 127, 140, 262, 264–65, 266, 282
  on Mary and the Church, 123–24
Sena, Michael, 100–101
Shaw, George Bernard, 66n.
Shema, the, 101
shrewdness of the serpent, 91, 225
  vs. nakedness, 76–78, 222–24, 226, 229
sin, 17, 24, 30–31, 35, 64, 183–84
  death in, 7, 19, 39
  effects of, 84–86, 87–88, 92, 213, 215, 219, 225–30, 232, 254, 256, 275
  forgiveness of, 5, 61, 89, 90, 133–35, 137, 176
  mortal sins, 133, 275
  original sin/the Fall, 71, 72, 76–78, 80–86, 87–88, 91–92, 94–95, 105, 105n., 112, 215, 218, 225, 227–30, 231, 233, 235, 238, 254, 256, 260–61
  renunciation of, 4, 161, 165, 169
  as social, 132
  venial sins, 133, 275
Sirach 14:8-10, 113
Stephen, St. and Paul, 8–11, 13, 19, 20, 24, 166–67, 168, 177, 178, 212

Ten Commandments, 104, 275
Tobit 4:7-11, 113
transparency, 84, 112, 223, 229
  and intimacy, 77–78, 80, 224

understanding as gift of Holy Spirit, 91

virtue, 94–95, 156, 213, 231
  chastity as, 95, 101, 109, 114, 116, 224, 235, 242, 248, 254–55, 257, 262, 263

wisdom
  as gift of Holy Spirit, 91
  of God, 43–44, 49, 51, 60, 64, 91, 181, 187, 192, 194, 196, 197, 200, 201, 206, 207, 213, 295, 298
  Paul on Jesus as power and wisdom of God, 43, 44, 192, 194, 195, 198

Zechariah, 117, 118, 257–59